```
||||||||||||||||||||||||||||||||||||||||||||
MW00988965
```

PINON HILLS HOSPITAL
313 Camino Alire
Santa Fe, NM 87501

INPATIENT
GROUP
PSYCHOTHERAPY

Books by the Same Author

Theory and Practice of Group Psychotherapy

Every Day Gets a Little Closer: A Twice-Told Therapy
  (with Ginny Elkin)

Encounter Groups: First Facts
  (with Morton A. Lieberman and Matthew B. Miles)

Existential Psychotherapy

INPATIENT GROUP PSYCHOTHERAPY

Irvin D. Yalom

Basic Books, Inc., Publishers *New York*

Library of Congress Cataloging in Publication Data

Yalom, Irvin D., 1931–
  Inpatient group psychotherapy.

  Includes index.
    1. Group psychotherapy. 2. Psychiatric hospital
care. 3. Crisis intervention (Psychiatry)
4. Psychotherapy, Brief. I. Title. [DNLM: 1. Patients—
Psychology. 2. Psychotherapy, Group   WM 430 Y19i]
RC488.Y28 1983   616.89'152   82–72411
ISBN 0–465–03298–2

Contents

Contents

Preface

The late 1960s witnessed a major shift in inpatient care—a shift away from prolonged stays in large, often geographically remote state hospitals to brief, but repeated, hospitalizations in small acute wards in community-based hospitals.

The shift in psychiatric hospitalization policy—together with major advances in psychopharmacology, the advent of crisis theory, the decreased reliance on somatic therapies, and the emergence of new mental health professions—has resulted in dramatic changes in the character and function of the acute inpatient ward. These changes have, for the most part, not been accompanied by corresponding alterations in psychotherapy technology. Group therapy in particular has failed to keep pace and to evolve adaptively to its new clinical circumstances. Inpatient group therapists have continued to use strategic approaches developed in another time for another setting.

In this book I argue that the clinical setting of the contemporary acute psychiatric ward is radically different from conventional group psychiatric settings and requires a radical modification of traditional group therapy technique. My goal is to propose a modified theory of group therapy and a corpus of strategies and techniques appropriate to the clinical exigencies of acute inpatient care. My intended audience is the "front line" clinician—the harried mental health professional who leads groups amidst the tumult often found on the acute psychiatric ward.

Acute inpatient wards vary greatly, but a prototypic contemporary ward (and the type of ward I address in this book) has the following characteristics: It has approximately fifteen to thirty-five patients whose hospital stay ranges from one to three weeks. The spectrum of psychopathology is very broad: major florid psychosis, borderline disturbance (with self-destructing behavior or brief psychotic decompensation), depression, substance abuse, eating disorders, geriatric psychiatric syndromes, acute crisis and decompensation (often with suicidal behavior) in relatively well-functioning individuals. The unit may be locked or open; if locked, the majority of patients could function on an open unit. The staff encompasses several professional disciplines (and often students from some or all of these disciplines): nursing, psychiatry, social work, occupational therapy, clinical psychology, recreational and activity therapy, movement, dance, music, and art therapy. These mental health personnel offer a variety of treatments: pharmacological, individual, group and family psychotherapies, milieu therapy, occupational and activity therapy, electroconvulsive therapy. The powerful invisible presence is the third-party payer—the financial denizen who has a shocking degree of influence over admission and discharge decisions. The pace of the ward is often frenetic; the turnover (of both patients and staff), rapid; the staff tension and dissension, high; the psychotherapy, fragmented.

I mean this book to be of immediate clinical usefulness to the inpatient group therapist. To that end I have drawn from all possible sources of information: my personal clinical experience

Preface

(as a staff member of inpatient wards and as the leader of a daily inpatient therapy group for the past three years), my own clinical research, and the clinical descriptive and research literature. I also draw from discussions with inpatient staff members over many years and from my personal observations of twenty-five inpatient units, which I visited in preparation for this work and where I interviewed the staff and observed many therapy group sessions. These inpatient units were located in private, community, and/or university hospitals. Any skewing in observations comes from their having been made of the best-known, most prestigious hospitals with excellent reputations, excellent training programs, and generous ward staffing.

Although the acute psychiatric ward I address in this text is common, it is by no means ubiquitous. The world of hospital psychiatry is vast, and there are many types of facility with which I have little familiarity. It is my hope that clinicians who work on such wards (and they include wards devoted to child, adolescent or geriatric care, substance abuse, chronic care, care of the psychotic unmanageable patient and the criminally insane) will find some of the tenets and techniques I describe immediately applicable and will adapt others to fit their own clinical settings.

Psychotherapists who lead *outpatient* therapy groups function autonomously: their skill and their decisions determine the course, the procedures, and the outcome of the group. Life is far different for the leader of the inpatient therapy group. The psychiatric ward offers a variety of therapies, which often overlap and compete with one another for patients, scheduling time, staffing, funding, and training and supervision resources. Consequently it is not the group therapist but the administrative staff who make such crucial decisions about the inpatient group as the frequency and duration of meetings, size, composition, co-therapy assignments, supervision, optional or mandatory attendance policy, and so on.

The destiny of the inpatient group is so heavily shaped by

contextual and administrative factors operating anterior to the actual group session that this book will proceed accordingly. Hence the first two chapters explore the interface between ward and small group and the final four chapters discuss explicit therapy strategy and technique.

In chapter 1, I discuss contemporary inpatient practice: the role of group therapy, structure of group therapy programs, the priority accorded it, composition and frequency of meetings, leadership, strategic focus. Since some inpatient units are uncertain about how much staff time and energy to invest in group therapy, I present the evidence, both empirical and rational-humanistic, for the effectiveness of group therapy. A lengthy survey and critique of the research literature would have deflected the purpose of this book: to serve as a clinical guide for the practitioner. But old academic habits die hard, and I proceeded, nonetheless, to review the research literature. The review, however, made for dull reading, and in the final draft my blue pencil spared only the most relevant research; I exiled the more exacting and tedious parts to the appendix.

In chapter 2, I propose several structural modifications necessary for inpatient work. After a brief summary of the principles of traditional group therapy, I describe the clinical setting of the inpatient group and the technical, structural modifications required by that setting—modifications in goals, composition, frequency and duration of meetings, size, confidentiality, subgrouping, and role of the therapist.

The structural changes required by the inpatient setting have far-reaching implications for the therapist's basic strategy and techniques—the theme of chapters 3 and 4. Many readers mistake the title of this book to be "impatient" group therapy. Chapter 3 suggests that the mistake may be prescient: a slow, patient, reflective, nondirective therapeutic approach has no place in inpatient work. Inpatient group therapists must adopt a shorter time frame, be active and efficient, and provide, in a number of robust ways, effective structure for the group. And

Preface

support, always support: all inpatient group work requires a foundation of support, and the leader must be familiar with a variety of techniques that facilitate the construction of a safe, trusting group climate.

Chapter 4 discusses the therapist's use of the here-and-now in inpatient group therapy. I present the rationale of the here-and-now, underscore its vital importance in all experiential group therapies, and discuss special considerations raised by the inpatient setting. Many group therapists avoid a here-and-now focus in inpatient groups because they make the error of equating interaction with confrontation or conflict. Chapter 4 emphasizes that the here-and-now focus may be used, even with deeply troubled patients, in the service of support, cohesiveness, and self-validation.

The final two chapters present specific models of group therapy meetings: chapter 5, a group composed of better-functioning patients; and chapter 6, a group composed of psychotic, poorly functioning patients. Although I describe these models in explicit detail, I do not present them as blueprints for others to trace; instead I mean them to illustrate the general strategy of a structured group meeting, and hope that others will fashion analogous procedures appropriate to their personal styles and clinical settings.

I focus exclusively in this text upon the central, indispensable ingredient of the inpatient group therapy program: the daily "talking" therapy group. I have sought to write a brief, clinically relevant guide, not a text of encyclopedic length or scope. Hence there is a great deal I do not discuss, including any of the wide variety of specialty groups (see page 5); ancillary group therapy techniques (such as video-playback, psychodrama, movement, dance, and art therapy); approaches required for certain specialized problems—the borderline, suicidal, aggressive, unmotivated, paranoid patients; or group-therapy-related topics (such as therapeutic training and supervision, staff T-groups, community meetings). I omit these important topics not only because of space considerations but because the precarious and confused field of contemporary inpatient group therapy calls for a contribution to basic, rather than to specialized, theory and practice.

It is a long journey from hastily scribbled observations of group sessions to a 340-page text, and many people have assisted me along the way. None more than Bea Mitchell and her glorious word processor. Neither ever blanched even at the sight of yet another final draft being demoted to penultimate status. I am grateful to David Spiegel, M.D., and Carol Payne, R.N., for their critical reading of the entire manuscript; to Vivian Banish for her valuable contributions to the model of the "focus group"; to my family for much support and for forgiving me, finally, for undertaking this work so soon after the completion of another lengthy project; to the patients and staff of the Stanford University Medical Center psychiatric unit (ward NOB) for their unflagging cooperation and assistance; to Marjorie Crosby for her generous sponsorship; to Phoebe Hoss for her editorial assistance; to Stanford University for providing me the freedom and the academic accoutrements required to undertake this task; and to all the staff of the many inpatient units who graciously permitted me to visit and to study their work.

INPATIENT
GROUP
PSYCHOTHERAPY

Chapter 1

Group Psychotherapy and the Contemporary Psychiatric Ward

If this were a treatise on outpatient group psychotherapy, it would be entirely appropriate to plunge directly into clinical waters, to begin the discussion of clinical strategy and technique immediately, in this very first paragraph. Not so for inpatient group psychotherapy! It is a major clinical fact of life for the inpatient group therapist that, unlike the outpatient therapy group, the inpatient group is not "free-standing" but is always part of a larger therapeutic system.

Hence, I shall begin by examining the relationship between group therapy and the therapeutic organization in which it is ensconced. The contemporary acute psychiatric ward offers, in addition to group therapy, a number of other therapies: psychotropic medication, individual therapy, milieu therapy, activity therapy, occupational therapy, family therapy, electroconvulsive therapy. These therapies are interdependent: decisions made about one therapy may influence any or all of the other therapies. Furthermore, different inpatient units may assign different priorities to the various therapies—an act that has far-reaching implications for the conduct of group psychotherapy.

First, let us investigate the role accorded to group therapy on the inpatient ward. Then we will consider the major problems that face inpatient group therapy programs and the solutions that wards have offered to these problems. Finally, I will discuss the effectiveness of inpatient group therapy.

Current Practice

Role of Group Therapy

To the best of my knowledge, every acute inpatient ward offers some inpatient group therapy experience. Indeed, the evidence supporting the efficacy of group therapy, and the prevailing sentiment of the mental health profession, are sufficiently strong that it would be difficult to defend the adequacy of the inpatient unit that attempted to operate without a small group program.

Many wards, however, are not heavily invested in group therapy and offer only a perfunctory program. Occasionally inpatient groups are led without formal sanction by the ward administration. I visited one university ward whose medical director, a psychopharmacologist, informed me that he had taken over the unit approximately a year before, had tried to use groups for the first three months, and, having concluded that therapy groups were ineffective in an acute setting, had

Group Psychotherapy and the Psychiatric Ward

"dismantled" the group program. However, when I interviewed members of his staff, I was informed *sotto voce* that the evening nursing staff conducted daily therapy groups concealed under the title of "rap groups." (Therapy groups, with some euphemism as a group title, are not, as I shall discuss, uncommon.)

In the literature there are occasional reports that remind us that some wards, until fairly recently, operated without a therapy program. For example, in 1974 an article by two psychiatrists described an experimental trial in which they conducted two group therapy meetings a week on an acute inpatient ward.[A]* The authors reported that the ward members overwhelmingly felt the groups were useful, did not complain of boredom, and invariably attended the group (despite the fact that groups were optional). Finally, the authors reported (with some astonishment) that the group therapy program had many advantages over the traditional medical morning rounds.

In 1975 a similar report by a psychiatric nurse described the establishment of a group program in a psychiatric unit.[B] The nurses on an acute unit perceived that a once-weekly therapeutic community meeting did not constitute effective group psychotherapy. Timidly, and without the support (or overt opposition) of the ward psychiatrist, the nurses began to develop a small therapy group program. They reported, with some surprise, that the small therapy group offered an important learning experience for patients, that the open discussion of feelings facilitated the functioning of the ward, that patients had strong negative feelings about the formality (including the starched white uniforms) of the nurses, and that the therapy group facilitated the patients' use of the other forms of available therapy.

What gives one pause is that these articles were written as recently as the mid-1970s. The fact that inpatient staff members

---

*All letter notations in this chapter refer to corresponding sections in the appendix (pages 313–35) where the relevant research is cited and, if appropriate, discussed.

independently discover the effectiveness of inpatient group programs is, of course, reassuring and corroborates my own views. Nonetheless, it also reflects the lack of attention given to group methodology in traditional psychiatric and nursing training programs.

Diversity of Programs

The single most characteristic aspect of contemporary inpatient treatment programs is their astonishing range and variation. When I visit *outpatient* clinics around the United States, I invariably find therapeutic group programs to be broadly consistent from one clinic to another. However, in contemporary *inpatient* units there exists a blooming profusion of types of groups, of leader strategies and techniques, of patterns of composition, and of duration and frequency of meetings.

One's head spins at such abundance: either it represents a great burst of creativity simultaneously erupting in inpatient hospitals all over the country, or it reflects significant and lamentable chaos in the field. Although many ward programs display considerable imagination and creativity—a creativity essential for continued professional development—I have little doubt that there is also an alarming absence of some stable center. There is no coherent body of inpatient group therapy principle and corresponding strategies and techniques that are consistent from unit to unit. This lack plays havoc in the education of young psychotherapists and encourages a dangerously speculative "every man for himself," "every woman for herself" approach to therapy which cannot help but be, in the long run, pernicious to the field and to patients' best interests.

Consider the types of therapy groups on inpatient wards. The wards I visited generally had traditional talking psychotherapy groups, which generally met from one to three times a week, and a series of other specialty groups, often meeting once or twice weekly and led by a member of the full-time staff or by a part-time mental health professional hired solely for that

Group Psychotherapy and the Psychiatric Ward

purpose. The range of groups offered by the wards I visited was astonishingly broad (even allowing for the fact that similar groups may be named differently on different wards) and includes: interactional groups, analytic groups, multifamily groups, goals groups, movement therapy groups, art therapy groups, massage therapy groups, transition groups, relaxation groups, guided fantasy groups, dance therapy groups, music therapy groups, horticulture group therapy, medication education groups, future-planning groups, therapeutic community groups, living skills groups, crafts groups, human sexuality groups, discharge-planning groups, problem-solving groups, rap groups, awareness-training groups, motor skills groups, assertiveness training groups, behavioral effectiveness groups, focus groups, Ann Landers groups, psychodrama groups, men's groups, women's groups, structured exercises groups, family-living groups, decision-making groups, puppetry groups, emotional identification groups, soap-opera discussion groups, task (project) groups, activity groups.

Another way that I can illustrate the diversity of group therapy programs is to describe the programs of three units with widely differing group programs. All three units were structurally similar: acute inpatient units of twenty to thirty beds with an average length of hospitalization of two weeks, and located in a general university teaching hospital. All three were well staffed and enjoyed excellent local and national reputations.

Ward A was run very much along the traditional medical model. The daily rounds were formal: the medical director and the psychiatric residents discussed the patients, with little participation expected from the nursing or the paramedical ward staff. The discussion focused primarily on pharmacological or electroconvulsive therapy, on esoteric questions about possible organicity as an etiological factor, or on post-hospital discharge planning. The ward group therapists contributed nothing whatsoever to the rounds, even though they possessed considerable and highly relevant information.

The medical director stated candidly that he had relatively little interest in group therapy. None of his residents led groups because he felt there was no adequate supervision available for them. Though there were available many social workers and psychologists who were experienced in group methods, he stated that it was a poor idea to have either medical students or psychiatric residents supervised by nonmedical personnel; that practice, he opined, provided a poor role model and discouraged many young physicians from pursuing careers in psychiatry.

The ward had a formal psychotherapy group led by the social worker; it met three times a week for an hour and was attended by approximately seven or eight of the best-functioning patients on the ward. These patients were chosen by the leader who, before each meeting, made the selection and circled the ward to invite or persuade them to come. The social worker, who was well trained in individual and family therapy, had little zest for group therapy and cheerfully canceled meetings whenever possible. Whenever she was absent from the ward, even on an extended vacation, no group was held. The nurses did not lead groups because of the medical director's decree that nurses not do psychotherapy. The occupational therapist used to lead therapy groups, but she was discharged, the head nurse informed me, because there were "too many staff people trying to give therapy to too many patients and no one willing to help fill the patient's day."

An art therapist and a dance therapist came in once a week to hold a group with the patients, but none of the staff members could describe what those meetings were like. A multifamily group met in the evening once a week but was poorly attended by the patients. A therapeutic community meeting was held twice a week for thirty minutes; in it, ward problems were supposed to be discussed, but the sessions were muted and perfunctory. Once a week the recreational therapist led a short community meeting in which she and the patients planned the week's activity.

Ward B offered a twice-weekly forty-five minute psychotherapy group led by two psychiatric residents and a psychiatric nurse, who selected for their group the ward's best-functioning patients (approximately eight of the twenty-two patients on the ward). The ward also held other groups:

Two community meetings weekly: one led by the chief resident; and the other, by the head nurse.

A multifamily group: forty-five minutes, once weekly, poorly attended.

A "social skills" group: forty-five minutes once weekly, for predischarge patients, led by two registered nurses (the content and procedure of these meetings were indistinguishable from those of the twice-weekly psychotherapy group).

An art therapy group: sixty minutes, three times a week, led by a leader hired specifically for this function.

A "daily living" group: three times weekly, led by occupational therapists and psychiatric technicians, who taught chronic patients such basic skills as cooking and personal grooming.

A "medication education" group: sixty minutes once weekly, led by nurses who provided information about the effects and the side effects of medication and helped patients talk about their fears about taking medication.

Ward C randomly divided its twenty-four patients into two teams. All patients of each team met twice weekly for forty-five minutes in a psychotherapy group led by two psychiatric residents and a psychiatric nurse. The Ward C medical director valued the group program highly and had on his staff five full-time mental health professionals interested in groups (music therapist, art therapist, dance therapist, recreational therapist, and occupational therapist). He had established an ethos on the ward of interdiscipline equality: all staff members were trained as therapists, and all roles were considered interchangeable, aside from physician and nursing functions of prescribing and dispensing medications.

In addition to the twice-weekly team therapy group, the ward offered a large number of other groups:

A multiple family group: once weekly.

A goals group: sixty minutes, twice weekly; all the patients of a team met to set personal goals for themselves for that week.

A therapeutic community meeting: forty-five minutes, once weekly.

A social skills group: once weekly, with a focus on grooming and conversation.

A dance therapy group: twice weekly.

A music therapy group: twice weekly.

A horticulture group: once weekly, led by the activity therapist, with a focus on learning to nurture.

A relaxation therapy group: for selected nonpsychotic patients.

An art therapy group: twice weekly.

A "medication-education" group: once weekly.

I selected these wards because they differ greatly along many variables: the prestige accorded to group therapy, the definitions of the role of the professional disciplines, and, above all, the number and the type of therapy group offered. But none of these wards is prototypical: each ward I visited had its own unique group program and body of staff mores governing the way groups were led.

Given the wide, often bewildering range of ward group therapy programs, it is imperative to select the salient group therapy issues which I can examine in a systematic fashion across many varied programs. I shall address several decisions that all wards must make about groups: the prestige of group therapy, the composition of groups, the frequency of meetings, leadership, the focus of the group.

The Prestige of the Inpatient Group

Wards differ considerably in the level of prestige accorded the group therapy program. At one end of the continuum was a ward on which the medical director led one of the therapy groups, supervised other groups, and participated in a weekly staff experiential meeting; at the other was a ward I mentioned previously on which the medical director, a psychopharmacologist, had dismantled the group program and the nurses were forced to lead clandestine evening groups.

If the ward administrators consider the group program to be unimportant or even countertherapeutic, there is little likelihood of the group's being an effective therapy modality. No inpatient group therapist can lead a successful group if the other members of the ward treatment team devalue group therapy. Staff skepticism initiates a process (commonly known as the "self-fulfilling prophecy") in which the ward team members operate in a fashion that causes their beliefs to be realized. Either explicitly or implicitly they communicate their sentiments to the patient community and adversely influence the patients' expectational set toward the group therapy experience. An unfavorable expectational set undermines psycho-\ therapy: a substantial body of research demonstrates that the greater the patient's initial belief that therapy will help, the better the ultimate therapy outcome.[C] The effect is more powerful in group than in individual therapy because of the contagion effect. Some group members who are skeptical and pessimistic about therapy rapidly convey their sentiments to other members; furthermore, they serve as "culture bearers" and demoralize succeeding generations of new members.

One can recognize such a ward easily: groups are held infrequently and for short periods of time; individual therapists interrupt the meeting and "call out" their own patients; the staff looks for reasons to cancel groups; the groups are led by unskilled and untrained individuals, often without supervision;

the groups are considered to be time fillers; the staff is uninformed and, at times, derisive about the various types of groups; the groups may have a variety of functions (for example, discussion, skill training, or discharge planning) but are not considered "psychotherapy" groups. In fact, sometimes the leaders of the groups are expressly forbidden to do "psychotherapy."

One medical director whom I asked about the group therapy program on his ward, stated that a therapy group met daily. He meant, however, I soon learned, that there were two small therapy groups a week, two thirty-minute community meetings a week, and one activity planning meeting a week, in which the patients decided upon their activities for that week. (He considered these all to be therapy groups.) He then continued, "There are lots of other 'mishmosh' groups led by nurses, O.T.'s, and dancers, but who can call them therapy?"

"Calling out" patients from the group therapy meeting is a clear sign that group therapy is undervalued. Some private wards are governed primarily by the private practitioners who hospitalize their patients on them. These practitioners specify whether their patients may attend the ward therapy groups; and if a practitioner comes to the ward to see a patient when the patient is in the group, the practitioner will, without regard for the disruption caused to the rest of the group, request that patient to leave the group immediately. The message to all the patients is abundantly clear: group therapy is a nice thing to do —as long as it doesn't interfere with therapy. The patient's faith in group therapy and in the group leaders—a necessary condition for successful outcome—is undermined, and the assumption that group therapy is ineffective soon becomes reality.

Other wards—for example, Ward C described earlier—value group therapy and build their program around it. All admitting physicians are well aware that their patients automatically enter the ward group therapy program, and that they, the physicians, must schedule their individual therapy hours accordingly.

Group Psychotherapy and the Psychiatric Ward

A particularly unsatisfactory program design is to be seen in some private hospitals where large numbers of patients are admitted by a few psychiatrists in private practice. Each admitting psychiatrist then leads—or, generally, hires a mental health professional (often a psychiatric social worker) to lead—groups of his or her own patients on the ward. This practice places the interests of a portion of the patients above the welfare of the entire community and is disruptive to any stable wardwide program. Since there may be several groups run by different people, all scheduled at the convenience of the group leader, it is not possible for the nursing staff to organize a program to include all members of the ward.

The Composition of the Inpatient Group

Psychiatric wards use two basic approaches to group composition. Some wards (for example, wards A and B) use the *level* model in which relatively well functioning patients are assigned to a "higher-level" group and the relatively regressed, psychotic ones a "lower-level" group.

Other wards (for example, Ward C) use the *team* model. In this model, the ward is divided into two or three teams, to one of which all newly admitted patients are assigned in rotation; and each team meets as a therapy group. The team therapy group will thus be very heterogeneous and contain at any given time patients at all levels of functioning, from chronic regressed psychotic patients to those who are relatively integrated but undergoing a severe life crisis.

Each of these approaches to therapy group composition—the level and the team—has advantages and drawbacks. Successful programs, as I will discuss in the next chapter, must find a way to reap the benefits of both.

The Frequency of Group Meetings

Rapid patient turnover presents a major problem in the group therapy program on every acute ward. If the group therapist is to develop any group stability whatsoever, there is, to my view, only one possible strategy: *hold group therapy meetings as frequently as possible.* Obviously, if the average length of stay on a twenty-bed ward is one to two weeks, then the composition of the group that meets only twice a week will be radically different from meeting to meeting. The group that meets daily will, of course, have a changing membership, but there will be enough carryover of members from one meeting to another to provide some measure of group stability. (More about this point also in the following chapter.)

Only a very few wards, however, hold daily meetings of their "official" psychotherapy group. The standard practice is to offer two or, at the most, three meetings a week of the major therapy group. The specialty groups (for the time being, I shall use this term to refer to the whole host of alternative groups [see page 5]) meet on the average of once or twice a week.

Why does the "talking psychotherapy" group characteristically meet so infrequently? Ward administrators offer several reasons, none of which are compelling. Some units report, for example, that they cannot hold groups more than twice a week because a rotating nursing schedule makes it impossible for the nurse group co-leaders to work the day shift with enough consistency to be able to lead groups more frequently. (Yet other wards find that it is not a difficult task to assign staff members to lead the group for a limited period—for example, two to three months—and to place the group leader(s) on a permanent day schedule during that period.) Some wards that are drastically understaffed report that they cannot offer frequent group meetings because of lack of staff and limited nursing time.* Although scheduling problems on a busy, "revolving door" ward may be significant, it seems that attitudes toward group

*Some of the most understaffed wards are caught in an unfortunate vicious circle: so much paperwork is required for a ward to meet official requirements for certification as effective that the nursing staff may not have enough time to provide the therapeutic experience that would, in reality, make a particular ward effective.

therapy are the primary determinant of group therapy frequency. If the clinical leaders of a ward value and endorse group therapy, then—*mirabile dictu!*—the insurmountable scheduling problems suddenly dissolve; and individual therapy demands and patients', nurses', and residents' schedules all easily accommodate to the group therapy schedule. Although co-leaders may be preferable, some units have learned they are not indispensable. A well-trained leader can "solo" most satisfactorily. The most understaffed ward that I visited offered a traditional therapy group only once a week but hired, at a modest rate, a consultant to lead a group four evenings a week.

Occasionally, no single group meets frequently enough because there are too many staff members vying for leadership. Often, as I will discuss in the next section, interdisciplinary rivalry propels each discipline to fight for its own therapeutic turf. In an effort to salve professional pride, each discipline is given a slot in the weekly group schedule, with the result that a patient's schedule may include many of the specialty groups I have cited. Indeed, some wards hold as many as three group meetings a day; and yet since no one single group meets more than once or twice weekly, the patient fails to have an ongoing, consistent group experience. Such a program is designed to meet staff rather than patient needs. Despite its intensity, the program may be countertherapeutic: it results in scattering rather than integration and fails to provide disorganized patients with the structure they require.

I believe that another reason inpatient groups are not held frequently enough is that group leaders are confused about how to lead them. Because the field lacks a coherent, commonly accepted schemata for inpatient group therapy, these leaders have received no adequate training. Consequently, inpatient leaders use an ineffective model, or each leader attempts to create an approach *de novo*. Either way, the majority of small inpatient group meetings are confused and ineffective. Therapists, no less than patients, suffer from this lack of rational therapeutic guidelines; the therapists want to lead inpatient therapy groups but, at the same time, are uncomfortable and demoralized about their work. Often they respond to this ambivalence by leading therapy groups only infrequently—a procedure that, unfortunately, makes the small group even more difficult to lead.

Group Leadership

The question of who leads the small inpatient group is complex. For one thing, the leadership issue often acts as a mirror reflecting many interstaff conflicts. A wide range of professional disciplines is represented by inpatient therapy group leaders: psychiatric nurses, psychiatric technicians, psychiatrists, psychologists, psychiatric social workers, occupational therapists, hospital chaplains, recreational therapists, activity therapists, movement therapists, dance therapists, art therapists, and students in all these disciplines. The most common group leader is the psychiatric nurse; and one of the least common, the psychiatrist (although approximately 50 percent of acute wards in university hospitals have groups led by psychiatric residents).

There exist enormous differences in attitudes toward the role of the various professional disciplines. On Ward C, for example, the boundaries between professional disciplines were blurred entirely, and all ward personnel were designated as psychotherapists. At the other extreme was Ward A, where it was explicitly mandated that no one but the psychiatrist and, to some extent, the psychiatric social worker could administer therapy. (In fact, as I have mentioned, the Ward A occupational therapist was discharged because of underground therapeutic activity.)

Thus, the debate about group leadership is often a debate about power, prestige, and professional territory rather than about a leader's competence. The issue is even more clouded by the fact that few, if any, of the professional disciplines receive any direct instruction in group therapy during their training, and virtually none of them receive any instruction in inpatient group psychotherapy.

The rivalry between disciplines has many repercussions for the overall group therapy inpatient program. In general, staff members want to lead groups and to enjoy the prestige of being labeled "therapist" and the satisfaction of being immediately effective in patients' recovery rather than engaged in the less satisfying role of time filling or maintenance. Decisions about number, types, and frequency of groups are often made on the basis of what will not ruffle the staff rather than of what will be most effective for the patient. I have, for example, witnessed inpatient groups that have as many as four or five professional leaders, not because more leaders are more effective (indeed, the reverse is often the case), but in order to placate representatives of each discipline. As I discussed previously, the same dynamics account for the policy of holding a large number of specialty groups rather than scheduling a single therapy group for daily sessions.

Such professional rivalry is often countertherapeutic. With many types of groups led by many leaders, there is often no forum available that permits the group leaders to communicate important events of the group to the ward staff. Staff members may have little interest in, or little respect for, the types of group led by other disciplines. It is often remarkable how little the most consistently present staff members (for example the full-time nursing staff and the ward psychiatrist) know about a patient's therapeutic experience in the many miscellaneous groups on the ward. This ignorance leads to a serious breakdown of communication between the nursing staff, the medical staff, and the admitting psychiatrist.

Frequently, the official title of the group conveys little information about what the group actually does. For example, one ward offered a formal psychotherapy group, which met only once a week, but also a thrice-weekly evening dance therapy group led by a professional dance therapist hired solely for the purpose of those three meetings. When I attended the dance therapy group and talked to the patients about their group experience, it became very clear that "dance therapy group" was a misnomer: the group was an intensive (and effective) psychotherapy group and only occasionally used some physical movement (that is, a brief nonverbal or gestalt exercise). The great majority of the better-functioning patients on the ward attended the group and valued it highly. The leader was a lay therapist with no official psychotherapy training but was exceedingly skilled and had been leading such groups for over fifteen years. As valuable as the group was to the patients, much potential benefit was lost by the lack of any established channel of communication between the dance therapist (she was only present on the ward for those three evening meetings), the full-time staff, and each patient's individual psychotherapist.

Failure to understand or to appreciate the groups led by other disciplines leads to considerable misunderstanding and distrust. At the end of a visit to one ward during which I had witnessed many therapy groups and offered a seminar, I spoke to an occupational therapy student who remarked with some bitterness that the movement therapist who, in her opinion, was the most important group therapist on the ward, was not respected enough by the ward staff to be included in the list of therapists for me to interview during my day's visit there or to be invited to my seminar. Earlier, when I had inquired about the content of the evening movement therapy group held twice a week, the nursing staff members described the group derisively, referring to it as a "touchy, feely," "weird" group which dangerously gratified needs. The log kept by the occupational therapy student, who had observed the group, was informative. On occasion, the dance therapy leader had recommended a "trust fall" or a "group hug"; but, aside from this, there was little emphasis on physical touching. Nonetheless, the rest of the ward staff picked up this very small detail and used it to disparage the

Group Psychotherapy and the Psychiatric Ward

group. This type of criticism is, of course, insidious; both intentionally and unintentionally, the staff members convey to the patients negative feelings toward a group format, thus rendering the group less effective.

It is a great misfortune that, in many university hospitals, including those with some of the leading psychiatric residencies in the country, psychiatric residents often do not lead groups. Those who design the residency curriculum offer several reasons for this lack. At one of the leading psychiatric residencies, each resident had seven individual patients on the ward as well as other ward administrative duties. The residents worked between twelve and fourteen hours a day, and the medical director said that there simply was not time left for them to do groups. I described earlier how Ward A's medical director commented that his residents led no groups because no medically trained personnel were available to supervise them. At another university hospital, the medical director said that psychiatric residents had, in past years, run groups, but that the changing nature of the hospital's population and shorter hospital stays made it impossible for them to run satisfying groups. The supervisors found it a necessary didactic device continually to remind these residents of what their strategy would be were they leading a "proper therapy group." Obviously the clinical facts of life are still not understood and accepted. Even though a short-term group is not ideal for learning group dynamics, it is the current fact of life on the inpatient ward and is likely to be so for some time to come.

Whatever the reason, the absence of inpatient group therapy training in psychiatric residency programs has serious repercussions: the administrative head of the inpatient unit is almost invariably a psychiatrist; and as long as psychiatric education fails to include training in group therapy, it will simply perpetuate the lamentable situation in which inpatient units are directed by professionals unknowledgeable and unsupportive of group therapy programs.

Psychiatric nurses—the mental health professionals who lead the majority of groups—have mixed feelings about the role of group leader. First, many have had no formal group therapy training and feel inadequate and threatened in the role. Though they much enjoy leading groups and appreciate such "assignments" by the physician, they also realize, with some resentment, that often the reason they are asked to lead groups is because the psychiatrist does not feel the group is particularly valuable.

Because nurses have had the primary responsibility for inpatient groups for two decades, they have naturally begun to claim ownership of the group program. A certain tension has set in in recent years with the influx of other mental health professionals (recreational therapists, activity therapists, movement therapists) who also wish to lead therapy groups. One unfortunate consequence of this competition is that group leaders who want expert supervision are reluctant to request it; they so fear takeover by some other discipline that they do not often openly discuss their needs and insecurities.

Many psychiatric nurses have led inpatient therapy groups for many years and have become highly skilled therapists. This, too, presents a problem: some nurses feel resentful that, despite their skill as therapists, they receive little of the prestige and the material benefits of the primary psychotherapeutic professions. These nurses are also, understandably, angered by the annual or semi-annual influx of psychiatric residents who feel too threatened by a nurse's expertise to take advantage of the opportunity of learning from one. Indeed, the tension between incoming first-year psychiatric residents and the competent psychiatric nurse is a constant feature of any acute psychiatric ward in a university hospital.

I have observed a particularly insalubrious pattern in some hospitals with a strong private-practice format. On their wards the great majority of patients are hospitalized (primarily for somatic or pharmacological therapy) by a few private practitioners who specialize in inpatient hospital work. The admitting physicians do not permit nurses to lead groups but, instead, appoint as group therapist a professional (on two wards I visited, a hospital chaplain and, on two others, a marriage and family counselor) who is well intentioned but obviously untrained in group therapy. This pattern at once reflected and instigated much nurse-physician tension. The nursing staff felt angry, demoralized, and undervalued; they opined openly that the private practitioners felt so possessive of their patients, and so threatened by the prospect of sharing (and perhaps losing) their patients to other psychotherapists, that they engaged a group therapist so inexperienced that he represented little personal threat to the practitioners.

I could continue at some length to relate sorry tales of unsatisfactory medical care, but I believe the point is by now obvious: interdisciplinary rivalry is invariably disruptive of patient care, and the "ownership" of the small therapy group is an issue around which much professional tension crystallizes. The assignment of the role of group leader is a delicate task; as I have stressed earlier, the small inpatient group is not an isolated island but part of an interdependent, complex archipelago.

Focusing the Inpatient Group

I can best begin the discussion of group focus in contemporary practice with a comment about what is *not* done. Of the scores of inpatient therapy groups that I observed, not one had an interactional focus: the groups did not work in the here-and-now. I believe, as I shall discuss at length in chapter 3, that an interactional focus is the *sine qua non* of effective group therapy. In all groups—even those composed of psychotic, disorganized patients—it is important to help members interact with one another and to understand, and generalize from, that interaction.

Group therapists who do not understand how to (or choose not to) use group interaction often flounder badly. I observed meeting after meeting where the therapist sought in vain for some effective focus for the group. The group therapist who, for whatever reason, does not focus on how members of a group relate to one another, has only a couple of other major options: the *then-and-there problem* orientation and the *common theme* orientation. Both of these options have serious shortcomings.

The therapist who focuses on then-and-there problems may examine the reasons patients come to the hospital, or the major life problems facing them in their outside lives, or their complaints or concerns about happenings on the hospital ward. Often the best that can come out of this type of approach is one patient will reveal something important about himself or herself and will feel accepted by the other patients, who may thus be encouraged to reciprocate by revealing something of themselves as well.

The most common mistake made by the group therapists whom I observed was to use a patient's presentation of a then-and-there crisis as a problem for the group to solve. This is almost always the worst possible option. It is rare that, through advice and suggestions, a group can provide some suitable solution to a patient's "outside" problem. First of all, the data presented by the protagonist is invariably inaccurate. Second, the patient has had considerable time to consider the various possible solutions both on his own and with the help of an individual therapist. In the span of less than an hour and with inadequate or skewed information, the group is rarely successful in being of use to that patient. Such an approach almost certainly ensures an experience of failure for the group: demoralization ensues, and the members' faith in the group dwindles.

To use the small therapy group for a discussion of ward complaints or administrative issues is inefficient practice. For one thing, the major individuals involved in administration are generally not in the small group; there are almost always other vehicles—for example, some form of ward community meeting —available for such discussion. But even more important is the waste of valuable therapeutic time: to transform the small therapy group into a gripe session or a business meeting is to collude with the patients' resistance and to allow a golden opportunity to degenerate into a leaden reality.

The second major option chosen by many group therapists is to focus the group discussion on common themes. For example, if one patient talks about suicide, or hallucinations, or loss, or distrust, or any other interpersonal or intrapersonal theme, the therapist can increase member participation by urging others to discuss their personal experience of, or attitudes toward, that theme. There are several disadvantages to this approach.

Often theme discussions are desultory and intellectualized since the majority of patients experience little motivation to discuss an issue that often does not represent a point of personal urgency for them. The meeting takes on the character of an issue-oriented discussion rather than of a relevant, person-oriented work session. Furthermore, theme-centered meetings often leave members with the sense that, though they have had an interesting discussion, none has gained any sense of mastery over his or her discomfort.

On many wards the very name of the group legislates, as it were, against an effective interactional approach. Often these names are entirely unrelated to the actual focus of the group. For example, one therapy group was called "life decisions"; another was called "family living"; another, "decision making." These names had been used for many years and no longer described what the group did. For example, I observed one meeting of a "family living" group in which seven of the eight members present were unmarried and living alone.

Time after time, I observed well-trained clinicians who were ineffective group leaders because they did not know how to turn the group's attention onto its own process. Take one example: A group meeting of nine patients led by a nurse and an advanced psychiatric resident began with two new members asking the leaders how the group should operate. The leaders, who assumed an extremely nondirective role, turned the question back to the group. Soon Morris, one of the patients, talked about the fact that he didn't see how the group could be useful because his problem was that he had lost his job, had no money, was forced to cut back in every way, and now found that there was nothing to cut back. Over forty-five minutes of a sixty-minute session were consumed by Morris's relating the entire history of the failure of his business to two baffled therapists and to eight other patients, some of whom seemed profoundly uninterested and the others insensate. The therapists' sole intervention during the session was to encourage any other people in the room who had financial problems to share them with the group.

Entirely overlooked, however, was the major fact of that group therapy hour: that is, Morris's impact upon the other members. Morris was like a broken record: he had, for many hours in other therapy groups and ward group sessions, talked about nothing else but his financial difficulties. The other patients found it extraordinarily exasperating to spend time with him: they avoided him in the group and on the ward as well. Morris's isolation was the real, but never expressed, theme of the meeting. The group could do little about his financial setbacks, but they could have done a great deal to teach Morris how he drove people away from him and contributed to his own isolation. (Indeed, his wife had left him, and his children and friends avoided him, not, as he believed, because of his financial failure but because of his obsessive, continual preoccupation with money and his self-absorption and insensitivity to the needs of others.)

The group leaders were well-trained individual therapists, and under no circumstances would they have wasted huge chunks of precious therapy time in individual therapy by focusing exclusively on a symptom. But this is precisely what they did in this group session. They failed to seize any of the obvious available interactional options: exploring, for example, the feelings evoked by Morris's repetitive and monopolistic rumination, the disengagement of the other members, the anger and frustration percolating in the group toward the therapists for not providing effective leadership. Over and over again, I have observed wonderfully ripe therapeutic plums spoiling on the tree because of the inability (or unwillingness) of therapists to focus on interaction.

To take another example: In the dozens of inpatient group meetings I have observed, I rarely saw a therapist focus the group's attention on an exceptionally important event for the members in that hour—namely, my presence. Each member no doubt had some feelings about a stranger observing the group meeting. What were the members' fantasies about my function there, or about my relationship with the therapist, or about what I might do with the material I observed? All of these questions were left unexamined.

Also, many other major group events occurred without examination. Members became bored or agitated and left the room without explanation; members stood up in the middle of the meeting and changed seats; members interrupted one another; members fell asleep; members deliberately baited the therapist; members made inappropriately hostile or affectionate overtones to one another. To allow these events to go unnoticed introduces into the group a sense of unreality, irrelevance, and futility—especially when each of these events may, in ways that I shall describe later, be turned to therapeutic advantage.

Many therapists fail to focus on interaction because of their lack of training in traditional group methods. The ability to facilitate member-to-member interaction and to help members learn from observing their own process is an acquired therapeutic skill that requires group training and supervision rarely available in most professional educational curriculums.

There is an additional reason: many therapists are frightened of an interactional approach. Many clinicians—and especially, it seems, program directors who are concerned about medical-legal issues and about maintaining a full ward census (and thus must be sensitive to the reputation of their ward in the psychiatric community)—equate the here-and-now approach with confrontation, conflict, encounter groups, the "hot seat," or heightened intensity. To my view, this is an erroneous assumption; and a major goal of this book is to clarify how the here-and-now approach leads to a supportive, encouraging, and facilitating group environment which, properly titrated, is appropriate for even the most acutely disturbed psychiatric patients.

Whatever the reasons, therapists who avoid the interactional approach find themselves drifting, confused, and without the sense of confidence that arises as a result of having a central coherent theory and a body of corresponding strategies and techniques.

All of these factors—the undervaluing of group therapy, the absence of a consistent, daily group, the confusion about proper composition, the professional rivalry surrounding group leadership and the lack of an effective focus—act in concert to limit greatly the potential effectiveness of inpatient group therapy. It is a tribute to the inherent power of the therapy group that, despite these handicaps, the format continues to be effective.

The Effectiveness of Inpatient Group Psychotherapy

Debate over Effectiveness

Despite the fact that group therapy has been well established for forty years, many medical directors of acute inpatient wards deeply question the effectiveness of inpatient group psychotherapy and choose not to provide it on their wards. At any given moment in the United States, there are probably as many patients engaged in group therapy as in individual therapy. One is hard put to find a clinical setting—from a vast variety of outpatient clinics, to prisons, chronic psychiatric hospital wards, psychological medical wards, schools for the delinquent, obesity clinics, stop smoking programs, and so on—in which group methods have not proven useful. Why, on the acute psychiatric ward, does a fundamental debate arise about the effectiveness of group therapy?

On some wards, group therapy programs are unsupported because of the specific clinical orientation of the ward administrators. Formal curricula in psychiatric residency programs or in nursing schools rarely offer training in group psychotherapy and almost never in inpatient group psychotherapy. Unless the medical director or the clinical nursing coordinator have had postgraduate education in group therapy, it is unlikely that either will have been trained in group therapy methods. Hence it is not to be expected that either one will heavily endorse a therapy mode with which he or she is personally unfamiliar.

On other wards the debate about whether group therapy is effective is, in reality, a debate about another issue entirely— the issue of professional territoriality. Traditionally, inpatient group therapy has generally fallen within the domain of the nursing profession. But what if the medical director or the admitting psychiatrists believe (and they often do) that nurses, occupational therapists, or any of the other paramedical disciplines are not qualified to do psychotherapy? In such instances, group therapy is declared—by dictum—ineffective, and the group therapy program is unsupported or devalued.

Significant substantive issues enter the debate as well. Many clinicians question whether group therapy is a viable form of treatment in the contemporary acute inpatient unit. They point particularly to two troublesome clinical facts of life on the acute ward: the brief hospital stay and the wide range of psychopathology (from mild neurotic disturbance to florid psychotic decompensation). How, these clinicians ask, can therapy groups be effective under such conditions? After all, membership stability and homogeneity of ego strength have always been considered prerequisites for the development of the cohesiveness and the therapeutic climate so essential for effective group functioning.

These arguments are not without substance. Shortly, I shall review some evidence that "traditional" group therapy—a treatment paradigm developed for other clinical settings—may indeed be ineffective when applied to inpatient work. *The contemporary acute psychiatric ward poses radically different clinical conditions and requires a radical modification of the traditional group therapy approach.* This task is formidable but not insurmountable. The mission of this book is to describe a therapy approach that is specifically responsive to these new clinical conditions.

If ward administrators are to invest time and energy in a group therapy program, they must be persuaded that there is a positive answer to the question whether inpatient group therapy is effective. Group therapists, too, must be similarly convinced of the efficacy of their approach. Earlier I commented that research evidence demonstrates that the greater a patient's initial belief that therapy will help, the better the ultimate therapy outcome. The same is true for therapists: if therapists, at the beginning of therapy, have a strong belief that the therapeutic process will help the patient, success is significantly more likely. Conversely, therapists who have deep doubts about the efficacy of their therapeutic approach will behave in ways that limit their therapeutic effectiveness.[D]

If one is to build an effective inpatient group therapy program, one's starting place, then, must be the belief system of the staff. Thus, I shall present the evidence for the efficacy of the inpatient group therapy approach. Since my aim is for this book to be a clinical guide for "front-line" practitioners, not a critique and analysis of research, I shall in this chapter present my conclusions about that efficacy and allocate description and evaluation of research methodology to the appendix.

Research Evidence

Researchers investigating the efficacy of inpatient group therapy have employed two basic methodological strategies: they have examined the relationship between outcome and the type of inpatient treatment program; and they have obtained the patient's retrospective observations about the value of inpatient group therapy. Let me review the findings of each approach in turn.

Outcome and Inpatient Group Psychotherapy

In the best of all possible research worlds, how would one design a project to provide a reliable measure of inpatient group effectiveness? One would study a massive number of patients admitted on an acute inpatient ward who would be randomly and strategically assigned to various types of therapy groups and to a control condition with no group therapy. All other parts of each patient's treatment program would be identical. Outcome would be systematically and objectively determined, and correlations measured between outcome and the nature of the therapy group experience.

But no such project has ever been done! Nor will it ever be done. Methodological problems are so overwhelming [E] that there is little rigorous research on inpatient group therapy on contemporary acute wards. Furthermore, because the inpatient unit has undergone recent drastic modification, much of the older inpatient therapy research is not relevant. Consequently, we must settle for studies that are less than perfect: either methodologically flawed or performed in different but related clinical settings.

One particularly important piece of evidence came about quite accidentally. A team of researchers [F] studied a large number of patients who had been admitted randomly to short- or to long-term hospital units. The researchers' intent was to determine the relationship between treatment outcome and length of hospitalization. Short-term patients, they learned, showed significantly greater improvement when compared with long-term patients.

Was it, the researchers wondered, sheerly the length of hospital stay that was responsible for the greater improvement of the patients, or were there other contributing factors? Very much to their surprise, the researchers found that the differences in improvement between long-term and short-term patients could almost almost entirely be accounted for by the significantly greater use of group therapy in the short-term units. Patients receiving group therapy, regardless of assignment to short- or to long-term units, improved to a significantly greater extent (especially in social skills) than did patients who received no group therapy.

The same researchers did a three-year follow-up on their patients and reported another intriguing finding: *the patients who had received inpatient group therapy were far more likely to obtain group therapy in their post-hospital outpatient course.* This is an exceptionally important finding because brief psychiatric hospitalization is effective only if it is coupled with adequate post-hospital therapy; and, as a considerable body of research demonstrates [G], group therapy is a particularly effective mode of after-care therapy.

Other studies demonstrated that inpatient group therapy on an acute open unit significantly reduced the necessity of transferring patients to locked units (although group therapy in itself did not affect the discharge rate) [H] and decreased recidivism for patients with the primary diagnosis of anxiety reaction (but not for alcoholics or chronic schizophrenic reactions) [I].

As little additional information [J] is to be obtained from pursuing the question whether inpatient group therapy is effective, a less primitive and more clinically relevant question to answer is, What types of inpatient group therapy are effective for what types of patient?

One well-designed research inquiry [K] compared the effectiveness of four types of group situation:

1. A "process/patient focused group": a supportive group in which the leader attempted to clarify and interpret the interaction between patients.

2. A "behavioral task group," in which the leader individualized behaviorally oriented therapy programs for each member.

3. A "psychodrama/gestalt group": an affect-evoking group in which each member of the group in turn was asked to identify and experience strong affect.

4. A control group consisting of no group therapy experience on the ward.

The researchers discovered that the groups differed significantly in effectiveness: patients in the "process/patient focused group" had significantly better outcome than patients in the other two types of group or in the "no group" control condition. The behavioral therapy group was relatively ineffective; and the psychodrama/gestalt group proved to be countertherapeutic: that is, patients attending that group showed an *increase* in symptomatology.

Other researchers have reported that inpatient group therapy led in traditional psychoanalytic style (that is, with an inactive, nondirective, insight-oriented leader) is ineffective in the inpatient setting [L]. It is an error, these studies indicate, to apply a clinical approach developed in one setting (long-term outpatient work) to another setting in which it is inappropriate.

Group therapy programs must be sensitive to specific needs of specific types of patient. There is strong evidence that psychotic patients are made worse by groups led by nondirective leaders who focus on insight and on affect evocation.[M]

In summary, the research evidence indicates that, overall, acute inpatient wards with group therapy programs are more therapeutic than those without them; that some group approaches are more effective than others (nondirective, unstructured, insight-oriented, psychoanalytic approaches seem to be less productive in an inpatient setting); and that psychotic patients may be made worse by traditional group therapy methods.

Inpatient psychotherapy, like all psychotherapy, apparently can be for better or for worse: proper group therapy can be of considerable therapeutic benefit, ill-advised forms may be countertherapeutic.

Patients' Retrospective Evaluations

Several projects have been reported in which patients, at the end of their hospitalization, were asked for their views about group therapy and also for their comparative evaluation of many of the inpatient treatment modalities[N]. (The other forms of inpatient therapy most commonly studied in these projects are individual psychotherapy, medication, one-to-one therapy with nurses, occupational therapy, activity therapy, community meetings.)

What do these investigations tell us? First, it is important to note that there is considerable variability. Inpatient wards offer a wide array of treatment modalities; and, almost in cafeteria style, different patients pick the modes of therapy that seem most useful to them.

Overall, there is research consensus that patients value most highly individual therapy with their psychiatrist. By no means, however, was individual therapy a runaway first choice. Even on inpatient wards where each patient was seen three to five hours weekly by highly experienced psychiatrists, fewer than 50 percent of the patients cited individual therapy as their most important form of therapy[O]. If wards offered a formal group therapy program with at least three group therapy meetings per week, then the therapy group was a strong second choice.

Another important finding reported in several studies is that the modes of therapy most highly rated by patients are based on relationship. The four top-ranking items are almost invariably individual therapy with admitting psychiatrist, group therapy, one-to-one talks with nurses, and talks with other patients. Therapeutic modalities that have a more impersonal basis (for example, crafts, ward activities, medication, or community meetings) are almost never considered highly therapeutic by the overwhelming majority of patients. Apparently hospitalized psychiatric patients seek some meaningful and supportive interpersonal exchange and repair.

Retrospective studies also demonstrate that different types of patients are benefited by different types of therapy group approach[P]. Borderline patients and patients with a neurotic mood disturbance value therapy groups particularly highly and generally report that they value their inpatient therapy group experience more highly than they do their individual therapy. Furthermore, they prefer groups that are more challenging, that expect patients to assume more responsibility for their own treatment, and that focus on the interaction between the members of the group.

Schizophrenic patients are less likely to rate groups highly. In one study[Q] they rated group therapy third of nine ward therapeutic approaches (after individual psychotherapy and talks with other patients). They prefer, in general, a group that is more supportive and places fewer demands on them and where they do not perceive themselves as being unable to perform the group task. Of the various types of schizophrenic reaction, paranoid patients are most commonly displeased with their group experience.

The results of one large study demonstrate in a particularly clear way the different preferences for groups among the various diagnostic categories[R]. On the ward studied, each patient in the study attended two groups daily: one, a team meeting, was composed of half of the ward members and was a supportive, low-key, low-challenge group; a second group was composed of the higher-level talking patients (a level group) who were challenged more and were asked to take more responsibility for their therapy than were those in the first group. (At the time of this study, the ward offered no lower-level group for the most psychotic, regressed patients.) The schizophrenic patients, on the one hand, and the patients with a borderline or with an affective disturbance, on the other hand, showed an exact reversal of choices. Of eleven ward therapy activities, those schizophrenic patients who attended both groups rated the team group third and the more challenging level group seventh. The borderline patients rated the level group first and the team group fifth; patients with an affective disorder rated the level group second and the team group fifth.

There is considerable consensus in the research literature that psychotic patients are most successfully treated in supportive, reality-focused, structured group therapy and require a sealing over rather than an opening up.[S] They are made more anxious by an unstructured group experience and do less well in groups if they disclose a great deal about themselves.[T] An extensive review of the entire clinical literature reaches the same conclusion: psychotic patients do far better in inpatient therapy groups that are reality- or activity-oriented rather than in insight-oriented ones.[U] A review of group therapy in day treatment centers yields the identical conclusion: group therapy aimed at insight and derepression is contraindicated for the schizophrenic patient [V].

Summing Up the Research Literature

From the research literature, we can draw these conclusions about inpatient group psychotherapy:

1. Group therapy is an effective treatment modality on inpatient units. It demonstrably improves outcome; upon discharge, patients value it highly; patients treated in inpatient groups are more likely to pursue a post-hospital treatment program.

2. The type of group therapy is of enormous importance. The

traditional group therapy approach, which was designed for long-term group therapy with neurotic outpatients, is ineffective and probably countertherapeutic on an acute inpatient ward. Major modification of group therapy technique is required for the acute inpatient unit.

3. Inpatient group therapy technique must be modulated to fit the type of patient population: different diagnostic groups require different group therapy approaches. There is strong evidence that psychotic and nonpsychotic patients require very different forms of group therapy.

Is Group Therapy Worth Doing? Other Arguments

There are other justifications besides research evidence for the existence of an active group program on the acute psychiatric ward—justifications with a rational-humanistic basis rather than an evidential one.

First, consider the reasons that patients enter the hospital. Though their presenting symptoms vary, a considerable portion of hospitalized patients have decompensated as a result of some interpersonal crisis, often a real or a threatened loss of a key interpersonal relationship. Furthermore, the great majority of patients are bedeviled by chronic interpersonal problems—for example, isolation and loneliness, poor social skills, sexual concerns, conflicts around authority, anger, intimacy, and dependency. If the ward staff members are to develop an empathic, therapeutic relationship with patients, they must address these interpersonal concerns.

The therapy group addresses them in two important ways. First, the group is the therapeutic arena *par excellence* in which patients learn to explore and to correct maladaptive interpersonal patterns. The group offers effective interpersonal instruction for the patients' post-hospital adjustment. Patients are helped to understand how their behavior prevents them from developing the interpersonal relationships they desire, and they are offered instruction in social skills.

Second, the inpatient therapy group enhances the ability of patients to relate to one another *during* their hospitalization. There is considerable research evidence that the relationships among patients are an important determinant of outcome.[W] Informal patient groupings and relationships contribute powerfully to the effects of hospitalization: patients can either support, nurture, and instruct one another; or they can threaten, alienate, and confuse one another. By focusing on the relationships among the patients, the therapy group augments the assistance patients derive from one another, rather than leaving to chance the development of constructive relationships among patients. Inpatient therapy groups, if properly led, decrease conflict between patients, facilitate the inclusion of isolated and withdrawn patients, promote a sense of cohesiveness and mutual respect, and break down interpersonal barriers of fear and stereotype.

Not only is inpatient group therapy the logical way to address a patient's pressing interpersonal needs but it is a form of therapy demanded by the clinical situation. On a typical inpatient ward, patients are totally immersed in a complex and powerful social system. To regard patients as windowless monads and to provide only medication and individual therapy is therapeutic negligence and deprives them of the considerable therapeutic potential inherent in that social system. The patient has sixteen waking hours a day. Rather than wasting these hours in time-filling, time-killing activities, the many skilled professionals who staff most psychiatric units can, with the proper support and orientation, provide important therapeutic aid.

Total immersion in a socially therapeutic system has been the keystone of effective psychiatric hospitalization since the moral treatment reformation two hundred years ago. Most recently, in the last ideological generation of hospital treatment, it was embodied in the principles of the therapeutic community. Although the crisis orientation and the rapid patient turnover of the contemporary psychiatric ward has rendered the therapeutic community (at least in its structural elements) obsolete, its ideological elements of patient support, responsibility, and social training persist and find expression in the small group therapy program.

Wards without active group programs not only fail to offer patients the full range of available therapy but are often staffed by personnel who fail to provide the supportive therapeutic milieu essential for psychological repair. The professional staff on an inpatient unit that has no group therapy program is generally a demoralized staff. Its members have been told, in effect, that the one-to-one therapist (usually a physician) is the effective treatment agent. Their role is to be custodial and managerial, to groom the therapeutic community, and to fill the patients' time between individual psychotherapy hours.

Invariably this situation breeds discontent. How could it not? The nursing staff are aware that they have the skills to be effective therapists, and that these skills, by fiat, must lie fallow. A discontented, demoralized staff, as every ward administrator knows, is no minor issue. Staff discontent breeds interdisciplinary conflict, patient neglect, high absenteeism, and staff turnover. Furthermore, there is persuasive evidence[X] that staff discontent and conflict, especially if covert and unexpressed (and wards without group therapy programs invariably are the same wards that fail to provide any ongoing vehicle for staff support, development, and conflict resolution), inevitably undermines the ward's therapeutic effectiveness.

Conclusion

In summary, an inpatient group psychotherapy program is demonstrably effective. Prospective and retrospective research indicates that inpatient group therapy makes efficient and effective use of the patients' time and of hospital and staff resources. Staff members actively participating in a group therapeutic program are likely to experience themselves as engaged, valued, and constructively challenged; hence, they are likely to contribute effectively to all aspects of the ward's therapeutic program. But specialized skills are required for effective leadership. Neither individual therapy nor outpatient group therapy training constitute sufficient clinical preparation for the inpatient group therapist. The acute inpatient ward constitutes a radically different clinical setting and requires a radical modification of group therapy technique. I hope, in the following chapters, to describe a strategy and a set of techniques which will enable therapists to lead groups effectively even in the most taxing inpatient settings.

Chapter 2

General Principles of Inpatient Group Therapy

In this chapter, after reviewing briefly the basic principles of "traditional" group therapy, I will consider the special clinical features of the acute inpatient ward and describe the necessary modifications in techniques for effective inpatient group therapy.

The last three decades have seen such a luxuriant growth of the group therapies that it requires great perspicacity and imagination to find, amidst the thicket, the primal trunk of "traditional" group therapy. But if there is a traditional group therapy, it is the long-term outpatient approach designed for patients with neurotic problems. Those professional curriculums that do include training in group therapy and the leading group therapy texts as well,[1] focus primarily on this type of therapy.

There are several reasons for this designated primacy. First, much more is known about long-term group therapy. It was the first widely practiced group therapy. Descriptions of this approach began to appear widely in the psychotherapeutic literature in the 1940s. Also, not only has a long skein of thoughtful clinicians observed and written about outpatient group therapy but the format has facilitated research. The groups are stable; the patients, generally motivated and willing to cooperate with research; and both therapists and patients sit still long enough to be studied.

There is no corresponding body of knowledge about inpatient group therapy, which is doubly afflicted in this regard. First, senior clinicians do not lead inpatient therapy groups and rarely remain long in inpatient settings: political and administrative turmoil generally results in rapid senior staff turnover or promotion of senior staff to administrative positions which remove them from direct contact with patients. Second, as I discuss in the appendix, the clinical setting of the contemporary inpatient unit thwarts rigorous research.

All things considered, however, the field is fortunate that a body of outpatient group therapy scholarship has accumulated because the principles of long-term outpatient group therapy are easier to generalize than those of any other single approach. Consider the range of the group therapies: assertiveness training groups, after-care groups, group psychoanalysis, groups of terminally ill cancer patients, substance abuse groups, stop smoking groups, gestalt groups, transactional analysis group therapy, and many, many more. The sheer number of approaches precludes the teaching of all of them in any single training curriculum. Hence educators have no better option than to teach a basic approach whose fundamental principles apply to the greatest number of variants *with the expectation that their students will adapt these principles to their unique clinical setting.* * I shall follow this didactic model.

*For more detailed discussion and for the evidence upon which these principles are based, see my text *The Theory and Practice of Group Psychotherapy.* [2]

Principles of Traditional Group Therapy

A suitable place to begin is the *clinical setting,* which is always instrumental in shaping the form of therapy. All clinicians know that certain fixed factors of the clinical setting (for example, degree and type of patient psychopathology, motivation, duration of treatment, financial resources) determine the *goals* of therapy. The goals of therapy determine the *therapeutic factors* which will come to play in the group and which, in turn, determine appropriate *therapist strategies and techniques.*

Clinical Setting

The typical outpatient group has six to eight patients and meets once or twice a week for approximately ninety minutes. Patients remain in the group for several months to two to three years. The membership turnover is minimal, and the same patients may meet together over several months. The patients are generally functional in their environment but may be acutely distressed and are hampered by underlying neurotic or characterological problems. Therapists attempt to compose a group that is heterogeneous for problem areas (type of symptom, type of personality problem) but homogeneous for ego strength (for example, a group made up of patients suffering from some neurotic or characterological disturbance will generally not include psychotic or severely borderline patients).

The therapist (or co-therapists) selects patients carefully, interviews them in one or two individual sessions, and prepares them adequately for the group therapy experience. The therapist remains with the group for at least a year and, generally, for the whole life of the group. The patients may see the group leader also in individual therapy, but generally their only contact with him or her is in the group.

Goals

The goals of long-term group therapy are ambitious and entirely analagous to the goals of long-term intensive individual psychotherapy. Group therapists hope that patients will not only obtain symptomatic relief but will also alter characterological structure. Patients are helped to identify and modify long-standing maladaptive interpersonal patterns of behavior—an outcome that not only affords resolution of a current crisis but so alters a patient's mode of experience and behavior that future crippling crises will not materialize.

Therapeutic Factors

I have always found it clarifies my own thinking about group therapy to ask a simple and naïve question: How does group therapy help patients? It is possible, by drawing from clinical research and clinician consensus, to formulate a set of basic *therapeutic factors* inherent in group therapy. (In an earlier text I referred to these factors as "curative factors,"[3] but "therapeutic factors" is a more realistic term.) These therapeutic factors provide a useful construct in that they span the entire field of the group therapies. These factors represent the core of therapy; and even though the group therapies may differ widely in their external form, all share basic mechanisms of change. Different groups, however (as a result of different clinical settings and different goals), accent different clusters of these therapeutic factors. Indeed, as we shall see, different patients in the same group may make use of very different factors. The therapeutic factors that I have proposed are:

1. instillation of hope
2. universality
3. imparting of information
4. altruism

5. the corrective recapitulation of the primary family group
6. development of socializing techniques
7. imitative behavior
8. catharsis
9. existential factors
10. cohesiveness
11. interpersonal learning[4]

Instillation of Hope

Therapy groups effectively instill hope in patients who are demoralized and pessimistic about therapy. Group members are at different points along a collapse/coping continuum and can gain hope from observing others, especially others with similar problems, who have profited from therapy.

Universality

Patients often enter therapy with the disquieting feeling that they are unique in their misery, that they alone have certain frightening or unacceptable impulses and fantasies. In the group, patients hear others share similar concerns, fantasies, and life experiences. The disconfirmation of the feeling of uniqueness offers considerable relief and a "welcome to the human race" experience.

Imparting of Information

Therapy groups implicitly or explicitly provide information to the members. Some group therapies (for example, Alcoholics Anonymous, Recovery Incorporated, discharge planning groups, or stress management groups) are specifically structured to include a didactic program. Other less structured groups provide considerable explanation and clarification to their members who, by the end of therapy, have learned a great deal about the meaning of symptoms, interpersonal and group dynamics, and the basic process of psychotherapy.

Altruism

When patients who have completed group therapy are asked to look back over it, they invariably credit other members as having been important in their improvement. Patients enter therapy demoralized and with a strong belief that not only are they unable to help themselves but that they have nothing of value to offer others. To learn that one is able to be useful to others is a refreshing experience: it encourages one to value oneself more, and it also dislodges one from a confining perch of morbid self-absorption.

The Corrective Recapitulation of the Primary Family Group

The group therapy situation resembles the early family in a number of ways, and patients have a tendency to re-experience old familial conflicts. However, the therapist constantly challenges maladaptive behavior patterns and does not permit them to freeze into the rigid impenetrable system that characterizes many family structures. Thus, there is not just a recapitulation but a *corrective* recapitulation of the primary family.

Development of Socializing Techniques

All therapy groups help patients develop social skills. Some groups do so explicitly by using such procedures as role playing, where members rehearse certain difficult social situations (for example, a job interview or asking for a date), while others offer constructive criticism. Other groups offer social-skills training implicitly through interpersonal feedback which offers members considerable information about maladaptive, "off-putting" social behavior. Members of long-term groups learn how to listen, to be responsive to others, to be less judgmental and more capable of experiencing and expressing empathy—skills that will be of great value in future social interaction.

General Principles of Inpatient Group Therapy

Imitative Behavior

Therapy group members often model themselves upon aspects of other members as well as of the therapist. Even if the modeling is short-lived, the process of trying out new behavior is an invaluable catalyst to *unfreezing*—that is, the dissolution of rigid patterns of behavior. Many less active group therapy patients are helped by *vicarious therapy*—through observing the therapy of other members who have a problem constellation similar to their own.

Catharsis

The open expression and release of affect is an important part of the group therapeutic experience. But it is a partial process; sheer ventilation in itself is rarely of lasting benefit. What is of great importance is that the group members learn *how* to express feelings and that the expression of feelings is not socially calamitous.

Existential Factors

The existential frame of reference in psychotherapy posits that, to a significant degree, anxiety and, hence, most psychopathology issue from the human being's confrontation with certain basic dimensions or "ultimate concerns" of existence: death, freedom (responsibility and willing), isolation, and meaninglessness.[5] Therapy groups deal with these themes explicitly, through the members' openly discussing and sharing their deep concerns, and implicitly through focusing on the process manifestations of existential concerns. To take one example, a group may exercise much therapeutic leverage by emphasizing responsibility assumption as it is manifested in the members taking responsibility for the functioning of the group and for each person's creation of his or her own role in the group. The ultimate concern of isolation, to take another example, is manifested in the group as patients grapple with loneliness and relationship. They learn, as I shall discuss shortly, not only what relationships can do but also what they cannot do. Relating intimately to others in the group will ameliorate loneliness but does not eliminate it; each individual must come to terms with the limits of relationship and learn to face the isolation that is inherent in existence.

Cohesiveness

Cohesiveness—the sense of "groupness," of being accepted, of being a valued member of a valued group—is the group therapy analogue of "relationship" in individual therapy. But cohesiveness is a broader concept and encompasses the patient's relationship not only to the therapist but to the other group members and to the group as a whole. It is the most universal of all the group therapy therapeutic factors; all therapy groups offer help to members by affording them the experience of belonging to a group. Most psychiatric patients, because of impaired interpersonal attitudes and skills, have had few intimate relationships, few opportunities for affective sharing and acceptance, and have generally had an impoverished group history. For these patients, the experience of sharing, of being accepted, and of successfully negotiating a group experience may be highly therapeutic.

Interpersonal Learning

The therapeutic factor of interpersonal learning is not a ubiquitous mechanism of change like cohesiveness: there are several types of group (for example, support groups of cancer patients, behavioral therapy groups, or inspirational groups like Alcoholics Anonymous or Recovery Incorporated) that do not engage this therapeutic factor. However, in groups that have as their aim the elucidation and the modification of interpersonal behavior, *this therapeutic factor is exceptionally potent. It is also complex and, of all the therapeutic factors, is the one most frequently misunderstood and underutilized in inpatient groups.* Hence I shall discuss it more fully than other factors.

Interpersonal learning is the group therapy equivalent of such individual therapy factors as self-understanding or insight, working through the transference, and the correctional emotional experience. Interpersonal learning involves the identification, the elucidation, and the modification of maladaptive interpersonal relationships.

To explain the rationale and the operation of this therapeutic factor, I must first describe three basic assumptions upon which it rests:

1. interpersonal theory
2. the group as a social microcosm
3. the here-and-now

Interpersonal theory.   First, let me establish that group therapy rests upon interpersonal theory. Basically, this theory posits that one's character structure is shaped by one's previous interpersonal relationships and that a patient's current symptoms are a manifestation of disordered interpersonal relationships. Individuals seek help with a wide array of complaints, but they have in common a major difficulty in establishing and maintaining gratifying and enduring relationships.

The language of group therapy is interpersonal. Each patient's complaint ultimately needs to be translated into interpersonal terms and then treated accordingly. For example, the interpersonal psychotherapy of depression is not based on treating depression: the therapist has no foothold, no leverage from that approach. The therapist instead examines the underlying interpersonal disorder (in depression it is frequently a disturbance of passivity, dependency, and catastrophic reactions to loss) and then treats the interpersonal problem accordingly.

The therapist's task in the group is to help the patient learn as much as possible about his or her distorted, disturbed interpersonal relationships and to alter them. But how does the group go about facilitating this process? How can a group of seven or eight members systematically investigate and alter each member's complex network of past and present relationships? Surely no therapy group has the time and patience for such an endeavor. To understand the interpersonal therapeutic endeavor, another concept is required.

The group as a social microcosm. The therapy group functions as a *social microcosm.* This concept states that, given enough time, one behaves *in the therapy group* very similarly to the way one behaves in one's outside social environment. Interpersonal maladaptive behavior that disrupts a patient's social adjustment is re-enacted as he or she interacts with others in the therapy situation. If, for example, one craves intimacy but attempts to attain it in such a demanding, ensnaring fashion that one finds oneself rejected and isolated in one's life, one will inevitably fall into the same pattern in the group. The patient who is, in life, self-effacing, or abrasive, or frightened of intimacy, or destructively competitive, will also be that way in the therapy group.

In other words, the part is reflective of the whole. In all therapy formats—group, individual, or family—therapists assume that the small piece of behavior that they witness in the therapy session is reflective of larger patterns of behavior. Although this principle is a key one in all forms of therapy, it assumes its richest form in the therapy group. Containing such a diversity of humanity (men and women, young and old, peers, competitors, authority figures, educated and uneducated, the wealthy and the poor, individuals from many walks of life), the group becomes a miniature social universe for each patient.

To summarize, the therapeutic factor of interpersonal learning is based on interpersonal theory which posits that psychopathology, regardless of its external symptomatic picture, has its source in disordered relationships with others. The patient suffers from disordered interpersonal relationships, and therapy consists of helping the individual develop adaptive, more gratifying interpersonal relationships. Furthermore, the group therapist assumes that the patient's maladaptive interpersonal patterns are re-enacted in the context of the therapy group. By helping each patient understand his or her patterns of behavior *in* the therapy group, the therapist helps the patient to understand broad patterns of interpersonal behavior in his or her outside social universe.

The here-and-now. These assumptions lead to the conclusion that the data required to illuminate the patient's life predicament is present in the therapy room, in the *here-and-now* group interaction. There is little need for the patient to provide the group with a detailed past history or a lengthy description of what has gone wrong in his or her life; much more accurate, "living" data emerge from observation of a patient's immediate interpersonal behavior in the here-and-now of the group. Furthermore, and this is a key point for therapeutic strategy, patients who correct maladaptive interpersonal patterns and risk new behavior in the here-and-now of the group, will ultimately transfer their learning to their outside lives.

It follows, therefore, that the group's major focus should be on the here-and-now, on the events that transpire right in the group therapy session. The primary task of the therapy group is shifted from an unrealistic task—that is, the solution of some "outside" problem—to an interior group task—that is, to helping each member learn as much as possible about the way he or she relates to every other member.

The here-and-now focus is so crucial in group therapy functioning that I shall discuss it at great length later (chapter 4), but it is important to note here that it is not only instrumental in facilitating the therapeutic factor of interpersonal learning but catalyzes other factors as well.

Consider, for example, cohesiveness. If a group is to be cohesive, its members must perceive it as effective: that is, they must believe that the group will enable them to accomplish their personal goals, and they must enjoy the activities of the group. A group focusing on the here-and-now, on its own interaction, is almost invariably a vital, cohesive group. There is nothing more deadening than a therapy group meeting in which a large group of people sit around unenthusiastically listening to one member discuss in great detail some aspect of his or her past or present life situation. Often the narrative is confused, generally it is inaccurate, and frequently it will have little meaning to the majority of other patients, especially to those who have had little opportunity to develop a close relationship with the narrator. At best, the listeners hope for a "taking turns" format: that is, they hope that in time their turn will come when they, too, will be allowed to present their life problems to the group for some group support or group solution. (Unfortunately, in an inpatient group with rapid turnover, the turn for many patients will never come.)

If the group focuses on the here-and-now, and the therapist has been explicit in informing the patients about why it is important to change interpersonal patterns, then members experience the group as relevant and effective. A group in which members continually express their observations of, and feelings toward, one another is a group in which no member of the group is very far from center stage. All members have the sense that they may be centrally involved at any moment in the group; and invariably the interactional group manifests a greater degree of patient interest, greater morale, better attendance, and, ultimately, far greater cohesiveness.

A here-and-now group also facilitates the development of social skills. Members obtain feedback and learn to see themselves as others see them. They discover, for example, what aspects of their behavior encourages others either to approach them and/or to avoid them. They learn that they have been unconsciously sabotaging themselves: that, though they wish very much to affiliate with others, their behavior has resulted in much unwanted isolation.

General Principles of Inpatient Group Therapy

Therapeutic Factors: An Overview

I have taken the group therapeutic process apart and discussed these eleven factors as though they were separate entities. Of course, they are not; they are intricately interdependent. Not only, as these last few paragraphs indicate, do the therapeutic factors facilitate one another, but different members of the same therapy group may value different factors. In fact, the same patient may value different factors at various stages of therapy.

Still, it is possible to make some generalizations about the comparative potency of the therapeutic factors in traditional long-term therapy. The factor that most successful group therapy patients deem most important is interpersonal learning in conjunction with catharsis and insight.[6] Patients acquire information about how they present themselves to others, begin to understand that their fixed interpersonal patterns are unrealistic in their present life situations, begin to discover previously unknown parts of themselves, and gradually try out new behavior. None of these steps are purely intellectual but are taken in conjunction with expression of affect and with a sense of being accepted by the group. Furthermore, patients discover that they, alone, must take ultimate responsibility for the way they live their lives. Thus, interpersonal-learning, catharsis, cohesiveness, and existential factors play the major role in the middle and the end stages of long-term group therapy; other factors less often cited by patients—such as universality, instillation of hope, and altruism—play a more important role in the formative stages of the group.

Note, too, that these factors develop over a long time. Often patterns of interpersonal behavior may become evident only very slowly. For example, an individual may be charming and generous early in a relationship, only to exploit others much later. Months may be required for the pattern to unfold, for the members to recognize and respond to it, for the protagonist to hear and accept the feedback, for one to understand some of the heretofore unknown sources of this behavior and gradually to experiment with new behavior. The entire pace of the group is measured; issues are worked through thoroughly and deliberately. Patients grow to know each other very well, and every nuance of behavior is examined. Termination is, of course, a major event. Leavetaking is hard and lengthy. Often many sessions are consumed by an examination of the dynamic issue raised by the act of terminating therapy.

Much more could be said about the basic principles of traditional group therapy. But my intent is not to give a full exposition but to offer an overview of traditional group therapy sufficient to serve as a backdrop for a consideration of the strategic modifications necessitated by the acute inpatient setting.

Clinical Setting of the Inpatient Group

However effective for outpatients, traditional group therapy is not effective for inpatients: *the contemporary acute psychiatric ward is a radically different clinical setting and demands a radical modification of group therapy technique.* Let me begin this discussion by examining the stark clinical facts of life that the inpatient group therapist must face:

1. There is considerable patient turnover. The average length of stay is one to three weeks. There is generally a new patient in the group almost every meeting.

2. Many patients attend the group meeting just for a single meeting or two. There is no time to work on termination. Some member terminates almost every meeting, and a focus on termination would consume all the group time.

3. There is great heterogeneity of psychopathology: patients with psychosis, neurosis, characterological disturbance, sub-

stance abuse, adolescent problems, major affective disorders, and anorexic nervosa are all present in the same group.

4. All the patients are acutely uncomfortable; they strive toward resolution of psychosis or acute despair rather than toward personal growth or self-understanding. As soon as a patients is out of an acute crisis, he or she is discharged.

5. There are many unmotivated patients in the group: they may be psychologically unsophisticated; they do not want to be there; they may not agree that they need therapy; they often are not paying for therapy; they may have little curiosity about themselves.

6. The therapist has no time to prepare or screen patients.

7. The therapist often has no control over group composition.

8. There is little therapist stability. Many of the therapists have rotating schedules and generally cannot attend all of the meetings of the group.

9. Patients see their therapist in other roles throughout the day on the ward.

10. Group therapy is only one of many therapies in which the patient participates; some of these other therapies are with some of the same patients in the group and often with the same therapist.

11. There is often little sense of cohesion in the group; not enough time exists for members to learn to care for or trust one another.

12. There is not time for gradual recognition of subtle interpersonal patterns, or for "working through," and no opportunity to focus on transfer of learning to the situation at home.

Goals of Inpatient Group Therapy

One of an inpatient group therapist's single most important acts is goal setting. The therapist must formulate goals that are consonant with the clinical conditions I have just described. There are two separate but parallel processes of goal setting. First, there is the silent process that occurs within the therapist's mind and provides him or her with the framework necessary for the construction of a plan of action for a particular patient and for the group as a whole. At the same time, the therapist deliberately helps each group member set explicit goals for individual work in the therapy group. In this section I shall discuss the therapist's internal, silent goal-setting process. In chapter 5, I shall consider the ways in which the therapist explicitly helps patients to formulate concrete goals in therapy.

I cannot overemphasize the importance of goal setting. Without appropriate goals, both therapist and patient drift aimlessly and anxiously through the therapy group session. The therapy group that pursues inappropriate goals is doomed to fail at the very outset. Earlier I described the goals of the psychotherapist working with neurotic patients in long-term traditional group therapy: that is, to relieve symptomatology and *also* to effect major changes in character structure. But for an inpatient group these goals are unrealistic, and inpatient group therapists who adhere to such ambitious goals rapidly become therapeutic nihilists and stamp themselves, or group therapy, as hopelessly ineffective.

Overly ambitious goals are not only ineffective but often anti-therapeutic. For example, a clinical report[7] described a twenty-six-year-old mother who was admitted with persecutory delusions that her family was under surveillance and in great danger. Her acute psychotic behavior was controlled well with psychotropic medication, and her psychotic behavior converted into an obsessive-compulsive concern about performing all of her household chores perfectly. When the group attempted to probe deeply into underlying dynamics (such as rage at her husband, early deprivation as a child, displacement of rage at her mother onto her husband, and so on), she became confused, and her psychotic thought disorder was exacerbated. The therapy group was far more helpful to her when it shifted tactics and offered support by reinforcing her obsessive-compulsive defenses.

What is required is a set of realistic goals—goals that acutely hospitalized patients can achieve in a sharply abbreviated time frame. But it is important to keep in mind that the goals of the acute inpatient group are *not* identical to those of acute inpatient hospitalization. Group therapists just as frequently make this error as they do the one of adopting long-term therapeutic goals. The goal of short-term psychiatric hospitalization on the contemporary inpatient unit is "to ameliorate the patient's problematic behaviors so that he can once again function outside the hospital."[8] The hospital ward has several effective modes of dealing with an acutely disturbed patient: for example, psychopharmacology, removal from noxious environmental pressures, alteration of self-destructive behavior, somatic therapies, milieu therapy, behavioral modification, relaxation therapy, provisions of limits and boundaries. Each of these therapeutic modes plays a role, but not all roles, in the patient's therapy. Group therapy is far less effective, for example, in rapidly reducing overwhelming anxiety than is psychopharmacology or biofeedback training or relaxation therapy. To set goals of amelioration of acute psychotic behavior for the small therapy group is unrealistic and will, almost certainly, result in the therapy group being, and being considered, ineffective.

So far I have considered inappropriate goals. What *are* reasonable expectations for the inpatient therapy group?

First, the ward staff has to be persuaded that psychotherapy has something to offer. Sometimes the ward staff concludes that since psychotic disorders have a genetic biological substrate, and since antipsychotic medication is widely effective, psychotherapy offers little more than an interesting way to pass the time. Yet, as I demonstrated in chapter 1, this conclusion is entirely unwarranted.

Consider this model which, despite its simplicity, may be helpful in providing a reasonable perspective on the role of psychotherapy. Let us suppose that an individual requires 100 points to be psychotic, and that two factors contribute to them: the genetic-biological substrate and the amount of stress experienced. Some individuals are unfortunate enough to have such heavy genetic-biological loading that the simple, irreducible stresses of everyday life are sufficient to precipitate psychosis. Most other individuals, however, may have some significant genetic-biological contribution, but it is only by virtue of considerable stress (emanating to a large degree from disordered, ungratifying, interpersonal relations) that they reach the (100-point) psychotic level. Psychotherapy, by helping one avoid and manage stress, can play a vital role in reducing one's propensity toward psychosis.

Engaging the Patient in the Twofold Therapeutic Process

A primary goal of the inpatient therapy group, and one that underlies many other goals, is to engage the patient in the therapy process. The therapist must keep in mind that the inpatient group experience is part of the twofold therapy process: *horizontal* (that is, a multifaceted therapy program on the ward) and *longitudinal* (that is, a post-hospital course of psychotherapy).

The Horizontal Process

Chapter 1 presents data that document the importance of patients' interaction. The small therapy group is a particularly effective instrument to facilitate these patient-to-patient relationships, especially among patients who are in the same group. The group may permit some patients to work out major disagreements. For example, roommates often may have tensions arising from close day-to-day living together. Other patients may work not on overt conflict resolutions but on difficulties that arise when they try to be intimate with others.

For example, one patient, Joan, spent most of her time on the ward reading in her room and emerged only for meals and mandatory ward activities. She rationalized this behavior by saying that her life as a high-level executive was extraordinarily harried and that her hospitalization offered her time, the first time in two years, simply to be alone and to read. Joan's major reason for hospitalization was her panic and fury over the threatened break-up of her marriage. In her therapy, however, it soon became apparent that the core issue in her marital difficulties was her fear and avoidance of intimacy. Thus, the setting of a goal for Joan of working on her difficulties in relating to other patients was doubly meaningful: it dealt with the core problem in her life and helped her to make far better use of the ward's therapeutic potential.

Another patient had tried to kill himself at the instructions of his auditory hallucinations. He, too, remained isolated from the rest of the ward patients because of his conviction that others would not tolerate his "crazy" thoughts. The small group task, then, was not to stop the voices but to help him deal more effectively with the consequences of his illness.[9] By sharing his experiences with the group, he soon disconfirmed his fear of ostracism and subsequently felt less oppressed by unnecessary, self-imposed isolation.

The Longitudinal Process

In chapter 1 and the appendix, I outline the evidence substantiating my conclusions that (1) brief hospitalization is effective only if coupled with effective aftercare therapy; (2) outpatient group therapy is particularly effective aftercare therapy; and (3) a successful inpatient group therapy program increases the likelihood that patients will participate in aftercare group therapy. Thus, an important goal of the inpatient group is to introduce patients to therapy and to provide a therapeutic experience so relevant, comfortable, and effective that they will elect to continue it.

Talking Helps

One elementary but important goal of the inpatient group is that patients simply learn that talking helps. They learn that unburdening and discussing their problems not only offers immediate relief but initiates the process of change. Through the therapeutic factor of universality, as I have said, one may learn that others are very much like oneself, that one is not unique, either in the wretched feelings or thoughts that one has, or in terms of the events of one's own life. To learn, often for the first time, that one's experience is, after all, human and shared by many others is enormously reassuring and one of the most potent antidotes to a state of devastating isolation.

Problem Spotting

A major goal of the inpatient therapy group is to help one identify problems in one's mode of relating to others. Although group therapy is not the most effective format to reduce anxiety, relieve profound depression, or ameliorate psychotic thinking and behavioral disturbances, it is the therapy setting *nonpareil*, to help individuals learn about maladaptive interpersonal behavior.

Note that inpatient group therapists must be content with "problem spotting." They help each patient to identify major problem areas and encourage each to work on these areas in the future, in post-hospitalization psychotherapy. In contrast to outpatient therapists, inpatient therapists do not have the luxury (or the gratification) of identifying major interpersonal problems, working through the meaning of these interpersonal symptoms with a patient, and then overseeing the process of change.

Consider this clinical situation, in a group that had established extremely explicit rules about the meeting starting on time and people not being able to come in late: A twenty-six-year-old patient, Mary, asked the therapist, a couple of minutes after the beginning of a meeting, whether she could go out and get a cup of coffee. The therapist shrugged off her request and mumbled that it was too late. A minute later, somebody commented that another member was on his way into the room, and Mary took this opportunity of asking again, since the group was waiting, if she could go out and get a cup of coffee.

The therapist focused at this point on process: that is, on what Mary's behavior told him about the nature of her relationships to others. The primary datum available was the therapist's great feeling of irritation. He commented to Mary that he felt really put in a bind by her request: on the one hand, he wanted her to have coffee and hated to play the mean, nay-saying adult; but, on the other hand, he was convinced that the rules about punctuality were good for the group. Did she know that she put him into such a bind? Did she know that she was asking him to treat her as a young child rather than as a twenty-six-year-old woman? "Perhaps," the therapist mused, "you do this to others as well. If so, mightn't this be an important issue for you to work on in therapy in the future?"

At this point a couple of other patients in the group said that Mary often put them, too, in the position of relating to her as if she were a young child. Mary acknowledged that it was indeed an important point; in fact, the departing message of her husband, who had recently left her, was that she had tried to make a daddy out of him. Mary's position was one of helplessness: she commented that she felt so out of control that she needed a daddy to take care of her. The therapist suggested that her formula was inverted: what seemed primary was her needing a daddy. Being "out of control," or veering toward being "out of control," was merely a mode (and an ineffective one, to judge from the therapist's reaction to her in the group) of locating and attracting a daddy.

That four- or five-minute interaction constituted the entirety of the work with Mary during that group session. And yet it was important work. The problem had been identified; it had been pointed out to the patient; others in the group helped Mary appreciate that it was a pervasive, important problem; she recognized its relevance in her current life crisis; the message was delivered to her in a sufficiently supportive, curiosity-evoking mode that she was motivated to continue work on this theme in her post-hospital psychotherapy.

John—a twenty-year-old, hallucinating, and delusional schizophrenic patient—provides another illustration of the group goal of problem spotting. The goal of John's inpatient group therapy was not the resolution of his thought disorder or the eradication of the hallucinations: that was primarily the task of antipsychotic medication. Where the therapy group could be useful was to help John recognize interpersonal problems that were fueling his discomfort and perpetuating his psychotic decompensation. John was a compulsive talker and exceedingly narcissistic. His continual interruptions and refusal to listen to others irritated the other patients and prompted them to avoid him whenever possible. The resulting isolation, of course, merely aggravated John's anxiety and thus deepened his psychotic decompensation.

An appropriate goal for John's therapy group was to help him understand that his behavior was maladaptive. The group therapists succeeded in this not through interpretation (John was far too stressed for that approach) but by prescribing roles for him in the group which taught him alternative, more selfless, modes of behavior. For example, they gave John the task of introducing new members to the group, of asking these members to tell something about themselves, of guessing how certain people in the group felt when they were interrupted or didn't get enough time to talk.

After a couple of weeks John's psychotic behavior diminished. At that point the therapists were able to help John see how his initial group behavior was self-destructive and how his current group behavior obtained for him the respect and attention he really wanted from others. The process was clear and relevant: John's identification of self-destructive behavior patterns was important problem spotting and constituted an entirely sufficient goal for his inpatient group therapy work.

Alleviation of Iatrogenic Anxiety

Another goal of small-group therapy is to help alleviate the anxiety connected with hospitalization. In addition to the primary dysphoria that exists anterior to, and necessitates, hospitalization, additional discomfort results from the hospital experience. Some discomfort issues from the general *process* of hospitalization, while other discomfort results from tension on a particular hospital ward.

First, consider the types of stress intrinsic to the process of hospitalization. Many patients experience great shame: hospitalization becomes a symbol of their failure to cope with life. Others are deeply concerned, often realistically, about the effects of hospitalization on their job status. They worry, too, about stigmatization: how will others—family members, friends, work associates, house mates—respond to them? Many patients have major economic problems which are aggravated by hospitalization.

Once on the ward, patients experience further dysphoria. They may be frightened by bizarre psychotic behavior on the part of other patients; they may have unrealistic expectations of the staff and thus be disappointed; they may be unsettled by the competition for staff attention; they may resent the acutely disturbed patients for consuming a disproportionate amount of staff time; they may be rattled by the endless staccato of admissions and discharges.

Another major source of patient anxiety is staff tension. Staff anxiety or unresolved staff conflict invariably takes its toll on the patient community. There is a demonstrably high positive correlation between intrastaff conflict and exacerbation of patient psychoses.[10] On the contemporary inpatient unit, staff tensions may run very high. There is, as I have said, much inherent frustration in working in a "revolving door" unit. Too often the ward staff members have little sense of being as fully therapeutic as they could be under less frenzied circumstances; they observe a large percentage of patients readmitted time and time again; often patients are unappreciative, since financial considerations necessitate premature discharge. There is often conflict and competition among the various professional disciplines as they vie for prestige, power, and recognition. And, of course, there are all the common countertransference problems. Staff members often feel helpless; they serve as vessels for projection and feel unjustifiably attacked by many patients; they find it difficult to deal with the manipulativeness and the splitting efforts of the many borderline patients on inpatient units.

Unfortunately these staff tensions are long festering: the contemporary inpatient unit has become so busy that it has lost sight of the importance of taking care of its own staff needs. I have seen many wards with rampant staff conflict and no existing vehicle for the staff to deal with these tensions. The staff T-group or support group has become, unfortunately, almost extinct.

Ideally, the therapeutic community meeting, not the small therapy group, is the place to work on the tensions intimately associated with hospitalization. In practice, however, the therapeutic community meeting is rarely used effectively for such purposes. The rapid patient turnover that leads to the instability of the inpatient group stability is even more problematic to the conduct of a large ward meeting. The patients feel threatened by the large number of people present in the community meeting; patients, because their hospital stay is too short to permit them to know and to trust the majority of the ward members, are unwilling to share much of themselves in a large ward meeting. The research cited in chapter 1, which examines patients' comparative evaluations of the helpfulness of various ward activities, demonstrates that generally patients consider the large community meeting on the contemporary ward one of the least helpful ward therapy activities.[11]

Obviously there is a great need for a creative reformulation of the large community meeting, but that is beyond the scope of this book. What is relevant here, however, is that the failure of the large community meeting to deal with these tensions leaves the small therapy group as the only suitable place to do so. This goal is an important one because frequently ward tensions can be so considerable that they derail the entire therapeutic process.

In small-group meetings, patients are not always aware of, or explicit about, their anxiety flowing from hospital events; often the group leaders must formulate these as sources of tensions for a patient. Therapists must make the assumption that major unsettling events on the ward invariably evoke dysphoria, and that the therapy group provides a forum for the discussion and dissipation of that dysphoria. A suicide attempt by one of the patients on the ward, a violent outburst, a transfer because of unmanageable behavior to another hospital, all of these evoke strong but not always expressed feelings. To help patients talk about these feelings may be an important goal of therapy, since it is a part of the general goal of helping patients understand that talking helps.

An illustrative clinical incident: Harold, a schizophrenic patient, was physically attacked by another patient on the ward who was immediately transferred to a locked unit. The group therapist noticed that Harold wore (and continued to wear for the next three days) the same shirt that had been torn in the attack, and, furthermore, that he moved his chair slightly out of the group circle as though he were courting an invitation into the group. In the small group Harold denied being upset by the incident and mused that it was curious that everyone else was so upset by it. The therapist persisted in his assumption that the incident was deeply upsetting; and eventually, the following day, Harold was persuaded to talk about the attack, his great fear of physical combat, and his strong feelings that there was too much sympathy for the attacker and too little for him, the victim. The therapeutic effect was excellent: Harold received the support he craved, and other members were able to discuss graphically their fears of physical assault.

In summary, appropriate goal setting is of crucial importance to the proper functioning of the small therapy group. Overly ambitious goals impair the effectiveness of the group and lower the morale of the therapist. Furthermore, the goals of the small group are *not* the same as the goals of short-term hospitalization. Some important and realistic goals for the small therapy group are: to engage patients in the therapy process (both horizontally and longitudinally), to help patients learn that talking helps, to spot problems, and to alleviate patients' anxiety associated with hospitalization.

Composition of the Small Inpatient Group

Psychiatric wards use two basic strategies to compose a therapy group. The first is the *team* approach, in which all patients are assigned, usually according to order of admission, to one of two or three teams, depending upon the size of the ward. All the patients on one team meet in a small therapy group. The second is the *level* approach in which a patient is assigned to a group according to his or her level of functioning: severely ill, psychotic patients are assigned to one group, and "higher-level" patients to another. Each of these approaches has its advantages and disadvantages.

The Team Group

The team small group is characteristically difficult to run. It contains a wide array of psychopathology, from psychotic, regressed patients to well-functioning borderline and neurotically depressed ones. Most therapists believe that, even from the team therapy group, patients should be excluded who—from all indications—will get nothing from it, will be unsettled by it, and/or will disrupt its functioning. Often a patient is too ill to come to the group for the first couple of days of hospitalization but, after medication has taken hold, is able to attend. Manic patients who are disruptive should be excluded as well as patients who are physically disruptive, very incoherent, or considerably brain damaged. Mute patients contribute little to the process, but it has been shown repeatedly that they absorb far more of the group than anyone supposes at the time. A patient's length of hospitalization is not a factor. Later I shall discuss that the therapist must consider the life of the group to be only a single session; many patients can benefit from attending only a single meeting.

Advantages of the Team Group

One important advantage of the team approach to composition is that it ensures that almost all patients are seen in groups. It provides the ward staff with considerable information about the mental status of each of the patients on the ward—information that should be communicated to the rest of the ward staff during rounds or nursing report. (Level group therapy meetings, as I shall shortly discuss, omit many patients. The contemporary practice on many psychiatric wards is to hold only the higher-level group meetings for better-functioning patients;

consequently the more acutely disturbed patients are often less known to the staff and receive no form of group therapy.)

Although acutely disturbed patients can distract and disrupt a therapy group meeting, their presence, at the same time, constitutes an advantage. Acutely disturbed patients create much disruption not only in the therapy group but on the ward at large. The small therapy group, especially with the demise of the community meeting as an effective forum, is the only possible place where social efforts may be made to ameliorate the disruptive behavior. In the therapy group the ward members can offer the disturbed patient constructive feedback, in carefully modulated doses, about the effects of his or her behavior on them. It is the task of the therapist to set the stage for that feedback; to create a supportive atmosphere; to help the feedback be perceived as supportive or educative rather than as attacking and punitive.

The small group is also a forum where the therapist can help the other members understand something about the experiential world of the acutely psychotic patient. For example, at one meeting a psychotic woman periodically stood up and shouted something inappropriate (for example, "you're pregnant," or "they'll kill us"). In each instance, the leaders of the group were able to help the rest of the group understand that this patient was responding out of anxiety and was reacting to frightening things that were being talked about in the group. One of the topics of the group that day had been the patients' concern about the possibility of a strike by the nursing staff. The discussion was unsettling to all the members but especially to that psychotic patient. The group thus could comprehend some previously incomprehensible, and therefore frightening, behavior. The more that patients are understood by one another, the less terrifying they become.

In the same meeting another psychotic patient suddenly shouted to two other patients, "Why don't you two get married?" The therapist, again, made sense of the incoherent communication by clarifying how much this patient was trying to help the others. Through her accepting, understanding, and gentle approach to the psychotic patient, the therapist provided excellent modeling.

Another way that the leader can facilitate the relationship between relatively intact members and relatively psychotic ones is to demonstrate that the latter have much of value to offer the group. For one thing, even the most acutely psychotic patients are generally able to offer accurate and often important observations about other members of the group. (They can do this much more easily and with far less risk than they can *receive* such feedback.) Thus, the leader can call upon such a patient to make observations about other members.

Psychotic patients, with their ready accessibility to primary process, can often express feelings, thoughts, and fantasies that other, more tightly defended patients may find reassuring, edifying, or liberating. The utterances of psychotic patients are often different only in degree from the typical mental processes of others. At some level, all patients harbor frightening, inchoate feelings and fantasies, and the ability of the more psychotic patients to identify and express these experiences may be more reassuring than frightening.

For example, in the first ten minutes of one meeting, several psychotic patients expressed considerable bizarre material. One patient talked about not really being there in the group, not really even being in her own body. Another talked about how obscene it was for her even to be talking to others in the group because she was too obscene a person to be in the company of others. One woman said to one of the male members that she liked the way that he was natural and very much himself, whereupon he burst into tears and told her that he loved her. Another person talked about feeling panicked by creepy feelings under her skin and wanting to cut herself to let the feelings out. Another woman talked of how her sense of herself was that she was a great wound stretching all the way down from her throat to her vagina, and how she longed for death as a respite. Despite the terrifying nature of this material, the session ended up being important for the members of the group, as they talked, for the rest of the meeting, about this bizarre material in a nonpsychotic fashion. One member, for example, said that she had always been afraid of the man in the group who had wept; but that seeing him weep made her feel much closer to him and made her realize how sensitive he was. Others in the group talked about their own feelings of depersonalization. Several talked about self-destructive feelings and shared episodes of death yearnings. The group ended up feeling close, cohesive, and—despite the content of the material—reassured by the experience of human bonding.

Disadvantages of the Team Group

The disadvantages of the team approach therapy group composition are far more readily apparent than are the advantages.

Despite the therapist's best efforts, such a groups is almost invariably characterized by considerable disruption. There are often outbursts from psychotic patients; some patients will be very restless and not able to sit still for the whole meeting. Frequently patients will have to leave the session. The comings and goings of members and the frequency of bizarre, incoherent remarks result in instability in the group. Patients who suffer from a lack of internal structure are often highly threatened by being thrust into a situation that seems to be out of control. It becomes very difficult for the therapist to impose a tight structure on the group and, at the same time, provide a level of work that is meaningful for all the patients in the group—both those on a higher level and those on a lower level of functioning.

Often it is impossible to find a level of work suitable for all patients: the leader either imposes so much structure that the work is too primitive and elementary for the better-functioning patients, or works with these latter patients and ignores the needs of the more disturbed ones. It is the rare therapist who does not choose the latter option; most therapists prefer to work with more integrated patients and to deal with more sophisticated issues—often issues that are closer to concerns in a particular therapist's own life. Consequently the therapist focuses largely upon those few patients in the group who are better integrated, and, for the most part, disregards the needs of the acutely disturbed patients. If the therapist focuses too extensively on the poorly functioning patients, the other patients will gradually resent the sicker ones, will devalue the group as not catering to their needs, and will soon invest little of themselves in the therapy process, often simply putting in an appearance.

Is there a way for the therapist to capitalize on the advantages of the team therapy group and to avoid its disadvantages? Indeed, there is. Almost all of the disadvantages can be avoided if the patients appreciate that the team therapy group does not constitute their *sole* form of group therapy. Patients will allow themselves to get what they can out of the team group, and not resent what they cannot get, if there is another vehicle of therapy available to satisfy their unmet needs. In other words, I advocate the use of *both* team and level therapy groups. But that's getting ahead of myself. Let me now turn to the characteristics, advantages and disadvantages of "level" therapy groups.

The Level Group

Many psychiatric wards offer two different types of level group—high and low.

The *lower-level group,* which is often referred to as a "support" or "focus" group, is provided for acutely psychotic patients. This group attempts to provide support and structure to help orient the patient to his or her temporal and spatial surroundings, to increase attention span, to facilitate socialization with the staff and other patients, and to enable the patient to take part in the ward program.

The better-functioning patients are assigned to a *higher-level group* which is primarily a "talking" psychotherapy group. This group offers an arena where considerable important work can be done. Patients often feel safer in this group than in the team group, learn to trust other members, and ultimately engage in greater self-disclosure than elsewhere in the treatment program. They identify problems to be addressed in post-hospitalization therapy and make important and therapeutic connections with other patients. In chapters 5 and 6, I shall present in detail clinical models of higher- and lower-level groups, respectively.

The ward staff generally assigns patients, shortly after admission, to one of these two groups. The assignments are based on observations made from the patient's first few hours on the ward and, if there is a team group, from the patient's behavior in its meeting. The assignment is not made solely on a psychotic-nonpsychotic basis. Some psychotic, actively hallucinating patients do well in the higher-level group. The triage is made on the basis of the type of therapy the patient needs: the more regressed, incapacitated, fragmented patient, who needs support, integration, and "sealing over," is assigned to the focus group; and the patient who is capable of verbally investigating his problems, to the higher-level group.

Some wards have attempted to provide an intake group for new members, who attend it for a few meetings before being assigned to a higher- or a lower-level group.[12] Turnover on most wards, however, is too rapid for that procedure to be feasible. Other clinicians have suggested several different "graded" groups to which a patient is assigned according to his or her precise level of functioning. But most clinicians find this measure impractical: the wards are too small, and their pace too busy; the definition of "level of functioning" is too imprecise; and the techniques of leading groups is too crude to warrant more than two level groups.

Another disadvantage of having groups of several different levels on a ward is the danger of instilling among the patient population a sense of being graded and evaluated by the staff. That issue does not generally arise with only two levels of groups. Patients sort themselves in a self-evident fashion. Severely psychotic patients are so obviously distressed and in need of heroic support that they are clearly identifiable by the entire patient community. Furthermore, severely psychotic patients rarely press for a more demanding group experience.

Often staff members have awkward feelings around group assignment which remain covert on most psychiatric wards. On one ward that I visited, the staff thought that the patients believed that the groups were really composed on the basis of age: that is, that in the lower-level group were the younger patients. This was obviously not the case, and frequently the age distribution in the two groups was almost entirely reversed.

When I first introduced a lower-level group for severely psychotic patients on a ward where there had previously been none, the staff feared that it would be seen as the group for backward "dummies" on the ward. This prediction was not fulfilled. Aside from someone calling it a "sandbox" group in the first week, the group was well accepted by the patient community. After only six weeks the lower-level group was perceived as an integral and highly valued part of the ward program. In most cases, patients recognize that some of their company are distinctly more disorganized than others; and for the staff to deny this is to undermine the patients' reality testing.

The name and description of the groups may facilitate ward acceptance. The staff usually refers to the higher-level group as a "psychotherapy group," and labels the lower-level one a "focus" or a "structured" or a "communication" therapy group; the latter is described by the staff as a group that attempts to facilitate communication and is designed for those patients who are confused, have relatively short attention spans, and profit more from a structured short group meeting rather than from a relatively unstructured group which freely explores and analyzes feelings.

Occasionally there will be patients who fall between the two groups and can benefit from neither. They are not psychotic but they cannot function in a higher-level therapy group: for example, patients who are exceedingly resistive, non-insightful, or psychopathic.

Advantages and Disadvantages of the Level Group

The advantages and disadvantages of the level group are the reverse of those of the team group. The major advantage of the level group is that it provides a more specific form of therapy. The therapist can pitch the group at a level appropriate for most or all the patients.

The lower-level group provides severely psychotic patients with a safe, supportive, highly structured environment. Moreover, it provides them with an experience of success. In the team meeting, psychotic patients are often unable to participate in the group task, are frequently disruptive, and perceive the other members to be irritated and impatient with them. The lower-level group is specifically geared to the level of functioning of psychotic patients and to their psychological defensive structure. The group is less challenging and is so structured that patients experience themselves as successfully engaging in the group task.

The higher-level group meeting is far more stable than the team meeting. Since there are no severely psychotic patients, the group is less disrupted, there are fewer bizarre outbursts and comings and goings. The attention span of each patient is longer, and the group is thus able to meet for a longer period. (Team groups generally meet for forty-five to sixty minutes; higher-level groups may comfortably meet for seventy-five minutes, whereas lower-level groups should not meet for longer than forty-five minutes.)

The level groups are generally experienced as more pleasant, relevant, and supportive than the team groups and consequently often assume the larger role in the goal of encouraging patients to pursue aftercare therapy.

The *disadvantage* of level-group therapy (if it is the only group program offered on the ward) is that it may increase the divisiveness on the ward. All the patients, the better integrated and the more psychotic ones, must live together on the ward, and some forum is required where ward tensions may be addressed. Not infrequently an acutely disturbed patient may create considerable antagonism or apprehension. If there is no group where the patients may learn to set limits, understand, and learn to communicate with the severely disturbed patients, then the ward atmosphere may be so bristling and unsupportive as to vitiate much of the therapeutic work.

The Team versus the Level Group

Two research projects conducted on the Stanford University psychiatric inpatient unit provide some interesting corroboration for the conclusion that the level and the team therapy groups perform different but important functions.[13] In the first project,[14] fifty-one consecutive patients were asked to evaluate the importance of eleven ward therapeutic activities, including the daily team groups and the level group (at the time of this research, a group was offered only for the better-functioning patients; no level group was provided for psychotic patients). All fifty-one patients attended the team groups; and thirty patients, the higher-level group.

The overall evaluation of the thirty patients who attended both groups showed that the level group was rated the second most important (of eleven ward activities) treatment modality (closely following individual therapy with their psychiatrist), and the team group was rated fourth. In summary, the results showed that *both groups were deemed important, and that different patients valued different groups.* The more severely impaired patients valued the team group, which was pitched more at a level for psychotic patients. The better-integrated patients valued the level group more—but *also* valued the team group (see appendix [N] for details).*

Shortly after this research project, the ward started a lower-level group; and eighteen months later, a consecutive small sample of patients (N = 12) who attended both groups (that is, team group and lower-level group) was asked to perform the same evaluation of ward activities.[15] The results were remarkably analagous to those of the first project. The patients valued *both* groups highly: the level therapy group was rated the second most valuable ward activity (closely following individual psychotherapy) and the team therapy group third (see appendix [S] for details). Another team of researchers studied patients' responses to homogeneous schizophrenic groups and found that the patients recorded considerable satisfaction, and that there was much therapeutic work as measured objectively (by the Hill International Matrix).[16]

The Stanford project also asked patients to indicate *how* each of the groups had been useful to them—that is, the relative importance of the various therapeutic factors.[17] The results demonstrated that patients experience different therapeutic factors operating in the higher-level and the team groups. For example, the members of the higher-level group rated "interpersonal learning" as the most important factor and "self-understanding" as also highly important. The same patients rated these two factors as far less important in the team group and instead emphasized such factors as universality and catharsis. Another project studied the therapeutic factors operating in lower-level, homogeneous schizophrenic groups, and reported similar results: the patients valued catharsis, universality, altruism, and cohesion and reported little help from such factors as insight or advice giving.[18]

*One diagnostic subgroup (the schizophrenic patients) rated the team therapy group as more effective than the level group, and patients with a major affective disorder rated the two fairly closely. It was the more verbal, psychologically minded patients (particularly the borderline ones) who rated the higher-level group as significantly more effective than the team group.

In a debriefing interview,[19] the patients compared the team and the level groups and commented that the former more often floundered, went off into many tangents, and was often too unstructured and too easily disrupted by highly disturbed patients. At the same time these patients valued the team group because it was warm and comfortable and gave the ward members a chance to sit down together and learn to know the people with whom they had to live. Patients valued the structure and the consistent interpersonal focus of the higher-level group; they recognized it as fast moving, hard working, and rewarding but occasionally too intense and demanding.

Group Attendance: Mandatory or Optional?

It is common clinical practice to make groups mandatory for patients on an inpatient unit. This is especially important in heterogeneous team groups and in the lower-level homogeneous groups. The clinical facts of life are that, if these groups were not mandatory, a significant proportion of patients would not attend. Patients who are withdrawn, frightened, depressed, hopeless, or drowsy because of medication, would, given a choice, opt to remain in their rooms, and an effective ward program would not be feasible.

Wards have different practices about recruitment. On most wards, the staff members will remind patients in community meetings of group assignments and, if necessary, round up the designated patients prior to the group meeting. Some wards list group assignments on a blackboard; other large wards use loudspeaker systems to remind patients of the hour of a group meeting and to specify which patients go to which group.

There is, in my opinion, a great deal to be said for making optional, rather than mandatory, the level group for better-functioning patients. (I shall discuss the advantages of optional attendance in detail in chapter 5.) If the group is run effectively, almost all patients who can benefit from the level group will attend with much regularity. If the ward places a high value on the group program, patients who are, in fact, sincerely interested in doing something about their mental health, gradually assimilate the ward values and soon have a difficult time justifying to themselves their failure to attend.

Every ward should, in my opinion, offer *both* a higher- and a lower-level group. In practice, however, some wards offer only a higher-level group; and, if the group is optional, occasionally patients who are too disturbed for the group will appear at a meeting. The group therapist must know the patients well (for this reason, one or both of the co-therapists should be a member of the full-time staff) and be able to make a rapid decision about whether a patient should be permitted to attend the meeting. The judgment should be made primarily according to whether the patient will interfere with the conduct of the group in any significant way. Highly disturbed patients who are not likely to be overtly disruptive may gain from the group purely by vicarious therapy. Patients who are distressed, who obviously will not benefit from the group, and who will interfere with its work (for example, heavily medicated patients who have difficulty staying awake, manic patients, organically impaired patients) should be asked to leave.

Rapid Patient Turnover: Implications for the Therapy Group

Frequency of Meetings

One of the unalterable facts of clinical life in the inpatient therapy group is the rapid turnover of membership. The average hospital stay in most acute units is one to two weeks. That means that a twenty-bed ward will have approximately one to two discharges and admissions every day. The inpatient therapy group, too, will rapidly change in composition, and there is virtually no way around this awkward fact. In hundreds of daily group meetings on an inpatient ward, I have rarely had the identical group composition for two (and almost never for three) consecutive meetings. Almost invariably, there will be a new member, or an old member has left. Nor can one ever expect any consistency in the turnover pattern since there is much variation around the mean hospital stay. The group therapist will have many patients for only a single session and also a few who may stay in the group for several weeks.

As I stated in chapter 1, there is only one logical clinical answer to this problem of membership turnover: to hold meetings as frequently as possible. If, for example, a group meets only twice or thrice a week, there will be such an enormous change of membership from one session to the next that the group can develop no sense of a separate group identity and no sense of continuity of the work culture. If the group meets five times weekly, the disruption created by membership turnover is not abolished, but it is minimized. Indeed if staff scheduling would permit it, there is much to recommend having a group meet seven days a week. (Often inpatient units fail to provide any therapeutic program on weekends.)

For three years, I once led an inpatient group that met four times a week, Monday through Thursday. A predictable sequence occurred in that group: The Monday meeting was tentative. On Tuesday and Wednesday the group gradually increased in intensity, and by Thursday the group was hard working, solid, and cohesive. Then came the three-day break; and by the following Monday, the group had slipped back to a tentative, testing, "Can we trust one another here?" culture. The sequence was so predictable that one could guess the day of the week by observing the group meeting.

In chapter 1, I suggested that one reason many contemporary wards do not hold group therapy meetings with sufficient frequency is that several professional disciplines actively compete for the opportunity to provide therapy groups; a compromise is reached by offering a large number of specialty groups, each of which meets once or twice a week. Specialty groups (such as sexual education or dance, art, or movement therapy) offer valuable assistance to many patients and enrich the therapeutic program. But if they are offered in lieu of daily therapy groups, then the group therapy program will produce an unfortunate sense of "scatter" and fail to provide a safe and consistent milieu for the work of therapy.

My recommendations for a comprehensive group therapy program are that two daily groups be offered for each patient: one team group (45 to 60 minutes) and one level group (the lower-level group lasting 45 minutes; the higher-level group, 60 to 75 minutes). If the ward is so understaffed that daily team and level groups cannot both be offered, *I recommend that daily higher- and lower-level groups be held.* In addition, specialty groups (the type depending upon the training and special interests of the staff) may be offered daily, especially during evenings and weekends.

Effect of Rapid Turnover on the Process of the Meeting

The rapidly changing membership of the group has some important implications for the therapist's basic strategy and tactics. I will discuss this in detail in chapter 3 but, for now, will underscore a few basic points.

First, the leader can, by increasing the frequency of the meetings, ensure that there will be a cluster of culture bearers who may help to provide a consistent, safe, trusting group atmosphere. But there is so much turnover of membership that therapists cannot assume that they can work through any particular theme with a patient in a subsequent meeting. Hence, therapists have to develop a new psychological temporal set: no longer can they view the life of the group in years, months, or even weeks. Instead, *the entire life of the group is a single session.* This temporal frame has, of course, major implications for therapist technique: the therapist must develop a sense of urgency, be active and efficient, and do as much in each session for as many patients as possible.

The rapid turnover is highly unsettling to therapists, especially since their formal group therapy training was based on stable groups: either long-term group therapy (where a constant circle of members settle in for a long duration) or brief "closed" forms (with a set number both of members and of meetings) of group therapy with stable memberships. It is, however, illuminating to study the *patients'* attitudes toward rapid turnover: the "revolving door" therapy group format may be far less disturbing to patients than to therapists. In a debriefing interview in the Stanford research project, fifty-one patients were asked how they felt about the rapid turnover in membership and the brief duration of their group therapy (see appendix [N]).[20] The overall results of this inquiry indicated that patients were less troubled by these factors than the researchers expected. For many patients, the inpatient therapy group was their first therapy group experience, and they had no long-term stable group therapy with which to contrast it unfavorably.

A minority of patients cited the expected drawbacks of rapid membership turnover. The group seemed unstable; new members entered daily; and patients often were cautious about trusting strangers with important personal material and did not feel connected to everyone in the group. They could not test out new behavior that they had learned in previous sessions, because they were not certain they could rely on favorable reactions from the new members. Many felt that the daily introduction and orientation of new patients wasted valuable time in the group, and that new members often slowed the group down to a more elementary level.

But these complaints were voiced by only a minority of the patients. A surprising number of patients alluded to distinct advantages of the inpatient therapy group format! Many gratuitously commented that the limited amount of time available increased their sense of urgency and provided them with a greater impetus to work harder and in a more concentrated and efficient manner. Some patients commented that seeing members leave continually increased the pressure on them to do something for themselves quickly. (It is well known that in a long-term therapy group the termination of a patient generally evokes, in the remaining patients, feelings of being left behind and increases the pressure on them to work more actively. In a short-term therapy group it appears, then, that the same dynamic operates.)

Some patients commented that the constant introduction of new members made for a sense of novelty, with new ideas and a wider, more interesting cross-section of reactions; the group never bogged down. The newcomers also provided the older patients with an opportunity to help others and a forum where they could practice important social skills with strangers. Other patients commented that the brief therapy format permitted them to see dramatic changes in a large number of patients over the few days of group therapy, and thus inspired hope in them and greater confidence in the efficacy of the therapeutic procedure.

A few patients remarked that the short duration of therapy produced a sense of personal regret—regret for not having used the group as well as they might have or as others did. With this regret came a resolve to use their next therapy modality more effectively. Many patients mentioned that it was painful to see so many individuals with whom they had developed a close relationship leave the group after only a few days. Nonetheless, the repeated sense of loss helped them to face and to deal with the various losses in their own lives. This is not an unimportant theme; the majority of patients entering the hospital are

General Principles of Inpatient Group Therapy

attempting to cope with some acute real or threatened loss in their lives.

Some inpatients, who had also been in long-term outpatient group therapy, made a rather striking response when asked about brevity of therapy on the inpatient unit. They pointed out that *brief* is a relative term! If one lives twenty-four hours a day with members of the group, then—even though therapy may last only a couple of weeks—the "duration" of therapy and the intensity of the experience may equal that of once-weekly psychotherapy over several months. A great deal of group therapy takes place outside of the confines of the group room. Work that has been started in the therapy group meeting is continued outside, as patients use the impetus of the group work to continue breaking down barriers between themselves and other patients.

Even with rapid turnover, still an "in-group" cadre of patients does develop. The therapist must not allow that core to exclude the new members. Attention has to be given to the assimilation of newcomers. Occasionally group members will attend to that, but generally it remains the therapist's task. Often groups may exclude new members by referring to the previous meeting (for example, a patient might report that the feedback given to her yesterday had been very useful in her meeting with her husband later that day). In such instances the therapist must take care to include the new members by, for example, simply checking with them to ascertain whether they understand what is happening and by asking older members to fill them in. This method may be tedious, but the assimilation of new members is imperative. If neglected, it will result in group fragmentation.

A clinical illustration: In a Thursday meeting, Don finally, after several days in the group, revealed his personal tragedy. For eighteen years he had had an exceedingly close homosexual love affair with a man who had suddenly died of a coronary one month before. The depth of his loss, and his shame and rage at the invasion of his privacy by the police (who for a time suspected suicide or homicide), was extraordinarily painful and had precipitated Don's deep depression. He had never in his life told anyone about his homosexuality or about his love affair. His revelation to the group was therefore momentous—a first-time disclosure; and the group's response to him was profoundly reassuring. The other members not only accepted and supported him but empathized as well, by commenting, "You must have loved him very deeply." Don was moved, grateful, and eager to pursue his work in the group.

The group did not meet on Friday or on the weekend. When it reconvened on Monday, two new members were present— one of whom was very needy, and the other highly judgmental and abrasive. Don tested the waters and searched in vain for the wonderful moment he had experienced in the previous meeting. Instead, the group atmosphere was defensive and, at times, acrimonious, especially the interaction involving the two new patients.

The leader's task in that meeting was complex. He had to aid in the assimilation of new members and at the same time provide massive support to Don, who had entrusted the group with so much at the previous meeting. The proper strategy involved labeling the atmosphere in the group that Monday and contrasting it with Thursday's group (which was then briefly described for the new members). The therapist suggested that much anger was present and directed at the new members, not because of who or what they were, but simply *because they were there*, because the group was not the same, and because Don and the group could not recapture the essence of the previous meeting. As the meeting developed, two events transpired: the new members, no longer unaccountably resented, were allowed into the group; and the idea of the lost, never to be regained, moment of the previous meeting facilitated further important work by Don and by others on the theme of loss.

The continually changing membership does, of course, make

it difficult for long-term patients to work through major problems. Often there must be a "backing up," an introduction and orientation of new members, a repetitive teaching of basic social skills, of how to give and receive feedback, of the difference between personal and impersonal behavior or between thinking and feeling. Thus, the occasional very long-term patient on the acute inpatient ward may find that he or she reaches a point of diminishing returns in the group.

The therapist must try to help patients benefit from what the group does have to offer rather than to allow them to frustrate themselves attempting to mold the group into something it cannot be. Even though "working through" is not possible in the inpatient group, a long-term patient may find it advantageous to describe a problem time after time to the newer members. These repeated restatements constitute a form of desensitization and eventually enable the one to think about one's life situation with less pain and to share it with others more freely. By the time a patient has described a deeply personal situation (that is, sexual assault, marital separation, the death of someone close) for the fifth or sixth time, the patient has gradually become more comfortable with that situation and is more likely to discuss it with other significant people in his or her life environment.

Size

Most clinicians prefer to have a group of between six and ten members—large enough so that there is sufficient interactional material to energize the group and yet not so large that there will not be enough time to encourage the participation of every member. Periodically, however, there may be wide fluctuations in size. At times the group may fall to as low as three members, but the very small meeting may, on a periodic basis, be very successful. Even though there is a very small group present on a particular day, it is good clinical practice to hold the meeting as designated. Remember that it is the therapists, not the patients, who are more often distressed about the small group size; patients often welcome a small group, knowing that they will receive more personal attention in it.

Other Differences between Inpatient and Outpatient Groups

Thus far I have emphasized two major clinical facts of life on an inpatient unit—the brief duration of therapy and the wide range of psychopathology—and discussed how these factors necessitate major modifications in traditional group therapy technique. There are still other less dramatic, but nonetheless significant aspects of the inpatient clinical setting that demand further modification of technique. I shall scan these factors all at once and then discuss each one separately.

1. The outpatient therapy group is generally an independent therapy entity. The inpatient group is not: it exists as part of a larger treatment system; events occurring elsewhere in the system may significantly influence the process of the group.

2. Traditional rules about confidentiality must be modified for the inpatient group.

3. Patients in an outpatient group generally have little contact with one another between meetings. Members of inpatient groups live together, share other types of therapy experience, and interact continually with one another between sessions.

4. The inpatient group therapist has access to considerably more information than that supplied by the patient.

5. Patients see the therapist of the inpatient group in other roles at other times during the day.

6. The severity of distress colors the group experience: hospitalized patients are more deeply troubled, desperate, demoralized, and nihilistic and are more often bereft of ordinary sources of environmental support.

The Inpatient Therapy Group: Its Relationship to the Rest of the Unit

The outpatient therapy group functions usually as an independent entity. Generally the members are strangers who come together only for one to two group meetings a week. Occasionally they share some overlapping membership; for example, they may all be patients at the same clinic, they may have been in other therapy groups together in the past, they may have had the same individual therapist, or they may currently all be in therapy with the same individual therapist. Often subgroups will form within the larger group: dyads or larger numbers of patients may meet outside the specified group therapy hours. But, as a rough rule of thumb, the less the subgrouping, the easier is the group to lead.

The inpatient group, on the other hand, never functions as an independent entity. It has a dense, complex network of connections with the larger inpatient unit in which it is imbedded. The staff of the inpatient unit also constitutes a complex system, consisting of a large number of groups to more than one of which each staff member is likely to belong: for example, medical versus nursing staff, professional versus nonprofessional, male versus female, high salary versus low salary, black versus white, psychiatric residents versus the clinical faculty, departmental versus hospital administration, nursing versus social service. These overlapping groups sometimes work well together; often, however, they do not, and they generate considerable friction on the ward.

The tensions of the inpatient unit are often evident in the small therapy group. In fact, one clinician referred to the small group as a "milieu biopsy" and provided the following clinical illustration:[21] A thirty-five-year-old asthmatic patient was part of a small inpatient therapy group but sat outside the group circle and near the door. Her reason for this was her fear that the cigarette smoke in the room would accentuate her asthma. Even when the group members stopped smoking, she remained outside the group, and the group therapists placed no pressure on her to become more of a member of it. Because group attendance was mandatory, she continued to come to the meeting, but the staff was singularly ineffective in helping her work in the group.

An examination of the ward system cast some illumination on this in-group event. Some months previously the medical director had left and had not yet been replaced by a permanent successor. Meanwhile the chairman of the psychiatry department, who was perceived by the ward staff as unfriendly to the ward, announced that the ward would begin to operate as a "psychosomatic" service. The staff felt highly threatened by this announcement; many of them felt that they no longer had the skills to deal with the medically ill patients.

Consequently the asthmatic patient personified the staff's dilemma. For one thing, staff members were uneasy about the patient's medical status and were fearful of precipitating an asthmatic attack. Furthermore, they displaced, onto this psychosomatic patient, many of the negative feelings they had toward the departmental chairman and acted out their resistance against him through the group therapy activities.

Another clinical example of the group as a "milieu biopsy" involves a group that was hostile and attacked one patient in particular because of her overly demanding attitude. Attempts to understand the dynamics of this group as an independent system were fruitless. But when the small group's context— that is, the larger ward system—was examined, the particular events of the meeting could be clearly understood. The ward had an unusually difficult weekend because the unit was understaffed, and there had been many new admissions requiring considerable nursing care and diverting attention from the older patients. The small-group meeting bore much of this tension, and the group scapegoated one patient who was the recipient of the resentment and frustration felt toward the many new patients and toward a staff perceived, unaccountably, as unwilling to provide for the patients' needs.[22]

Every inpatient unit goes through periods of demoralization. Often it is difficult to delineate the reasons with great clarity; generally it is a combination of factors, some relating to the patient ward composition and some to staff morale. Occasionally there is an influx of unmotivated, passive patients who sap the ward staff's energy and provide little gratification. In addition, the staff members may experience burnout or considerable tension among themselves. During these phases the small therapy group will often reflect this resistance to work. It is important that the group therapists apprise themselves of the state of the ward before they begin to change their group techniques in any radical fashion or to doubt their effectiveness.

There are other occasions when the patient community is in great conflict with the ward staff and attempts to "split" the therapists, to play one off against the other. At times, during such occasions, the small group (especially if led by a consultant who is not part of the full-time staff) may be highly lauded by the patients as a mode of criticizing the remaining ward staff. The group therapist will, during these times, hear comments to the effect that the small therapy group is the only useful function on the entire ward or that the group therapist ought to play a more active role in other ward activities.

Patients are exquisitely sensitive to events on an inpatient unit, and massive patient resistance to the ward therapeutic program may be generated by any of a large number of events: acutely disturbed patients on the ward who require large proportions of staff time; the presence of disruptive manic patients; the admission of several "repeaters" (whose presence often undermines a patient's faith in the staff); the failure of the staff to meet unrealistic expectations may be unsettling to patients; the presence of "splitting" borderline patients who mobilize the anger of the patients toward the staff; the obvious failure of the staff in the treatment of some patients—as evidenced by a suicide attempt on the ward or a patient's being transferred to a chronic institution.

Though the small group may reflect ward tension, it is not the task of the small group to heal these tensions. The ward must provide other forums for such work (such as therapeutic community meetings, staff meetings, staff "T-groups," patient planning groups, or "burnout" workshops). The small inpatient group is most effective if the ward system is in good repair and the group may address itself to what it does best—the goals delineated earlier in this chapter.

The group leaders' motivation is obviously highly influential. Are the leaders disgruntled psychiatric residents who are forced to lead groups as part of their duties on their clinical rotation? Are they perceived to be interested primarily in making money? Is a leader a senior clinician who is using the group for training of the student observers or for research purposes? In chapter 1, I described a hospital ward on which the groups were led by a sensitive but untrained clergyman—an individual who had been appointed to lead the groups by the patients' referring physicians. All the nurses on the unit agreed that this group leader had been selected because he constituted no threat to the referring physicians: there was little possibility of his "seducing" patients away from them. If the nurses felt this so strongly, surely some derogatory messages must have been transmitted to the patients.

The relationship of the therapy group to the individual therapy program is extremely important. In an ideal situation both individual and group therapy can be offered daily to the patient; and, to the extent possible on a busy ward, they should enhance each other. Some of the time in individual therapy should be devoted to working through patients' resistances to group participation and to helping them explore their relationships with other members of the group. In a reciprocal fashion, the therapy group should spot problems and open up areas that the patient can investigate in depth in individual therapy.

Some inpatient wards are organized in such a way that individual therapists prescribe which activities their patients attend, including group therapy meetings. My experience has been that this invariably proves to be an unsatisfactory model: it disrupts and undermines the operation of the ward group therapy program. The ward program must have primacy; and although the counsel of the individual therapist should be sought, it must be the ward team which makes the decision about which aspects of the program may be inappropriate for a particular patient.

To be avoided at all costs is the situation where group and individual therapy are perceived as competitive. For example, the individual therapist who schedules individual sessions without taking into consideration the ward group program, may need to call one of his or her patients out of a therapy group meeting for an individual session. Obviously, as I have said, this practice is disruptive and demoralizing for the group and conveys the message that group therapy is a relatively unimportant activity. A ward with a well-constructed therapeutic program must communicate to the individual therapist what hours are available for individual therapy and convey also the message that certain hours, especially the group therapy hours, are inviolable.

Not only do the values of the ward and the ward atmosphere influence the events and dynamics of the small-group meeting, but the reverse is true as well: the events of the small-group meeting may have a significant influence upon the atmosphere of the larger unit. Sometimes the small therapy group evokes powerful feelings in the members—feelings that need to be integrated during the remainder of the day. The group leader who is not a member of the full-time ward staff must communicate the major issues raised in the group to the ward staff—in either a written or, preferably, an oral report.

On wards with more than one therapy group, an arbitrary assignment of some patients to one group and some to another may disrupt the cohesion of a subgroup of patients which has formed naturally on the ward.[23] This disruption may have repercussions upon the patterns of socializing among the patients during the day. Often pressure may be put upon the ward staff to reassign patients so that those in the subgroup may all belong to the same therapy group. Generally speaking, this pressure should be resisted, since the presence of a closely knit subgroup or clique within a larger therapy group is generally disruptive.

In summary, the small group on the inpatient unit does not act as an independent entity; its functioning is intricately interwoven with those of the entire psychiatric ward. The two are interdependent: the dynamics of each influences the dynamics of the other. Furthermore, one can learn a great deal about each system through a thorough knowledge of the events and dynamics of the other.

Confidentiality

The rules about confidentiality differ in the inpatient group situation from those in the outpatient group. In the latter, strict confidentiality must always be established. During pre-group interviews with each patient, the therapist generally states this explicitly by commenting to the effect that "just as it is important for strict confidentiality to be maintained between individual therapist and patient, so is it equally important for the therapy group as a whole." If members of a therapy group believe that their revelations will be repeated to other unknown figures, the necessary trust and freedom to disclose will never develop. In my experience of over twenty years of leading outpatient groups, the issue of confidentiality has rarely raised problems; I have rarely seen violations of this pact.

General Principles of Inpatient Group Therapy

Some outpatient groups may modify the confidentiality rule to the extent that it is considered permissible for members to discuss some events of their therapy with a spouse or a very close friend. But in these instances the group is generally careful to insist that the individual talk about his or her *own* experience in the group, not about the experience of others, and never reveal, under any circumstances, the name of another person.

In the inpatient group, it is not possible to maintain the same rules of confidentiality; and an entirely different pact must be established. The events of the small group must be communicated to the rest of the ward staff and to the individual therapists as well. The group membership changes every day. Patients who are not present during a meeting in which one patient reveals a great deal will have to be filled in the following day. Furthermore, there are often observers watching the group who are generally other members of the ward team.

Still, in order to develop the trust necessary for effective therapy, it is essential for patients to be able to rely upon professional confidentiality. Thus, in inpatient groups, confidentiality must still exist but with a different *boundary.* Confidential material revealed in the small group remains confidential, but to the *whole unit,* not to the small group alone. All group disclosures are the property of the entire ward. In fact, it is not uncommon for small-group members to use the group as a means of communicating difficult things to other members of the ward staff. For example, in one meeting a patient discussed her homosexuality and stressed that she was fearful that she would frighten other people away. In particular, she emphasized that she was greatly comforted by hugs from staff members or other patients and was fearful that the fact of her homosexuality would cause others to keep their distance from her. Her revelation in the small group was thus a communication to patients and ward staff who were not present in the group but whom, she was certain, would be informed of her concerns.

Contact between Members Outside of the Therapy Group

Socializing outside the group and "subgrouping" have been called the Achilles' heel of group therapy. In outpatient groups, subgrouping may disrupt the work of the group by interfering with its primary task: the open and deep analysis of the interpersonal relationships between each member and every other member, including the therapists. If a dyad or a small clique of members form friendships outside the group, they may begin to value these friendships more than they value the work of the therapy group. These members are then reluctant, in the formal therapy group meetings, to "betray" confidences with which they have been entrusted in subgroup discussions. Such withholding can become so pervasive as to make the effective work of the therapy group grind to a halt.

Subgrouping in outpatient groups occurs with great regularity. The great majority of psychiatric patients have had a dearth of intimate relationships in their lives and thus treasure an intimate relationship with some other member of the group. It is a precious commodity that group patients are often loath to jeopardize for some intangible promise of personal growth.

It is important to note that subgrouping in outpatient groups is high gain as well as high risk. Frequently, in meetings outside the group, members make observations about one another that, when shared with the group, greatly facilitate the group work. Thus, it is not the subgrouping *per se* that is destructive to the group work but the conspiracy of silence around it. The outpatient group runs most effectively when there is little or no socializing between members between group meetings; and when—if there be such contact—the members take the responsibility for discussing it openly in the group.

The inpatient group faces an entirely different situation in regard to subgrouping. Inpatient group members interact with one another throughout the day, often, indeed, sleeping together in the same room. It makes little sense to discourage such socializing or to expect, within the limited time of the inpatient group therapy meeting, that patients share all important aspects of their interaction with one another. The only reasonable therapeutic approach is to confront the existing clinical situation and to search for ways to turn it to the group's and the patients' advantage.

Rather than discourage extra-group socializing, the inpatient group therapy leaders often encourage it. One may, for example, assign certain patients the task of discussing at length outside the group an issue that first emerged in it. If, for example, a patient has great difficulty in disclosing some intimate material to others, the therapist can facilitate self-disclosure by asking the patient to select someone in the group in whom to confide following the session. If patients resist extra-group socializing, the therapist examines this resistance and raises the question of what keeps individuals away from one another. The therapist may ask a patient to select some other member with whom he or she would like to be closer, and then helps analyze the factors that get in the way of the development of that closeness.

The rationale of this approach rests on the assumption that, as I have said, the great majority of psychiatric patients experience great interpersonal isolation in their lives. By encouraging socialization in the hospital, the therapist simultaneously facilitates patients' work on the issue of isolation in their outside lives and also helps them make better use of the therapeutic resources on the inpatient unit. Earlier I presented evidence to suggest that a significant proportion of patients are benefited through their interaction with other patients on the ward. The more inpatient therapists can facilitate that process, the more useful will they be to their patients.

Often patients are so desperately lonely that they look upon the hospital as a source of friends and expect once they have left the hospital, to continue their relationships with other patients. As a general rule, these expectations are not realized; and although there are exceptions, hospital friendships seldom develop into enduring relationships. It is important that patients be given a frame of reference so that they do not consider the impermanence of hospital relationships to be a failure. Patients must be helped to understand that the therapy group is a dress rehearsal for life: a place where one learns *how to* form friendships, not a place where one finds friends.

Forming close relationships with other patients on the ward not only enhances each patient's social skills but it also provides each with an invaluable internal reference point. Once having formed an intimate relationship, even a short-term one in a therapy group or on an inpatient unit, one is imbued with a sense of confidence that one has the capacity for closeness; one also develops a deeper appreciation for friendship's power to enrich life.

As I have said, the outpatient group therapist abhors tightly knit cliques in the therapy group because they spawn secrets or pacts that interfere with the analysis of the group interaction. Inpatient group therapists have a different set of concerns. First of all, because of the brief duration of hospitalization, the clique will have a brief life span. Furthermore, inpatient group therapists often regard cliques more as a boon than a curse. For perhaps the first time in their lives, some patients experience what it means to be part of an in-group. It is often helpful to encourage patients to discuss what that feels like or to discuss what made it possible for them to feel close to the other people in the clique. But whenever there is an in-group, there is a corresponding out-group; and the therapist must attend to those who feel excluded from the clique—both to help those in the clique to learn to be more inclusive and those out of it to learn to express their feelings and their disappointments more explicitly.

Inpatients frequently find themselves in the bind of having been told important things in confidence by other patients and then participating in a group with these same patients who choose to withhold these issues from the therapeutic work. When patients were asked in debriefing research interviews[24] what important things were *not* talked about in the group, the most frequent answers were the use of alcohol and other drugs during hospitalization and sexual attraction and relationships between patients. Patients generally are less conflicted about suicidal intent. A patient who knows that another patient is saving up pills or planning a suicide attempt, is generally able to confide this to one of the staff members—usually individually rather than in a group setting.

Romantic pairing occurs not infrequently in inpatient settings, though perhaps less frequently than previously, in the days of longer hospitalizations. On rare occasions, especially if both members are strongly committed to the group therapeutic task, it is possible to do some useful work on the strengths and the problems of these relationships. Generally, however, it is too much disclosure to expect of patients; and the group therapist does well to accept that it is an issue that the group cannot deal with and that his or her time can best be spent working on other achievable goals.

If there is a pair whose feelings are not mutual—that is, one individual is much enamored of another who does not reciprocate—then it is sometimes possible to examine this situation in the context of the inpatient therapy group. The therapist may help one of the patients learn some of the reasons that the other may be wary or even threatened by his or her advances. For example, one female member discussed the fact that she was attracted to a male patient who cared deeply for her, but she was frightened by his oft-repeated comment that their relationship was the only thing keeping him from suicide. That felt like too big a burden for her to bear; and, despite her attraction to him, she refused to allow herself to become involved. Another patient learned that he drove away women by falling in love with them so quickly that they perceived, quite correctly, that a significant part of the attraction was transferential in nature (that is, his love developed too quickly and with too little knowledge of them). Another patient learned that her over-dependence on her therapist discouraged a would-be suitor, who complained that she related to him only on her therapist's instructions; and he felt that when he and she were alone, there were not two but three people present.

In debriefing research interviews, fifty-one patients were asked whether living together all day long made it more or less difficult to work together in therapy groups.[25] Seventy-five percent of the patients felt that there was no problem living and working together in therapy groups. Many patients, indeed, felt that it constituted a distinct advantage! The therapy group bridged feelings of isolation, drew people closer together, and helped them feel as though they were living in a family. The group broke down superficial, inhibiting social barriers and allowed the patients to relate to one another on deeper levels.

The 25 percent who thought living together constituted a disadvantage for group therapy, commented that they did not want to be in therapy twenty-four hours a day, and that it was difficult relating "therapeutically" in the group and "socially" in their interactions the rest of the day. They also felt thrown into conflict if someone told them something in confidence and then told the group something else. For example, one patient confided a secret to another member and was on the point of telling it in the group but then declined to do so, leading the group on a wild goose chase for over fifteen minutes. The patient who had known the secret felt extremely frustrated at having to bite his tongue in the group and also angry with the other patient for wasting that much group time.

The Inpatient Group Therapist's Other Sources of Information about the Patient

The outpatient group therapist has patients in therapy for much longer periods of time and consequently knows his patients at a much deeper level than does the typical inpatient group psychotherapist. But the latter often has available a great deal of information about the patient that the patient has elected not (or not yet) to disclose to a particular therapist. Sources of information include the psychiatrist's admitting history and examination, the progress notes of the patient's individual therapist, nursing notes, and information the patient has shared in one-to-one discussions with various members of the ward staff.

As I stress throughout this book, the inpatient therapy group is best conducted as an interactional group, with primary attention given to the analysis of the here-and-now interaction as it unfolds in the group. Consequently outside information or past history is not generally necessary to the functioning of the group; and the ancillary information at the group therapist's disposal does not, as a general rule, constitute a major problem. Indeed, it is often difficult for the therapist, especially if he or she is not a member of the full-time staff, to assimilate all the charted information on all the patients who may attend the group on any one day. Generally, it is advisable for at least one of the co-therapists to be part of the full-time staff and have access to information that is available at daily intake conferences, nursing reports, and rounds.

Occasionally, however, outside information will be essential for the functioning of the group and for the therapeutic work of a particular patient. Consider these three clinical situations that occurred in the same group:

Barbara, fifty years old, had attended approximately five group meetings and had done no therapeutic work whatsoever. She invariably presented her needs to the group in such a vague fashion that the members never were able to find a way to be useful to her. She stated that she needed to find some useful way of spending her time, some form of spiritual rebirth, a reformulation of her hierarchy of values, and so on. She was an imposing woman, obviously upper class, and well educated.

This demeanor intimidated others and discouraged them from interacting closely with her. The therapists, however, had at their disposal (from the nurses' notes and the report of her individual therapist) some important and relevant information. Barbara was confronted with a catastrophic situation in her life: her husband had squandered all of the family financial resources and had deserted her, leaving her without any source of income. Her two children had become totally alienated from the family and had had no communication with her for several years. She had just lost her home; she had no money, no job; her goods were in storage; she had no idea where she was going to live when she left the hospital.

Lester was forty years old. He had come to the group daily for approximately two weeks and had expressed a wish to work on two problems: his alienation from his two sons and his failure to be moved by the tragic lives of any of the other patients on the ward. Lester did little productive work in the group. He was repetitious and evasive. He, too, intimidated many of the patients in that he was articulate and obviously well educated. He was a physician's assistant, but the patients on the ward thought that he was a doctor and referred to him as such; Lester did not trouble to correct their misconception.

The therapists had additional information about Lester to which the group was not privy. First, although there was indeed an estrangement between Lester and his sons, it was of many years' standing and was unrelated to the current crisis which had necessitated hospitalization. The immediate precipitating stress for Lester's hospitalization was a minor criminal charge (he had kept a rented car for so long that he was accused of car theft); he had entered the hospital in a depressed state on the very day that he was scheduled for trial.

Lisa was a twenty-four-year-old anorexic who had had a prolonged hospitalization as part of an anorexic program and had attended the group daily for over four weeks. She attempted to work in the group on her self-loathing, her negative feelings about her physical appearance, and her great fear of being judged by others. The group had never been useful to her, and the group therapists felt so stymied and frustrated that they often avoided working with her in the group. What Lisa did not mention in the group was that she had seen a series of individual therapists and had been so resistive and antagonistic to them that each broke off therapy after a brief time. At the time that she was in the group she was so persistently abusive to her individual therapist that he had arranged for a psychiatric nurse to be present at each of their therapy meetings.

Now, in each of these three situations, not only were the patients—Barbara, Lester, and Lisa—stuck in their therapeutic work but the group, too, was blocked and ineffective. This sense of ineffectiveness undermined the faith of other group patients in the therapeutic process. To make matters worse, there were patients in the meeting who served as confidants to Barbara, Lester, or Lisa but were reluctant to "betray" a fellow member by revealing material he or she obviously did not want discussed. These patients felt trapped, irritated, and frustrated with the therapy group. Some, indeed, chose to skip meetings.

What should group therapists do in such instances? First, it is important for you to exhaust every means at your disposal to help patients provide the missing information to the group. As a last resort, you may always comment to the patients that they seem to be stuck in therapy and that the group seems to be unable to be helpful to them. You may raise the question of whether there is important information the patient is not sharing with the group which would be helpful to them in their therapeutic work.

If all else fails, then I believe it is the proper task of the therapist to find a supportive, constructive way to reveal this material to the group. Obviously, you have to use your clinical judgment. If, for example, the patient is a paranoid schizophrenic, then generally no circumstance warrants such a disclosure on the part of a therapist. The patient will almost invariably respond adversely to your disclosure, thus rendering impossible even the most tenuous therapeutic alliance.[26] But, if in the judgment of the group therapists, the concealed information is vitally important to the success of the therapy, then you must disclose this information. The initial sense of embarrassment or resentment is transient and more than compensated for by the ensuing therapeutic progress.

It is important that the therapists disclose the material in a manner that does not appear to the patient as a betrayal or a humiliation. Consider Barbara, the first patient. The therapists steered her into a discussion of pride—what it meant to her, the advantages of her pride, and the price it often extracted from her. Barbara and the group together discussed how her demeanor and her pride created a gulf between herself and others. The therapists then revealed that they had information that she was in a desperate, real-life situation; and yet they were struck by the fact that Barbara would not allow others either to know about this or to help take care of her.

The group therapists took a similar approach with Lester. They emphasized that his life work was the taking care of others but that he concealed his own needs in such a way that he never received any caring for himself. What would it mean for him, the therapists wondered, to disclose the real events surrounding his hospitalization? What would it mean to the role he wanted to assume on the ward? What would it mean to his pride system? What was it like for him to come to the group every day and to know that he was holding back information that, in effect, might make it impossible for him to satisfy any of his own needs?

Lisa's group therapists broke the impasse by sharing what they knew about her problems in working with her individual therapists. The group therapists maintained a therapeutic posture by allowing Lisa to investigate whether the group might be able to help her with those problems. What, the therapists mused, did it have to do with her feelings about authority figures, perhaps especially males in an authority situation. Why did she seem so timid and retiring in the therapy group and yet apparently so boldly angry at her individual therapist? Was it possible that she was angry at the group therapists as well and that some stifling of this anger was getting in the way of her working in the therapy group?

In each of these instances the therapists' revelation of the material was gentle, supportive, and facilitative of further work. In each instance also, the therapists found that this strategy was personally liberating and enabled them to work more effectively not only with the particular patient involved but with the rest of the group as well. Sitting on information vital to the progress of therapy is often highly disconcerting and involves therapists in a silent anti-therapeutic conspiracy with the concealing patient.

The Inpatient Group Therapist in Other Roles

Outpatient group therapists generally see a patient only once or twice a week in the therapy group. Occasionally they may need to see a patient in crisis in an individual session. Some group therapists also undertake to see their group therapy patients in long-term individual therapy. Group therapists may dispense medications or see group patients in couple or family therapy as well. In general, however, it is most desirable for the outpatient group therapist to assume only the pure role of group therapist; therapy runs far more effectively and smoothly in the absence of additional roles to complicate the process.

Inpatient group therapists do not have the luxury of limiting the roles that they play with patients. Generally the inpatient group therapist is a member of the ward staff and, as such, must interact in many ways with each patient. It is essential for the inpatient staff to provide a firm structure and to set limits. Often this limit setting will result in unpopular acts—acts that evoke considerable anger from the patient population. Every inpatient unit has periods in which patients and staff are polarized, and an adversarial relationship may reign for days and sometimes weeks. The group therapist does not escape these feelings and must be prepared to deal with them in the therapy group.

A clinical vignette is illustrative: Christine, a twenty-five-year-old borderline patient, had been a regular member of the group for two weeks and had come to ten consecutive group meetings. She was an attractive woman who had a poignant way of presenting her life situation and enjoyed considerable support and sympathy from the rest of the patients. Christine had a tendency to act out and, during her hospital stay after she heard some bad news about her job, made a suicidal gesture by putting a plastic sack over her head.

Her act generated considerable dissension among the staff. Some staff members had the feeling that she had been working well during her hospitalization, and that the act was clearly a gesture since there were other people nearby and she had made quite a few attention-seeking sounds. On the other hand, the unit was an open one, and there was an explicit ward rule stating that a patient who made a suicide attempt while on the unit would have to be transferred to a closed unit. Furthermore, Christine's individual therapist was concerned about her suicide potential and urged that she be transferred. Consequently, arrangements were made to transfer her immediately to a locked unit.

The group meeting that day was exceedingly tumultuous, with the group members feeling extremely angry toward the ward staff and toward the group therapists as representatives of the staff. The patients accused the leaders of being cruel, arbitrary, legalistic, uncaring, and inhumane. Furthermore, the patients regarded the leaders as rigid in their refusal to make exceptions to rules made a long time ago. The feeling among the group members was unanimous; all ten patients in the group that day felt sympathetic with Christine and placed pressure on the group therapists to reverse the decision for transfer.

What recourse did the group therapists have? First of all, they could not reject their roles as members of the ward staff. Even should they have disagreed with the decision to transfer Christine, it would have been unwise to voice these feelings. Such evidence of staff dissension and of staff susceptibility to splitting will in the long run be unsettling to the great majority of patients, for whom firm, consistent, external structure will facilitate recovery from a state of inner disorganization. In an instance such as this, the strategy of the inpatient therapist is considerably different from the more personalized, transparent approach of many therapists engaged in long-term outpatient treatment. I do not mean to say, however, that therapists cannot express personal dismay and regret at what has happened. As a general rule, if a therapist has conflicted feelings, it is almost always advisable to share both sets of feelings. Thus, the group therapists could discuss their caring for Christine, their dismay that her course of therapy should be disrupted in such a manner, their hope that she would be able to get into immediate and effective therapy in the new institution. But, at the same time, the therapists had to discuss their concern about Christine's potential lethality, and their belief that Christine's individual therapist knew her best and needed to be heeded in such a situation. They could also share their "systems" concerns: that is, the belief that the rule about no suicide attempts on the open unit was important and, in the long run, beneficial to the great majority of patients.

When a patient, especially one who is well liked by other patients, is ejected or transferred from the ward, much anxiety is evoked in the patient population. Such an ejection evokes deep anxiety—anxiety stemming from the fear of rejection by the primal group. The therapist needs to help the group members appreciate the distinction between two situations: (1) the ward staff not liking the patient, throwing the patient out, abandoning the patient because he or she is bad or unlovable; and (2) the ward staff assuming proper medical and psychiatric responsibility for the treatment of the patient. If one treatment setting proves inadequate or unsafe for a patient, then it is a proper exercise of basic medical responsibility to shift the patient to a more appropriate setting—just as it is appropriate to change medication or any regimen of treatment that has proved unsafe or ineffective.

Generally, if anxiety is extreme, patients will not be able to hear this distinction for some time; and therapists will need to persevere and to repeat their stand and their feelings on many occasions. One of the most difficult things for a neophyte therapist to learn is that, though setting limits is difficult and unpopular, it is beneficial and vastly reassuring to the patient in the long run.

Another issue that often arises for nurse group therapists is that, they—in their daily, ongoing contact, and especially in their one-to-one conversations, with patients—tend to be more revealing about their personal lives than seems appropriate in the role of group leader. Consequently, nurses frequently feel they must juggle two different presentations of self. If the nurse co-leads the group with a therapist who does not play a role in the day-to-day life of the ward, the group members perceive the two co-therapists in quite different ways. If there are patients for whom this situation is problematic, the very best course to pursue is for the group leaders to discuss it openly. Thus, they present good models for the patients, emphasizing that there is no danger in self-disclosing and in free discussion.

Hospitalized Patients: More Deeply Troubled, More Demoralized, More Bereft of Ordinary Sources of Environmental Support

It is obvious that the inpatient group psychotherapist almost invariably works with patients who are more severely ill than those with whom the outpatient group psychotherapist works. But also important is the fact that the very act of being in a hospital further determines the character of the patient's response in therapy. For many patients, as I have said, hospitalization signifies failure and defeat—affects that compound the stress, disorganization, and demoralization that they have experienced in their life situations.

Hospitalization also compounds the sense of isolation and estrangement of many patients who are isolated from their families and friends. Although isolation from a noxious environment is generally beneficial, it also has many disadvantages. For one thing, the group therapists cannot expect, as they would in an outpatient group, for patients to transfer in-group learning to out-group situations, to try them on for size, to report back to the group the results of their attempts to transfer learning, and further to modify such learning when appropriate.

For many patients, the hospital setting augments and legitimizes the emergence and the surrender to dependency feelings. Patients are placed in a dependent position by being fed, by having minute attention given to their physical needs, by having few realistic housekeeping obligations expected of them in return. Consequently, dependency is very evident in the inpatient therapy group, and the therapist must develop methods of countering these dependent cravings.

Inpatients commonly face enormous environmental stress. A substantial number of them have no secure home, job, social-support system, financial security; many do not know where they will live when they are discharged from the hospital a few days hence. It is essential that the therapist recognize the magnitude of these problems; but, as I discussed in the section on goals (see pages 52–62), it is essential that the therapist not make the error of asking the group to deal with problems for which groups are not effective.

The sheer level of stress frequently limits the type of work that can be done. Often the inpatient therapist has an awareness of important insights into the defensive structure of a patient. Indeed, there is often so much primary process available that the analytically trained, insight-oriented therapists often feel as if they were in a candy store of psychodynamic sweets. They must continue to keep in mind, however, that a wide gulf exists between the therapist's discovery of the patient's psychodynamic themes and the patient's capacity to use these insights. One of the fundamental pillars of good psychotherapy is timing: there are times when the patient can make good use of insights, and there are times when he or she is not yet able to hear or to integrate interpretations. Not only are premature interpretations ineffectual, they are often unsettling, and they impede therapy by misdirecting attention from the therapeutic work that is possible in the group.

The great majority of patients in the inpatient group are in crisis; they are highly dysphoric; they search for comfort and survival rather than for growth. Clustering at the top of every therapist's hierarchy of values are such qualities as personal growth, self-knowledge, and self-actualization. Naturally, we therapists wish these qualities for patients as well, and it is difficult to curb our desire to help patients stretch. Yet hospital work often requires a bridling of such well-intended soaring wishes. The inpatient therapist must help to lay the foundations of safety and security and leave the architecture and masonry of the upper stories and spires to the therapist who will treat the patient after discharge.

Chapter 3

Strategies and Techniques of Leadership

In the previous chapter I considered some of the clinical facts of life faced by the inpatient group psychotherapist. Inpatient clinical exigencies—such as the brief duration of treatment, the severity and range of pathology, and the relationship between the small group and the larger ward—demand that group therapists modify their approach toward such structural issues as composition, frequency, duration and size of meetings, goals of therapy, extra-group socializing, and confidentiality.

In this chapter I shall discuss the implications of these clinical facts of life for the inpatient group therapist's basic strategy. It is my intent here to describe strategies and techniques that are generally applicable to all forms of inpatient group therapy. In chapters 5 and 6, respectively, I shall present a detailed model of two types of inpatient groups: the higher- and the lower-level therapy groups.

The Single-Session Time Frame

Outpatient group therapists have a longitudinal time frame: they build cohesiveness over many sessions; they observe patterns develop over weeks and months; they patiently work through issues repetitively over a long series of meetings; they continue to work on themes from one week to the next (in fact, as a general rule, the stronger the sense of continuity from meeting to meeting, the more powerful does the group become).

But, on the inpatient unit, the rapid turnover of group membership, the brief duration of hospitalization, and the changing composition from one meeting to the next—all dictate a fundamental shift in the therapist's time frame. Rarely does the group have two consecutive sessions with identical membership. Indeed, many members will attend only a single session.

Inpatient group therapists cannot work within a longitudinal time frame; instead, *they must consider the life of the group to last a single session.* This necessity suggests that they must attempt to do as much effective work as possible for as many patients as possible during each group session. The single-session time frame dictates that inpatient group therapists strive for efficiency. They have no time to build the group, no time to let things develop, no time for gradual working through. Whatever they are going to do, they must do in one session, and they must do it quickly.

These considerations demand a *high level of activity*—far higher than is common or appropriate in long-term outpatient group psychotherapy. Inpatient group therapists must structure and activate the group; they must call on members; they must actively support members; they must interact personally with patients. There is no place in inpatient group therapy for the passive, inactive therapist.

Structure

Nor is there a place in inpatient group psychotherapy for the nondirective leader! Many outpatient group therapists prefer to provide relatively little structure to the procedure of therapy; instead, one permits the group members to search for their own direction, and one studies the varying responses of the group members to the ambiguity of the therapy situation. But, as we have seen, the time frame of the inpatient group therapist does not permit this luxury.

The outpatient group therapist also can depend upon a stable group membership to provide a durable norm skeleton for the group. But, as I also have discussed, the inpatient group therapist cannot depend on that source of structure; instead, the therapist himself must provide a norm structure.

Furthermore, the nature of the psychopathology confronting the inpatient group psychotherapist demands structure. The vast majority of patients on an inpatient unit are confused, frightened, and disorganized; they crave and require some externally imposed structure. The last thing a confused patient needs is to be thrust into an enigmatic, anxiety-provoking situation. Numerous clinical observers have noted that confused patients feel deeply threatened by being placed on wards that themselves appear confused.

Keep in mind the experience of a confused patient who enters a psychiatric unit for the first time: he or she is surrounded by large numbers of deeply troubled, irrationally behaving patients; the new patient's mental acuity may be obtunded by medication; he or she is introduced to a bewilderingly large staff whose specific roles are often undifferentiated; because many staff members are wearing street clothes, the new patient may confuse them with patients; furthermore, since the staff is often on a complex rotating schedule, the patient's sense of external constancy becomes even further eroded.

An externally imposed structure is the first step to a sense of internal structure. A patient's anxiety is relieved when he or she perceives a clear external structure and is provided with some clear, firm expectations for his or her own behavior. A debriefing interview with patients as they were being discharged from an inpatient ward focused on their reactions to their therapy group situation.[1] A recurrent theme voiced by the overwhelming majority of patients was the preference for leaders who provided active structure for the group. Patients appreciated leaders who got the ball rolling in the beginning of a meeting and provided clear direction for the procedure of the group. They preferred leaders who assured equal distribution of time, who actively circled the group inviting individuals to contribute, who actively focused the group's attention on work, who prevented rambling patients from derailing the group's work, who provided the group with a clear sense of the basic group task and direction. Patients, with only rare exceptions, desire a strong, spunky, active, and structured group leader.

These interview results are strongly corroborated by empirical research, which demonstrates that members and therapists as well consider structured group meetings as far more therapeutic than unstructured ones.[2]

Modes of Structure

Group leaders provide structure for the group by delineating clear spatial and temporal boundaries; by adopting a lucid, decisive, but flexible personal style; by providing an explicit orientation and preparation for the patient; and by developing a consistent, coherent group procedure.

Strategies and Techniques of Leadership

Spatial and Temporal Boundaries

Consistent, well-delineated spatial boundaries beget a sense of inner stability. It is important that the group meets in a room of appropriate size—a room that provides comfort but is not cavernous. I prefer to meet in a room that is largely filled by the group circle. It is exceptionally important that the group meet in a clearly delineated space, *preferably in a room that has a closed door.* Because of space limitations, many groups have to meet in a very large general activity room or in a hallway without clear demarcation. It is my experience that such settings place these groups at a considerable disadvantage, and it is preferable to find a room off the ward than to meet in a space whose boundaries are incomplete or unclear.

The ideal seating arrangement for the group is a circle. Therapists should avoid a seating arrangement in which any member of the group cannot see every other member (for example, three or four patients sitting in a row on a long couch). Such an arrangement will invariably discourage the member-to-member interaction so vital to the therapy group and will, instead, encourage the patients to address the therapist rather than each other.

The therapist should endeavor to have as few interruptions in the group's time as possible. All late arrivals and premature departures of members during a meeting should be discouraged. In the ideal situation, of course, all members are present at the beginning of the meeting, and there are no interruptions whatsoever until its conclusion. Debriefing interviews with patients make it clear that patients invariably resent interruptions caused by late-comers. The therapist must model promptness and be on time for each meeting. The more disorganized patients will often need reminding and escort service into the room. If patients are napping, the staff should awaken them at least ten to fifteen minutes prior to the meeting.

The staff must be active in ensuring prompt attendance for

the team meetings and for the lower-level groups. But another strategy entirely may be applied to the higher-level groups which, for reasons I discuss in chapter 5, may function better with an optional attendance policy. In higher-level groups I have, for many years, preferred a policy of not permitting late-comers (regardless of their excuse) to enter the session. Once the door is closed, the group space is inviolable. Naturally some resentment is experienced by members who come three or four minutes late and are not allowed to enter, but the advantages far outweigh the disadvantages. The therapist demonstrates to the patients that he or she values the group's time and wishes to make maximal use of it. The great majority of the group members will appreciate the decision not to allow late-comers to enter; and the patient denied entrance will sulk briefly but invariably be prompt the following day.

Most leaders feel uncomfortable at being such strict gate-keepers; it runs against the grain of clinical training to refuse admission to a patient seeking therapy. These feelings exist simultaneously with the therapist's belief that such limit setting is ultimately therapeutic, not only for the group but for the late-comer as well. If the therapist has two coexisting, conflict-ing sets of feelings, it is always a good policy to share both sets with the group members. Furthermore, it is advisable to seek out the tardy patient after the meeting in order to reassure him or her that no rejection was meant, to explain once again the rules of the group, and to issue an invitation for the next meeting.

There is an additional benefit to a "no late-comers" policy. Considerable social-psychological research indicates that if there are barriers to admission, and if one has to make an effort or a sacrifice to enter the group, one invariably perceives the group as more desirable. Such conditions increase the patient's expectational set; and, as I discussed in chapter 1, there is con-vincing evidence that the higher the expectational set of the patient, the more successful will therapy be. In other words, if the patient values therapy and believes that it will be helpful, it will, in fact, be more efficacious.

It is also desirable that the members of the meeting not leave early. Dealing with early "bolters" is more complex than dealing with late-comers, since highly anxious patients (especially those with claustrophobic tendencies) are likely to become more anxious if they perceive that they will not be permitted to leave the room. Therefore, the therapist is well advised simply to express the hope that members can stay the full meeting. The therapist who, before a meeting starts, sees any clearly hyperactive and agitated patients should inquire whether they feel able to sit in the group for the duration of the meeting. If the answer is No, the therapist may suggest that they not attend the group that day but, instead, return the next day when they feel more settled. In lower-level groups (to be described in chapter 6), patients may frequently have to leave early but should be supported for the time they have been able to remain in the group. Often contracts may be established between patient and therapist whereby the latter agrees to stay a few minutes longer each day.

If a patient is disturbed by some event during the session and decides to leave, the therapist cannot, of course, physically prevent him or her from doing so. Depending upon the particular situation, however, the therapist does have a few options available. Occasionally the therapist can reframe a situation for the patient in a way that appeals to the latter's personal therapeutic goals. If, for example, the patient has a long history of fleeing from conflicted situations and has already expressed a desire to change this maladaptive pattern, then the therapist may be able to exert some leverage by reminding the patient of his or her resolution. The therapist might, for example, say something to this effect: "John, I can see how terribly uncomfortable you are, and it may not be possible for you to stay in the group feeling as bad as you do. On the other hand, though, I think it would be awfully important if you could stick with it and stay in the group for a while longer today. Remember that one of the things you want to change about yourself is the way you have dealt with other people when you have felt uncomfortable or angry. Here's a wonderful opportunity to try and make the change. If you leave, you'll only be repeating what you've done so often before."

If the patient seems more diffusely anxious or restless, the therapist may encourage him or her to stay by simple reassurance or by suggesting that he or she remain for the rest of the meeting but simply as a listener. If the patient is frightened, the therapist may suggest that the patient change seats and sit next to one of the co-therapists in the room. It is occasionally useful to invite the patient to observe the group for the remainder of the session from a seat outside the group circle or, if one exists, from the observation room. If it is impossible to keep a distraught patient in the room, one of the co-leaders must leave the room with the patient and inform another member of the staff of the patient's distress.

A prompt ending of the group is rarely problematic, since space demands on most inpatient units are heavy, and the room is usually needed for some other activity. On the whole, this limitation is for the good. Occasionally the end of a session may find the group in the midst of a crucial issue which absolutely demands that the session be extended for a few minutes. Generally, however, a prompt ending is as important as a prompt beginning to create a sense of consistent structure for the patients.

Personal Style

The therapist's style of communication greatly contributes to the amount of structure the group provides to patients. Acutely troubled, frightened, and confused patients are reassured by a therapist who is firm, explicit, and decisive yet who, at the same time, shares with them the reasons for his or her actions.

Not uncommonly, disruptive events happen in inpatient groups. Patients may become tangential or confused or belligerent or otherwise disruptive in a number of other ways. Ideally, it would be desirable for the group members to be able to deal with these crises on their own in order to increase their sense of mastery and personal and group autonomy. Generally in outpatient groups, the group therapist prefers to permit the crisis to run much of its course and scrutinizes the group's attempts to rescue itself; ultimately the leader's intention is to help the group members analyze their deep reactions to the disruptive events.

In inpatient groups, however, it is almost invariably an error for the therapist to be passive or nondirective in the face of some major, disruptive event. Patients are too frightened, too much in crisis, too highly stressed to be able to deal effectively with such events. They are reassured and experience the group environment as immeasurably safer if the therapist is able to act firmly and decisively in such instances. If, for example, a manic patient is veering out of control, nothing is to be gained by allowing the patient to continue on that course: he or she will not feel better as a result of the runaway behavior, and the rest of the group will feel irritated at the patient and cheated of their therapy time. The therapist's stance must be firm and decisive. You may suggest to the manic patient that it is time to be quiet and to work on learning to listen to others; or if the patient has insufficient inner control, you may have to ask the patient to leave the group.

Patients will be much relieved by such firm intervention by the therapist. Occasionally some patients might feel concerned or threatened by a therapist's decisive behavior; but this response is often ameliorated by a process discussion of the incident and of the therapist's response. Often it is good modeling for the therapist to comment on any of his or her own contradictory feelings. For example, you may comment on having felt

113

uncomfortable at silencing a patient and concerned about having thereby possibly hurt that patient, but mention also your strong feeling that it was the best thing to do for the patient and for the group. It is often advisable to solicit feedback from the group. Do the group members feel you are being too strict or too stern? Do they feel you as rejecting? Do they have some relief when you intervene?

At other times the group will engage in long intellectual, impersonal discussions, which the therapist regards as unproductive. In outpatient groups, the therapist often has the option of patiently commenting about what the group seems to be doing. In inpatient groups, it is advisable to be more directive and less subtle with such interventions. The group welcomes, and is facilitated by, direct intervention such as: "It's clear to me that what we're talking about is a very important issue for a number of people in the group. But I also have a very strong feeling that this isn't the best way to use the group. Groups are much more helpful by focusing on some of the feelings that we have about relating and communicating with others, and I think it would be better if we could get back to . . ." (at this point the leader can supply some clear option available to them for discussion).

Therapists must feel assured that they have a coherent, cognitive framework for the group's goals and procedures—a framework and an assurance that they convey to the patients. It is not feasible or clinically useful to be explicit about every benefit of the group format: some therapeutic mechanisms are rendered less effective if made absolutely explicit (such as the raising of self-esteem by group acceptance). Furthermore, some therapeutic factors (such as altruism and universality) require a degree of spontaneity and are less effective if explicitly orchestrated. Nonetheless, there are many benefits of the group that can be lucidly described. The leader who shares, in an understandable way, the theoretical rationale underlying his or her actions, not only provides useful structure to the patients but also enlists them as allies in the therapeutic work.

Patients who have developed a clear picture of the group goals and of the task necessary to approach them are more likely to invest themselves in the work of therapy. Research corroborates that patients report high levels of satisfaction with a group session if they feel that the meeting dealt with important, relevant issues and progressed toward clearly formulated goals.[3]

Dynamically oriented therapists are not educated to be directive and explicit about the goals and procedure of therapy. They are trained to observe the patient's response to the formlessness of the therapy hour, to study the patient's free associations, and to facilitate easy, nonjarring transitions in the therapy hour. But inpatient group therapists must learn to be direct and explicit. They must be explicit in the orientation statement they make in the initial minutes of each meeting, and continue to be explicit throughout the session.

Orientation and Preparation

The first minutes of the group provide an opportunity for the therapist to create considerable structure for the session. The therapist provides an official beginning to the group and launches the meeting on its way. It is a time to introduce, orient, and prepare the new members for group therapy. Even if there are no new members, it is a time nonetheless to restate briefly the goals of the group and its procedure. The provision of external structure, as I have stressed, promotes the acquisition of internal structure; and the beginning of the group is the place to begin building that structure. If observers are viewing the group, the therapist should always so inform the patients at the very outset of the meeting.

A typical orientation in a higher-level group session (see chapter 5) where a new member is present, might begin with addressing the new member thus:

"John, I'm Irv Yalom* and this is the afternoon therapy group which meets daily for one hour and fifteen minutes beginning at two o'clock. My co-therapist is ———, and she will be here four of the five meetings for the next four weeks. On the fifth day another psychiatric nurse will take her place. The purpose of this group is to help members to understand their problems better and to learn more about the way they communicate and relate to others. People come into the hospital with many different kinds of important problems, but one thing that most individuals have in common here is some unhappiness about the way that some of their important relationships are going. There are, of course, many other important problems that people have, but those are best worked on in some of your other forms of therapy. What groups do best of all is to help people understand more about their relationships with others. One of the ways that we will try to work on relationships is to focus on them in this group and especially to focus on the relationships that may go on between people in this room. The better your communication becomes with each of the people here, the bet-

---

*There is great variation around the country about how patients and therapists address one another. In the informal climate of California, most group patients and therapists address one another by first name. In more formal settings, the patients are often addressed by first name; and some therapists (generally psychologists and psychiatrists) are addressed as "Doctor," whereas other therapists (that is, nurses, social workers, activity therapists, occupational therapists) are addressed by first name. In a few very formal settings, the patients are addressed as "Mr." or "Ms.," and all the staff as "Mr." or "Ms." or by professional title. Having lived in California for many years, I feel most comfortable on a first-name basis with patients. There will be some patients who prefer to call me "Dr. Yalom" or even find it extremely difficult not to do so—a difficulty that is sometimes worthy of investigation. Whatever the practice used by the group therapist, I would urge some therapist-patient consistency and equality. If the staff members insist on their last names being used, then the patients should be addressed by their last names as well. If some members of the staff are to be called by their first names, then all members of the staff should be as well. The old hierarchical division between the "doctor" and the ancillary therapist makes little sense in the group therapy situation and is in fact contradicted by the egalitarian way that they relate to one another in the group. Furthermore, not infrequently, the co-therapist (nurse, social worker, occupational therapist, activity therapist) is a more experienced and skilled group therapist than the doctor.

ter will your communication become with people in your outside life.

"It's important to know that observers are present almost every day to watch the group through this one-way mirror. [I point toward the mirror and also toward the microphone, in an attempt to orient the patient as clearly as possible to his spatial surroundings.] The observers will usually be medical students or other members of the ward staff. No one else will be allowed to observe the group without my checking that out with you before the group starts.

"We begin our meetings by going around the group and checking with each person and asking each to say something about the kinds of problems they're having in their lives that they'd like to try to work on in the group. After the go-round we then try to work on as many of these problems as possible. In the last ten minutes of the group, we stop our discussion and check in with everyone here about how they feel about the meeting and about the kinds of leftover feelings that should be looked at before the group ends."

Such an introduction serves a number of functions: it provides some temporal, spatial, and procedural structure; it breaks the ice of the meeting; it serves as a formal beginning; and it also constitutes a brief preparation for group psychotherapy.

Group Therapy Preparation

A compelling body of research literature demonstrates that if the patient is systematically prepared by the therapist for group therapy, then the patient's course in the therapy process will be facilitated.[4] (Similar evidence exists, incidentally, for individual therapy as well.)[5] In long-term outpatient therapy groups it is standard practice for therapists to prepare a patient for the impending group therapy experience in individual session(s) prior to the patient's entry into the group.[6]

In preparation for *outpatient* group therapy, the therapist provides patients with a clear explanation of how the group will work and what the members can do in the group to facilitate their therapy. The therapist gives a brief introduction to the interpersonal theory of psychotherapy, instructing patients about the pervasive importance of interpersonal relations and about how disturbances in relationships underlie their current symptoms. The therapist informs patients about how the process of understanding their relationships to other members of the group will provide them with exceedingly valuable insight into how each of them creates his or her own maladaptive interpersonal environment. Patients are forewarned about certain stumbling blocks of the group: puzzlement, discouragement, frustration at not having the amount of personal attention one would like. Patients' misconceptions about group therapy are discussed; and, if possible, the therapist attempts to augment the patient's confidence in group therapy by emphasizing that groups do not constitute an inexpensive, second-rate therapy. In fact, the therapist emphasizes that, by providing a rich arena in which they can learn a great deal about how others perceive them and how they relate to others, group therapy represents a unique and particularly effective therapeutic modality.

In the hustle and bustle of inpatient work, there is no time for the luxury of such a lengthy preparation. Consequently, group therapists have to prepare patients for group therapy in any way possible during the brief time available. It is often advisable for the therapist to share the task of preparation and orientation with some of the members. The therapist may, for example, ask one of the older members to tell the new member(s) about the purpose and procedure of the group. The therapist then may ask some of the other patients whether there are any additional points they want to contribute; and if the therapist feels there are still some points that have not been stated, he or she can then state them. This approach increases not only the participation of members but also their tendency to experience the meeting and the procedure of the meeting as their own rather than something that is imposed upon them.

Patients who come from the lower socioeconomic levels of society, and are unsophisticated about psychotherapy, particularly profit from an intensive preparation. A researcher systematically prepared such patients admitted to an acute psychiatric ward and compared their progress in the therapy group with similar patients who were not systematically prepared.[7] Data from the first five group sessions demonstrated that the prepared patients worked much more effectively: they volunteered more, communicated more frequently, engaged in self-exploration more frequently, initiated more statements in the group.

In another study, patients were assigned for their first four days of hospitalization to a special group designed to pre-train them for group therapy.[8] The training procedure offered in the intake group was demonstrably successful in helping patients integrate more quickly into the group and to work well in their therapy. Unfortunately hospital stays are too short on most acute wards to allow for such pretraining groups, and the preparation must be done in the initial part of the therapy group rather than in a special group.

One important function of the preparation is that it helps to eliminate discrepancies in expectations between therapists and patients. A study of patient and staff expectations on one inpatient ward demonstrated that patients expected that the staff would approve of their seeking advice, whereas the staff hoped instead for more self-direction on the part of the patients.[9] Such a discrepancy between the patients' and the staff's expectations will invariably breed confusion and impede the formation of a therapeutic alliance. It is absolutely essential in short-term therapy that patients be given explicit procedural directions.

Explicit preparation for the group also reduces the patients' apprehension and makes it more possible for them to participate in the group without crippling anxiety. It is to be expected that patients will be anxious in a therapy group. Individuals with life-long disabilities in interpersonal relationships will invariably be stressed by a therapy session that urges them to discuss their relationships to others with great candor. Most concur that a certain degree of anxiety is necessary for therapeutic growth; anxiety increases vigilance and motivation to work in the group. But too much anxiety freezes the group work. Primary anxiety—the anxiety stemming from a patient's psychological disorder—will be an inevitable accompaniment of group work, and there is little the leader can do to ameliorate it in the initial stages of the session. But the leader can do a great deal to prevent secondary anxiety—anxiety that stems from the patient's being thrown into an ambiguous therapy situation. Considerable research demonstrates that ambiguous group goals, methods of goal attainment, and expected role behavior will increase the members' anxiety, frustration, and uninvolvement with the group.[10]

A Consistent, Coherent Group Procedure

Clarity and structure are so important that many clinicians prefer highly structured, explicitly programmed groups. One ward has instituted a procedure in which patients go through a series of "step groups," each of which is designed to teach a specific set of behavioral skills.[11] For example, the most elementary group emphasizes good eye contact, learning to listen and understand others, et cetera. The next step teaches patients to ask open-ended questions, to make questions into statements, to reflect feelings. The next step teaches learning to give and accept feedback, and to self-disclose. Clinicians using such programs report that they are far more effective than unstructured groups.[12]

My impression is that a heavily structured approach is particularly indicated for groups of more poorly functioning patients. In chapter 6, I shall describe in detail a structured model for such a group.

Keep in mind, however, that it is the *process* of providing structure, rather than the *content* of the structure, that is the key issue. An interesting project elucidates this point.[13] Researchers assigned patients to three types of group: (1) carefully programmed groups oriented toward problem solving; (2) groups that simply read comedies together, with fifteen minutes set aside at the end of each session to discuss the play; (3) a third control sample, in which the patients attended no groups on the ward.

The behaviorally oriented researchers were considerably invested in demonstrating the superiority of a programmed, problem-solving group mode for the small inpatient unit. They found, however, that the play-reading group was as helpful as the problem-solving group in most important dimensions. The control, no-group therapy, sample showed significantly less improvement than did the other two groups. One important conclusion issuing from the study is that the specific task given to patients may not be of such paramount importance as the fact that there *is* a task—that there is some structure, and the patients are not thrown into an anxiety-elevating, ambiguous situation.

Structure is as important to a therapist as it is to the patients. Leading a group is anxiety provoking. The therapist is exposed to many powerful and often primitive emotions. There are many patients vying for the leader's sole attention; and the leader will inevitably disappoint and frustrate some of them, who may then respond angrily and ungratefully. Group therapy with psychotic patients particularly is intrinsically anxiety provoking. The work is slow, often unrewarding, and generally perplexing. Furthermore, group therapists are exposed. No secret therapy sessions behind closed doors for them: their work is painfully visible to large numbers of people.

One of the fabled definitions of psychotherapy is attributed to Harry Stack Sullivan: "A situation in which two people meet together, one of whom is less anxious than the other." The therapist who falls prey to these many sources of anxiety may violate Sullivan's law, become more anxious than the patient, and—by definition—cease to be therapeutically effective.

Ambiguity is as anxiety provoking for the therapist as for the patient, and the therapist's chief defense against the anxiety intrinsic to the practice of psychotherapy is the sense of structure provided by a therapeutic model. It is less important *which* model than that there *be* a model. By developing a cognitive framework that permits an ordering of all the inchoate events of therapy, the therapist experiences a sense of inner order and mastery—a sense that, if deeply felt, is automatically conveyed to patients and generates in them a corresponding sense of clarity and mastery. Research demonstrates that patient satisfaction with a group therapy session is significantly and positively correlated with the therapist's self-ratings (for the same meeting) of personal satisfaction, interest, and understanding.[14]

One of the most powerful structure-providing techniques available to the therapist is the creation of a consistent, explicit sequence to the therapy group meeting. Although groups, depending upon their composition (that is, whether they are level or team groups), will have different sequences, natural lines of cleavage appear in the great majority of inpatient group therapy sessions.

1. *The first few minutes.* I have already described this section of the meeting in which therapists launch a meeting, introducing and orienting the new patients and briefly preparing them for group therapy (see pages 115–20).

2. *Definition of the task.* In this phase therapists attempt to ascertain the most profitable directions for the group to take in a particular session. It is often unwise to plunge, at great depth, into the first issue advanced during the session. In doing so, therapists may miss other possibly more important and productive agendas. Therapists can discover the task of the meeting in many ways. They may simply listen to the first several comments that the patients make. Therapists may suggest some

systematic "go-round," in which each patient is asked to say something about what he or she would like to examine, work on, or accomplish in that meeting. Once the therapists feel that they have some representative overview, they then move on to the next stage of the group. (See also pages 212–42.)

3. *"Filling" of the task.* This phase comprises the bulk of the group time. Having acquired a broad view of the various relevant issues of the members, therapists attempt to address these issues and to involve as many patients as possible in the discussion. (See also pages 243–52.)

4. *Ending the meeting.* In the last few minutes therapists indicate that the work phase is over and that a short period of time should be spent on reviewing the meeting. Several options are available: therapists can check with each of the patients about his or her satisfactions and disappointments in that session; or therapists can elicit comments from the inactive patients to find out how they experienced the meeting; or therapists can attend to jagged edges of the meeting—that is, unfinished business or possibly ruffled feelings requiring attention before the patients leave the room; or, finally, therapists may choose to give some review or summary of the work the group has accomplished during a session.

Disadvantages of Structure

Are there any disadvantages in providing structure? Indeed, there are! Providing too much structure is as harmful as providing too little. Although patients desire and require considerable structuring by the therapist, excessive structure may retard their therapeutic growth. If the leader does everything for patients, they will do too little for themselves. Thus, in the early stages of therapy, structure provides reassurance to the frightened and confused patient; but persistent and rigid structure, over the long run, can infantalize the patient and delay assumption of autonomy.

Empirical research provides persuasive, corroborating evidence of this paradox. In 1972 my colleagues and I studied the impact of leader behavior upon member outcome in a large number of encounter groups.[15] (The subjects in this study were not hospitalized patients but well-functioning young adults. Nonetheless, the group dynamics can be extrapolated to a considerable extent.)

Two findings in this project are particularly relevant. The researchers measured the amount of structure each leader provided (by counting the number of structured exercises used) and studied the correlation between the amount of structure and the outcome of the members. The findings indicated that there was a *positive* correlation between the amount of structure provided and how competent the members deemed their leader to be immediately at the end of the group experience. In other words, at the moment of termination, the more structure the leader had provided, the more competent the members judged the leader to be.

A related finding, however, demonstrated an *inverse* correlation between the amount of structure the leader used and the overall outcome of the group members at the six-month follow-up. In other words, the *more* structure the leader provided, the *less* positive growth was demonstrable in the group members six months after termination of the group. These two findings suggest that, *though members are pleased by a leader who provides the greatest structure, they are less likely to undergo significant growth when working with such a leader.*

A second major finding of this study stems from an intensive study, by research observers, of the leader's behavior along two dimensions: (1) *total activity*—number of words spoken, number of interventions made; and (2) *executive, managerial activity*—managing the time, providing structure, setting limits, and so on. It was found that each of these two kinds of structuring behavior was related, in a *curvilinear* fashion, to overall positive outcome both at the end of the group and at the six-month follow-up. This finding means that too much *or* too little leader activity or leader managing behavior was detrimental to growth. *The law of the golden mean prevailed.* Too little of this behavior resulted in an aimless, drifting group; too much limited the growth of the members.

Thus, group leaders face a dilemma. On the one hand, they must provide structure; but, on the other hand, they must not provide so much structure that patients will not learn to use their own resources. The basic task of the therapist is to *augment the advantages* of structuring the group and to *minimize the disadvantages.* There is a solution to this dilemma—a general principle, which I shall emphasize numerous times throughout this book: *the leader must structure the group in a fashion that facilitates each patient's autonomous functioning.*

Support

Short-term hospitalization is effective only if it is coupled with effective aftercare therapy. One of the major goals of the inpatient therapy group program is to increase the desire in patients to continue therapy after they have left the hospital. In fact, if the therapy group does nothing else but encourage the patient to pursue post-hospital psychotherapy, especially group psychotherapy, it will have been an effective intervention.

Thus, it is imperative that patients perceive the therapy group as a positive, supportive experience, one that they will wish to continue in the future. The therapist must create in the group an atmosphere that is perceived as constructive, warm, and supportive. Patients must feel safe in the group. They must learn to trust the group. They must experience the group as a place where they will be heard, accepted, and understood.

The inpatient therapy group is not the place for confrontations, criticism, or the expression and examination of anger. There is considerable clinical consensus that, if the inpatient therapy group is to accomplish its goals, these sentiments must be avoided.[16] There will be patients who may need a certain degree of confrontation. For example, sociopathic or manipulative individuals do not often profit from a therapeutic approach that is continuously supportive and empathic; but it is far better that the group therapist "miss" these patients than run the risk of making the group feel unsafe to the majority of patients.

A vast body of research literature demonstrates conclusively that, both in individual and in group therapy, positive outcome is positively correlated with a supportive and empathic relationship with the therapist.[17] To take one example, consider an extensive encounter group project that studied different types of group leadership and correlated leader behavior and member outcome.[18] Whereas there was a curvilinear relationship between such leader characteristics as activity and directiveness (that is, too much *or* too little of such leader behavior was counterproductive), there was a highly significant *positive linear correlation* between leader support and member outcome (that is, the more leader support that was offered, the better was member outcome).

Not only does considerable empirical evidence support the importance of a positive, nonjudgmental, accepting therapist-patient relationship, but there are numerous retrospective views of psychotherapy in which patients underscore the importance of a therapist's liking them, valuing them, and noticing and reinforcing their positive characteristics. Many years ago I entered into an unusual therapeutic contract with a patient. For reasons not germane to this discussion, the patient agreed to write a discursive and impressionistic summary of the way that she experienced each therapy hour. She handed these, sealed, to me each week. I agreed to do the same thing and wrote similar weekly summaries. (Years later, the patient and I published our summaries together in a book called *Every Day Gets a Little Closer: A Twice-Told Therapy.*[19] It was extremely illuminating to compare my views of what was helpful in therapy with the patient's views. All my elegant formulations and interpretations? The patient never even heard them! Instead, what she remembered and valued from the therapy hours were the subtle, almost unnoticed (by me) personal, warm, supportive remarks that I made to her about such things as her appearance, about how well she was dealing with a particular situation, about the degree of vitality or spontaneity she expressed in a given session.

Some personal therapeutic experience is a fundamental ingredient in the education of every mental-health professional. I would suspect that when each of the readers of this book reflects back upon their own therapy, they appreciate the overriding importance of the therapist's acceptance and support. Certainly it is true that what I remember and value from my own therapy, decades ago, are the warm, caring, affirming statements that my therapist made to me.

In a therapy group situation, the therapist's personal support takes on an added dimension. Not only does the therapist interact with his or her own person upon each of the members of the group, but the therapist's actions shape the norms (the code, or the unwritten rules) that influence how all the members behave. Therapists create norms in many ways: they explicitly set certain rules, they reinforce certain types of behavior in the group and extinguish others (either through explicit disagreement or discouragement or implicitly by inattention to certain types of comment). But one of the most important modes through which therapists shape the norms of the group is through their own behavior upon which patients pattern themselves.

Despite the enormously important role that "support" plays in the ultimate outcome of psychotherapy, relatively little attention is given to it in conceptualizations of psychotherapy or in training programs. Support is often taken for granted; it may be considered superficial; it is often assumed that "of course" therapists will be supportive to their patients. Many therapists conclude that support is equivalent to paying compliments, and that such a simple act hardly needs any detailed discussion in therapy training. My goal in the following pages is to demonstrate that the provision of support (and the creation of a supportive group atmosphere) is not a simplistic, automatic process: as much as any other act in psychotherapy, it requires attention, sensitivity, and a sense of proper timing.

One need only attempt to formulate a definition or a comprehensive description of a therapist's "support" to become aware of its multifaceted nature. The therapist supports the patient by expressing, either verbally or nonverbally, personal acceptance, valuing, or liking of the patient. The therapist supports by treating the patient with respect and dignity. The therapist supports by identifying and reinforcing the patient's strengths and virtues. The therapist supports by refraining from undermining defenses but instead by bolstering them and by encouraging patients to employ defenses that are at least one step more effective than the one they are currently using.[20] The therapist supports by encouraging behavior in the patient that will result in the patient's being more highly valued by others (and conversely, the therapist discourages behavior that will result in the patient's being unsupported or rejected by others). The therapist supports by empathizing as deeply as possible with the patient. By understanding and sharing the patient's inner world, the therapist enables the patient to feel less alone and to feel understood. The process of being deeply understood by another conveys also that the therapist values the patient enough to want to enter the patient's world and to understand the nuances of the patient's experience.

Support is *not* something that therapists "of course" provide. As a matter of fact, many intensive training programs in psychotherapy unwittingly extinguish the therapist's natural proclivities to support the patient. Therapists become pathology sniffers—experts in the detection of weaknesses. In extreme form this tendency results in the therapist's regarding positive qualities with suspicion: kindness, generosity, diligence, moral responsibility—all may be approached in a reductionistic fashion and be interpreted as psychopathology. Furthermore, therapists are so sensitized to transferential and countertransferential issues that they hold themselves back from engaging in basically human supportive behavior with their patients. I remember vividly a heated discussion I heard twenty years ago in an analytic conference about the pros and cons of the therapist's helping a patient (an old lady) on and off with her overcoat! Therefore, learning how to give support in inpatient group therapy often entails a degree of "unlearning" of professionally taught postures and attitudes toward patients which obstruct the therapist's natural human inclinations to provide support.

Acknowledge the Patient's Contributions

An example of provision of support occurred in a meeting in which a severely disturbed borderline patient was present for the first time. The patient, whom I shall call Lorna, began the meeting by talking about her pervasive sense of unreality. She stated that she didn't know who she was, where she started, where other people ended; if she heard someone say something, she immediately took those to be her own feelings and had no trust whatsoever in the validity of any of her personal experiences. The therapist encouraged her reality testing early in the meeting by helping her to experience herself experiencing feelings. For example, Lorna commented that she was bothered by the microphones in the room because she thought there was a hum (observers behind a one-way mirror were watching the group). As soon as she said this, other members said they heard the hum as well. The hum had been caused by auditory feedback, which the observers corrected by turning down the volume. The therapist intervened by pointing out to Lorna that it was she who had heard the hum, that it was she who didn't like the hum, and that it was she who had raised an objection to it. The objection had obtained objective support and affirmation by the others in the group, who appreciated Lorna's having raised the objection; and, furthermore, it had been effective and resulted in the correction of the situation.

Later in the group Lorna offered some feedback to Bob, one of the men in the group, who had been very blocked and stuck in therapy. She stated that he seemed very small to her, and she was surprised to see how tall he really was when he stood up. Lorna's comment opened up many things for Bob, who then began to talk about how he didn't want to be a big grown-up person, how he felt small and fragile inside, and how he especially wanted women to see him in that way. Soon other people talked about their observations about Bob's posture, his carriage, and his mannerisms—observations that were deeply instructive to Bob.

Still later in the meeting, the group seemed stuck in trying to understand some communication difficulties between two of the other patients in the group. Lorna volunteered the observation that she felt that it was "illegal" to talk about the vibes that she sensed between two of the members. She wasn't sure why, but she felt she was an intruder, that it wasn't her place to ask them anything. Her comments opened the way to others to express similar feelings. Soon the two members talked about the fact that there had been a "small romance" going on between the two of them, and that this romance was making it very difficult to be in a group together.

Toward the end of the same session, Lorna talked about the fact that people seemed to be looking at the therapist surreptitiously, and she had a sense that everyone in the group was vying for his attention. This remark propelled the other members into an extremely constructive discussion of their wish to please the therapist.

The therapist supported Lorna by emphasizing the contributions she had made to the group. He explicitly stated how impressed he was at her great sensitivity, at her ability to come into a group for the first time and unerringly to put her finger on so many important issues that had blocked the group for several meetings. Was she aware of this ability of hers? he wondered. Did she give herself credit for her interpersonal skills and her ability to help people grow and understand themselves? In addition to support, the therapist helped the patient re-establish her ego boundaries, by emphasizing that it was *she*, Lorna, who had such sensitivity and had been so helpful to others.

To a large extent as a result of this meeting, Lorna reintegrated very quickly and began to re-establish her sense of self-worth and her personal sense of identity.

Take the Patient Seriously

Another example of support involved a patient, whom I shall call Charles, who experienced great difficulties in relating to the therapist; instead, he engaged in considerable pairing and considerable subtle undermining of the therapeutic staff. The therapist knew that Charles had a long history of conflicted attitudes toward authority figures, beginning with a powerful father whom Charles felt had often humiliated him. In the group Charles felt that the therapist slighted him and did not take him seriously. For example, Charles accused the therapist of never listening to, or respecting, any of his (Charles's) observations or suggestions to the other patients (especially some of the female patients) in the group. If the therapist made his own observations, and especially if other members found these observations helpful, Charles felt defeated and angry.

One possible mode of responding to Charles would have been for the therapist to interpret his behavior: that is, to interpret Charles's competitiveness with the therapist for the women in the group as a compensatory mechanism to deal with Charles's sense of impotency vis-à-vis the therapist. Even though there was much clinical data to support this interpretation, it would have been countertherapeutic. Instead, rather than interpreting Charles's behavior, the therapist was far more helpful to him by supporting his attempts to find new ways of responding to older males in roles of authority. It was, indeed, a healthy adaptive step for Charles to be openly critical of the therapist and to attempt to compete with him. It was important for the therapist to let Charles's comments matter to him and to take them seriously; whereas to have offered him an interpretation would have been to defeat him.

The therapist's task was to listen to Charles's comments, to accept those that were accurate, and to reflect openly upon them in the group. For example, the therapist wondered aloud in the group about whether it might not be true that he (the therapist) got so involved with his own ideas and observations in the group that he tended not to value highly enough some of the observations of Charles or other members. He validated Charles's comments and commented that he, too—the therapist —had blind spots which would persist unless others, like Charles, were willing to point them out to him. The therapist continued to let Charles matter to him and in subsequent meetings solicited feedback about himself from Charles and others in the group, especially about comments that might be seen as disrespectful or inconsiderate. At the same time the therapist was more open with some of his dilemmas. For example, in one meeting when Charles complained that he had not been given enough time, the therapist shared the difficult choice facing him during the session: although he knew that Charles was under considerable internal pressure and was working well in the group, he, the therapist, was concerned about three of the silent members who were deeply troubled that day but unable to ask for time from the group.

Discourage Self-Defeating Behavior

Often it is a significant therapeutic challenge to find a way to help everyone feel valued and supported by the group. Not infrequently patients present themselves in such objectionable fashion that the group response will inevitably be so critical that they end up feeling even more rejected and defensive. When the therapist identifies such behavior, it is important to intervene quickly before animosity toward such a patient builds too high.

For example, one elderly patient, Martha, had frustrated the other patients on the ward for several days. She persevered about the pain in her leg, wept incessantly, and was so repetitive that the members of the group openly referred to her as a "broken record." Any attempts in the group to deal on a more directly cognitive level were unsuccessful. For example, the therapist asked her what that feedback meant to her. Had she ever heard it before? How did it feel to be referred to as a broken record? All such inquiries merely aggravated the behavior which resulted in further rejection by the group—a vicious circle that could in no way be helpful to Martha or the group.

The therapist then tried another approach, which was far more useful. He intervened to help Martha behave in a way that allowed her to be valued by the group. Martha had had some training as a counselor and, although not sensitive to her own behavior, was very sensitive about others. Consequently, the therapist "dereflected" her and asked her if she could share with the group what perceptions she had about the personal struggles and pain that the other members of the group were having. Martha, somewhat reluctantly, went around the group, picked out several people, and described, with great sensitivity, her perceptions of their primary life issues.

One very troubled schizophrenic boy in particular felt deeply understood by Martha. Later in the group when he talked about his isolation, the therapist asked this patient to look around the room and select someone with whom he felt he might become closer and thus penetrate his isolation. He selected Martha, who then walked across the room, sat next to him, and held his hand for the remainder of the meeting. This was a dramatic turn of events since, not only did Martha walk rather buoyantly across the room and stop talking about the pain in her leg, but she was able to remain in the room for the entire meeting (which she had never done previously because of her pain).

To Understand All Is to Forgive All

The group can often accept particularly irritating behavior if the therapist provides a cognitive framework that permits the members to reframe a patient's objectionable behavior. For example, Mabel, at sixty-two years of age, had had many surgical procedures on her hands and talked about them endlessly. It was extremely difficult to derail her from her somatic preoccupation. When the therapist encouraged her to describe her life situation, it became clear that she felt she had given everything to her children and had received nothing in return. With the therapist's encouragement she also described her sense of unworthiness and of being inferior to the other members of the group and of the ward.

The therapist commented that he felt very strongly that when Mabel talked about her hands, she was really saying something else: that is, "I have some needs, too, but I have trouble asking for them. Therefore when I talk about my hands, what I'm really saying is, 'Pay some attention to me.'" After two or three such interpretations Mabel hesitantly agreed with the therapist's formulation and also to his request that henceforth whenever in the group she talked about her hands, he would immediately translate that into the real, interpersonal statement of "Pay more attention to me." It was a successful ploy and helped to integrate Mabel into the group—a difficult task to accomplish with a somatizing, ruminating patient.

Support the Monopolist

Monopolization is bad for both the group and the monopolist. The group's time is used unproductively, and the monopolizing patient is ultimately harmed because the other members of the group develop resentful feelings toward him or her which reinforce the monopolist's feelings of worthlessness and self-hatred.

Unless a group contains some particularly assertive members, it may not deal directly with a monopolist for some time. Often members of a group are reluctant to interrupt or to silence the monopolist because they fear that they will incur an obligation to fill the silence. There is the obvious rejoinder of "All right, I'll be quiet, *you* talk." People do not talk easily in a tense, guarded climate.

Instead, groups often smolder quietly or make indirect, hostile forays. Usually oblique attacks on the monopolist only aggravate the problem and fuel a vicious circle. The monopolist's compulsive speech is an attempt to deal with anxiety; as the monopolist senses group resentment, that anxiety rises, and the tendency to speak compulsively is correspondingly increased.

One of the basic principles in dealing with a monopolistic patient is that generally the flow of words does not result in others' knowing the patient more closely but constitutes, instead, a barrier to knowing that patient. Thus, the therapist's primary job is not to silence the monopolist, *not to hear less from the patient but to hear more*—but more on a personal level, not more of the words that act as a smokescreen and prevent the patient from being known or seen by others. Each therapist, according to his or her personal style, may convey this message to the patient in a different way. But the patient who gets the message that the therapist is interested in him or her and wants to get closer, will then feel supported rather than attacked.

Encourage Positive Behavior

It is important to help a patient show more positive parts of himself or herself so that they will be supported not only by the therapist but by the other members. In one group, for example, Robert, a sexually obsessed young man, talked continually about how much he wanted sex from women. Despite the fact that he was physically attractive, he presented himself in a way that so repelled women that at the age of twenty-seven he still had had no sexual relationship. The women in the group provided him feedback about their adverse reactions to his crude sexual overtures and his failure to express any interest in the nonsexual parts of themselves. Robert responded to this feedback in a highly self-defeating fashion: he immediately launched into a discussion of his many bathroom obsessions. In lurid detail he described his unusual excretory habits—all of which, of course, repelled the women in the group even more.

The therapist was struck by the fact that Robert inevitably presented himself in the worst possible light. One obvious tactic would be to make the interpretation that Robert so feared sexuality that, by presenting himself in a gross manner, he ensured that he would never have to be exposed to a sexual encounter. But Robert had conveyed on many previous occasions that an interpretive approach was not useful. The therapist, instead, found a way to be directly supportive. He commented that he was aware that Robert rarely talked about those aspects of himself in which he took some pride. What were the parts of himself that he really valued? Robert then began to talk about his love of music. He startled the other members by disclosing that he had been a concert violinist. From that moment on, they experienced Robert in a different way, and the therapist extended that process by suggesting that Robert bring his violin to the hospital to play some evening for the patients.

Often the only way to make contact with a withdrawn schizophrenic patient is to focus on strengths. One can comment upon or analyze the frozen external gates of the person indefinitely without ever budging them. For example, in one session Tom, a severely ill, schizophrenic young man, was extremely rigid in his facial expressions and his movements. The group had, in this session and on previous meetings, remarked upon his forbidding exterior. They gave him considerable feedback about how they were unable to know if Tom was angry or pleased with them. In this particular session there was a young woman, Luella, who resembled Tom in many ways. She, too, was very stiff and wore a heavy persona. She talked during the session about her vocation as a model and how she had always been taught to "stage" her appearance. Tom seemed very interested in what she was saying, and the therapist asked Tom whether he saw similarities between himself and Luella. Tom proceeded to describe his own personal need for perfection which interfered with his work. He was a professional artist and, for the first time during his hospitalization, talked about his work and responded openly to questions that members asked him about his painting. His frozen mask melted; he opened up and talked about several of his other interests.

At the end of the session, the therapist commented how much he liked what Tom had done in the meeting and how much closer he felt to Tom and how much better he felt he knew him. The other members of the group responded similarly. Luella blushed and, taking a great risk, said that she found Tom very attractive. She also commented that she'd never said that to a man before, and Tom responded that no one had ever said that to him. Both members were strongly supported by the therapist and by the other members for their risk taking and their openness in the session.

Identify and Emphasize the Patient's Value to Others

Therapists must learn to be as sensitive in identifying and pointing out positive aspects of the individual as they are in locating pathology. For example, one fifty-year-old woman, Sonia, with multiple sclerosis was deeply depressed. She spoke at length in a group session about her disease and how her physical handicap had robbed her of any purposeful service in life. She felt that she was useless and could no longer serve her husband or her son. She had so organized her life around service that it now seemed pointless to continue living.

The therapist and the group were enormously supportive of her by underscoring how important and helpful she had been to patients on the ward. Several people had earlier gratuitously commented how significant she had become to them in only a very few days. The therapist helped her realize that she didn't have to "do" anything to justify her existence. Her sheer presence, her listening, her support were important on the ward and, undoubtedly, in her home as well.

Do Not Support One Patient at the Expense of Another

When one patient does good work and receives support from the group, take care that it is not at the expense of another patient.

The following incident is illustrative. Linda opened a session by revealing how difficult it was for her to communicate to other people. One of her common patterns was to become angry, often inexplicably, and drive people away from her. Later in the meeting another member, Ron, commented that he felt uncomfortable at the prospect of receiving feedback in the group. The therapist wondered what he feared. Ron said he feared the dropping of the other shoe. "What would that be?" asked the therapist. "In your worst fears what might be said?" Ron said he feared someone would say that he was loathesome. A couple of minutes later, the therapist asked Linda how she was feeling about what Ron had said, and she replied angrily that she didn't even know what Ron was talking about because he seemed so "spacey," so much in a daze all the time.

The group spent several minutes working with Linda's peculiar response to Ron. What finally became evident was that Linda did not know what the word "loathesome" meant and responded to that with anger toward Ron. Linda then went on to make an important disclosure: that is, that a major reason for her reluctance to communicate closely with others was that she was convinced that she would be found stupid by other people.

When she approached a danger point—a point at which she feared her stupidity was becoming evident—she found a way to terminate the interaction, often by becoming irritated or angry.

This was a first-time disclosure for Linda, and it represented exceedingly important work. The group gave her tremendous support for the risk that she had taken. Ron was silent throughout all this; and when he was asked about his response to Linda, he blocked and then ultimately took off on a highly intellectualized tangent which was very difficult for people to follow. The therapist attempted to help focus Ron on his immediate feelings toward Linda, and asked whether he might not have felt closer to Linda as a result of this disclosure, but Ron continued to intellectualize. The therapist asked others how they might respond if they were Ron at that moment, and they were able to be much more simple and straightforward through comments to the effect that "Linda, I really feel closer to you now." "I feel I understand you." "I like your honesty," et cetera. When Ron was asked whether he could hear the difference between this message and the way he had first responded to Linda, he nodded in agreement.

In the summing-up phase of the group during the final ten minutes (see pages 259–73), the therapist raised the question whether Linda might have felt very good about what had happened but that Ron may have felt defeated by the meeting —that is, that he had failed. Ron nodded strongly in agreement with this. Knowing that Ron took much pride in his intelligence, the therapist was careful in his summing-up comments to speak to that strength. He commented that here was one instance in which Ron's considerable intelligence had gotten in the way of something else he wanted—that is, a closer relationship to others. The therapist commented that he really liked Ron's mind, his ability to use words and to think through abstract concepts, but that he, the therapist, hoped Ron would allow the group to help him develop this other part of himself more. That type of comment felt useful to Ron, and he left the group feeling supported and opened up rather than defeated.

Do Not Attack a Patient

It is obvious that therapists must avoid attacking patients. Therapists are in a position of great power. Not only are they imbued with much wisdom and power by patients but also, as group leaders, they are able to mobilize considerable group power. Despite the clear nature of this imperative, it is striking how often therapists are aggressive to patients. Generally such aggression occurs when one patient is being cruelly attacked by another, and the therapist defends the one attacked by, in turn, attacking the aggressor.

In one meeting, for example, Norman, who was very aggressive, harshly attacked another patient, Nancy, who consumed Pepsi-Cola nonstop on the ward while lamenting her inability to stop. The attack continued for quite some time. Finally, the therapist, his patience exhausted and his protective instincts aroused, berated Norman thus: "How can you go tell someone in such a cocky manner simply to stop drinking Pepsi when you yourself cannot control your alcohol drinking?" Although Nancy felt supported, Norman felt extremely defensive, especially since he had not yet revealed his alcoholism to the group.

What constructive options were available to the leader? How could he have supported the attacked patient without at the same time wounding the attacker? One of the first issues for the therapist to consider is whether there was any positive aspect to Norman's behavior. Indeed, in this case, there was! One must always give a patient the benefit of the doubt in terms of motivation. There were, after all, several silent patients in the meeting—members who had not responded in any way to Nancy. Norman might be given credit for his wishes to be helpful to the Pepsi addict. The therapist might, for example, say, "Norman, I'm aware that you have a strong wish to be helpful to

Nancy. I see you very frustrated, even angry. But it seems to me that your frustration comes out of a desire to be helpful."

If the patient acknowledges this (and he or she usually does), the therapist might extend the inquiry by raising the question whether the patient has accomplished what he or she hoped to do: that is, was Norman being useful to Nancy? Could he, for example, ask Nancy what she felt? Generally, Nancy will then say that she felt defensive and hurt by his attack. At this point the therapist might reflect back to Norman that it seems as if he has obtained a result that he hadn't wished for. Is there some other way, then, that he could have attempted to be helpful to Nancy?

Another tack would be to help the attacking patient be more self-reflective and establish some positive connections between attacker and attacked. For example, the therapist might comment that he sees Norman as being a little tough on Nancy and wonders whether that's not a reflection of how tough he is on himself. Are there, for example, parts of himself or aspects of his behavior that he would like to change by sheer will power and, like Nancy, is frustrated by being unable to do so?

These strategies are equally supportive to Nancy but do not constitute a put-down or an attack on Norman. On the contrary, they are supportive and point the way for him to begin some personal therapeutic work.

Make the Group Safe: Give the Patient Control

One reason patients are reluctant to work in a therapy group is they fear that things will go too far, that the powerful therapist or the collective group might coerce them to lose control—to say or think or feel things that will be catastrophic. The therapist can make the group feel safer by allowing each patient to set his or her limits and by emphasizing the patient's control over every interaction. Thus, the therapist can repeatedly "check in" with the patient through such questions as: "Do you want to pursue this further? Am I pressing you too much? Shall we stop now or would you prefer continuing to explore this? What questions can I ask that would be most helpful to you now?" Each of these approaches puts the control of the interaction in the patient's hands.

Treat the Patient with Respect and Dignity

These vignettes all illustrate variants on the same theme. The therapist must learn to be supportive and generous to the patient. It must become second nature to the therapist to identify strengths and to reinforce them by commenting on them. The therapist must learn to tell patients what he or she likes about them, to comment favorably upon any kind of progress, and to underscore the positive aspects of a patient's behavior rather than the negative ones, to focus on the tumbler being one-third full rather than two-thirds empty. If, for example, one patient is interacting with another and remains, to a large extent, aloof and distant, the therapist can help that patient interact more closely by commenting upon the positive aspect of his or her behavior (for example, upon the intention to communicate, upon the risk the patient is taking, or upon how much better the patient is doing than in the previous meeting) rather than by commenting on what the patient is *not* doing.

In behavioral terms, I advocate operant rather than aversive conditioning. I am reluctant to use behavioral terms, however, because of the very negative implications such language conveys about the nature of the therapist-patient relationship. It is exceedingly important that the therapist not relate to the patient as an object. When that happens, all the compliments, all the "operant cues," all the reinforcement in the world will not be perceived as truly supportive. Above all, the therapist must treat the patient with dignity and attempt to empathize as deeply as possible with him or her.

Often the therapist's comments about a patient's nonverbal behavior may, if not carefully couched, result in a patient's feeling like an object. For example, in one meeting one very anxious patient, Otto, attempted to share his distress and his despair with the group but engaged in considerable blocking and denial. Throughout the meeting he nervously tore away at a tissue box, and the therapist, in an effort to confront him and to decrease his denial, called his and the group's attention to the demolished box. The therapist wondered whether Otto's actions might reflect some anger as well as anxiety.

Otto left the meeting extremely upset and refused to return the following day to the group. He told his individual therapist that his experience in that session recapitulated one of the most humiliating experiences of his life. When he was ten years old, he had had extensive surgery done to repair hypospadius (a congenital deformity of the penis). He remembered, with great anger and shame, the many clinical conferences in which he was put on display and examined by groups of doctors on their surgery rounds.

Nonverbal behavior is an exceedingly important source of information for the therapist. Nail biting, posture, seating arrangement, gestures—all can convey important information about a patient's internal events. Unless the therapist is inordinately sensitive, however, verbal observations about these nonverbal cues are often experienced as objectification (that is, feeling that others regard one as an object). In the great majority of cases, nonverbal cues should be used as sources of information for the therapist, not as subjects for explicit discussion.

A Structured Approach to Support

All of the comments I have made in this section about support are even more pointedly relevant to groups of particularly severely disturbed or regressed patients. Most of the structure imposed by the therapist in such groups is designed to provide support to each of the members—support both from the therapist and from the other members as well.

In chapter 6, I will present in detail a model for lower-level groups, but here I shall describe one illustrative exercise. In this exercise, each patient is asked to write his or her name on a blank sheet of paper and then to write down two strengths: two things about oneself that one likes and does not want to change. The papers are then passed in turn to each person in the circle, who adds something that he or she likes about the person whose name is at the top of the paper, and passes it on. The exercise continues until the papers make a complete circle of the room, and each has returned to its original owner. In the rest of the exercise, each person reads aloud the list of strengths that others have perceived in him or her, and talks about those that he or she likes most of all and about those that are a bit surprising. Not only is this exercise particularly powerful and supportive of the patients; but since the therapist must participate as well, it provides excellent training in the discrimination and expression of patient strengths.

Conflict in the Inpatient Therapy Group

The strategic approach to conflict is, to a large extent, determined by the identical considerations raised in my discussion of support. Support and conflict are incompatible in the inpatient therapy group. Many, probably most, psychiatric inpatients have significant problems with anger: either they express anger in destructive fashion; or they are so threatened by anger that they stifle it and suffer such consequences of internalization as somatic illness, self-hatred, and depression.

Yet, despite the omnipresence of anger, there is much agreement among clinicians that small inpatient therapy groups cannot and should not be asked to deal with overt rage.[21] As one experienced clinician comments, "We have learned from bitter experience never, never to explore angry feelings or to encourage the expression of such feeling for its own sake."[22]

Strategies and Techniques of Leadership

Anger and conflict, even under the best of circumstances, evoke considerable discomfort. In the long-term therapy group, for example, considerable cohesiveness must be established before the therapist can begin to facilitate the overt emergence of conflict. Unless there is firm bonding between the members of the group, prolonged conflict will result in group fragmentation and premature termination on the part of many of them.

Some wards offer a discussion group for the ward staff—a group forum for them to discuss their own interpersonal tensions and conflicts. The staff members who participate in such groups know firsthand how extremely uncomfortable it is to deal with conflict, especially conflict with those with whom one lives all day. Those wards that do not offer such a group are generally embarrassed by their failure to do so: they are aware that a major reason for avoiding such discussion forums is that they are uncomfortable at the prospect of dealing explicitly with existing conflict. If professional mental-health workers are not able to deal openly with conflict, we should not expect severely disturbed inpatients to do so.

Sources of Conflict

A significant number of patients enter the inpatient therapy group with much anger—anger at having to be in the hospital, anger at themselves for having failed, anger at other people whom they perceive as having betrayed, abandoned, or mistreated them. Paranoid patients may enter the group with considerable resentment that their special qualities have not been recognized and that others conspire to deprive them of what is rightly theirs. Substance-abuse patients may be profusely angry at being unable to procure the drug they require for their comfort. Young adults and older adolescents often bridle at the limits imposed upon them by the ward staff.

In addition to these sources of anger originating within each of the group members, the inpatient therapy group has to cope with another source of anger—anger that arises from interpersonal and group dynamics. One of the most common sources of anger is *transference* (or *parataxic distortion*): a phenomenon in which one responds to another on the basis not of reality but of some image of the other that is distorted by one's past relationships and one's current interpersonal needs and fears. Thus, one may see in others aspects of significant individuals in one's own life. Should this distortion be negatively charged, then antagonism is easily initiated.

A particularly common form of distortion in therapy groups is the *mirror reaction*, which occurs when one encounters some other person in whom one sees traits of one's own—often suppressed traits of which one is very much ashamed. In other words, a person may hate another because one sees in that other some hated personal (conscious or unconscious) traits of one's own.

Rivalry may be another source of conflict in small inpatient groups. Patients must compete with one another for time and attention. This rivalry may be even more pronounced than in outpatient groups because of the time pressures inherent in the inpatient group. Often in long-term outpatient group therapy, members are content to wait, to allow others to consume a large proportion of the meeting because they are confident of the *quid pro quo:* they know that if they give to other members, their turn will come, and the group, in some future meetings, will reciprocate. But inpatient group members know that their turn may never come. Their personal stay in the group (and the stay of the people to whom they have given time) is so short, possibly only a day or two, that the time given will never be reciprocated.

Often this anger of rivalry is covertly expressed through displacement or a generalized irritability. Sometimes, however, groups flash past the boiling point and express it overtly. In one group, for example, the other members were furious at two unruly adolescent members. When the former finally expressed their anger, they directed it not toward the adolescents' rude behavior but at their having taken so much valuable time from everyone else in the group.

Occasionally anger emerges from the patients' competition with one another in the group for some particular commodity. Hospitalization enhances the emergence of regressive, dependent, demanding wishes. Patients may vie for the largest share of the therapist's attention or for some particular role: the most influential, the most sensitive, the most disturbed or needy person in the group. A patient may become angry because his or her (unrealistic) expectations of therapy have been frustrated: the patient was not chosen by the therapist as the favorite child; the therapist has somehow disillusioned the patient and failed to meet his or her expectations. The group members who are unable to confront the therapist directly with these disappointments may displace their anger onto a scapegoat, further increasing the general level of conflict and anger in the group. Because of the short-term, crisis nature of the inpatient group, these sources of conflict tend to be less pronounced than in the long-term outpatient group; but their emergence, in some form, must be anticipated.

Whatever the sources, the consequences of conflict in the inpatient group are very grave. Mutual trust is eroded, the group feels unsafe and the self-disclosure necessary for therapeutic work dies stillborn. A group in conflict cannot achieve one of the major goals of the inpatient therapy group: an introduction to therapy as a supportive, pleasant, and constructive experience, which patients will wish to continue after they leave the hospital.

Dealing with Anger

There are several important therapeutic guidelines for dealing with anger. First, there is no place in the small inpatient therapy group for conflict evocation. Inpatient group therapists must not make the error of concluding that, since many patients have problems in the sphere of anger, the therapist should find methods to help these patients "get their anger out" and deal with it in therapy. *The inpatient group therapist's aim must be rapid conflict resolution, not conflict evocation.* There may be some need to help a patient who is suffused with anger to express, displace, or sublimate that anger. But the small group is not the place for such help. A patient can work on that task in one-to-one settings or in some form of physical exercise, such as punching a punching bag. Significant conflict between two patients may be worked out in a meeting consisting of those two patients and one or two members of the ward staff.

I do not mean to say that the inpatient group therapist should pretend that anger does not exist. Your task is to find a way to help patients deal with anger in a fashion that does not disrupt the safety of the group atmosphere.

One recommended mode of working with anger is to help patients translate rage into something that is safer and less threatening—some affect that may be worked with comfortably in the group. If patients announce to the group that their chief problem is anger, either too much or too little, and they want to work on that in the group, I usually suggest the following steps: I first comment that it is generally too difficult to work on rage in the therapy group. It's often too scary and too uncomfortable for everyone concerned. I then proceed to comment that one of the reasons it is so painful to deal with anger is that many individuals let it build up inside of themselves until it is so great it feels as though it will erupt like a volcano: at that point it frightens the individual, and it frightens others. The best way, I continue, that anger can be worked with in the therapy group situation is to express it when it is still very young—so young that it has not yet become anger but is still irritation or annoyance or assertiveness. I urge these individuals, then, to express "young" anger—that is, irritation, annoyance, or assertiveness—as soon as they become aware of it.

To help group members express these affects, I first ask them to express their irritation or annoyance in the safest possible way—that is, not toward another group member, but toward an issue or a procedure. I ask them, for example, what irritation they might have about the procedure of this meeting or about the way that I, the therapist, am leading the group in this session. It is far easier, let us pray, for the therapist to deal with anger than for any of the group members to do so. Generally patients are not able to comply at the first request, and it is necessary to return to them several times during the session and inquire whether they are experiencing irritation.

Only later, and then very carefully, do I encourage members to express irritation that they may experience toward some other individual. I urge them to find some way to express their annoyance or irritation toward another which will not be painful, which will not close the other individual down but, instead, will open him or her up. I encourage them also to keep in mind that their task is to express a small, nascent feeling which has not grown into a huge, ponderous chunk of irritation or anger.

When a patient does express irritation at another patient, the therapist must monitor the process carefully. Some patients are so conflicted in the sphere of aggression that acknowledging and expressing irritation is extraordinarily painful. Other patients may be so insecure and vulnerable that the mildest criticism may be experienced as catastrophic. The therapist must be sensitive to both possibilities and proceed accordingly.

The patients who have the most difficulty expressing anger are often the decompensated, severely obsessive-compulsive patients. Such patients usually have a core of rage that they experience as so dangerous that a brief exploration of it in a short therapy group is not generally therapeutic.

For example, one patient, Rose, discussed at great length her problems in a group meeting. There were many obvious clues that anger was a core dynamic for her: she shared her profound feelings of grief about the recent death of her dog and her guilt that, through her negligence, she might have been in some way responsible for the dog's death. Her words made it clear to everyone that the dog had been an incredible burden upon her for some years. There were other stresses, including divorce, that Rose faced in her life, and the care of a chronically ill, incontinent, irritable dog would have taxed the patience of Mother Teresa. (The matter was hardly improved by the fact that the dog had originally belonged to her husband who, when he left Rose, left the dog as well.) Without doubt, Rose had death wishes toward the dog and, at some level of awareness, experienced some relief when the critter finally expired.

Sensing that Rose was choking on her unexpressed rage, the therapist urged her to examine her irritation minutely and to take a risk and express some of that irritation she might be feeling toward one of the members of the group. Rose hesitated, then finally took a risk and, turning to a nineteen-year-old patient in the group, blurted out, "There's no reason at all why you should need to be in the hospital. You're young, good-looking, in good physical health, and strong. Pick yourself up by your bootstraps and get on with your life!"

Although her words and her tone were relatively mild, it was apparent that Rose was uncomfortable about this confrontation and immediately afterward attempted to undo it by commenting that her contemptuousness was one of her big problems: she knew it was a foolish thing to say because people couldn't get well by willing themselves to get well! If that were so, she would have been out of the hospital a long time ago. She pointed out that she, too, had lots of problems when she was nineteen years old, et cetera.

Rose's discomfort increased. No amount of reassurance by the group could check it. She was not even comforted when the young woman whom she had addressed reassured Rose that not only was she not crushed but she now liked Rose much better. After the group Rose's anxiety increased to panic, and she was unable to sleep the entire night. She refused to come back to the group for subsequent meetings.

In retrospect, it is apparent that the therapist misjudged Rose's capacity to tolerate the expression of anger. A more salubrious strategy would have been to have requested something safer from her—that is, irritation at some issue, some aspect of her past life, or some feelings about the procedure of the group.

Patients commonly are afraid to express anger, even in small amounts, because they believe that it will set into motion a catastrophic event. Generally, if patients are not as vulnerable as Rose, it is advisable to help them express anger in some attenuated form so that they learn that their calamitous fantasy is but a fantasy and will not materialize.

Let me describe an example involving two patients whom I shall call Peter and Ellen. Peter had always had a great deal of difficulty asserting himself and in saying anything critical to anyone. He was, he claimed, weary of warily walking on eggshells and hoped that therapy would help him change. The group therapist encouraged him to take a chance, to start that process by trying to make one negative comment about something that had been irritating to him in the group that day. Peter complied and took a chance. But it was not the gentle one the therapist would have hoped for; instead, Peter turned toward Ellen, a twenty-one-year-old anorexic-bulemic patient, and said, "I think that you're taking too much time in the group today!" To this, Ellen responded very adversely, putting her hands to her head and sobbing for at least five minutes, despite all efforts of the group to console her.

The meeting at this point seemed to be heading toward catastrophe. The therapist's rationale, in asking Peter to take a risk by expressing some minor negative feelings, was that Peter could discover that such an act would *not* result in the catastrophe that he anticipated in his fantasy. Ellen's response was the last thing the therapist hoped to hear: the event seemed to be confirming rather than allaying Peter's fears.

The therapist saved the day by doing some excellent modeling for the group. He approached the whole incident in a confident, matter-of-fact manner and demonstrated to the members that anger and upsetness were not "too hot to handle." First, he checked out how the members of the group felt about the time distribution. How many people in the group felt that Ellen was taking too much time in the group meeting? It turned out that one other person agreed with Peter, whereas six others disagreed. Three members opined that Ellen was too unselfish and was not taking *enough* time in the group. The split "vote" was an interesting commentary on an issue that was exceedingly important for both Ellen and Peter: Is it possible to please everyone? (On even a relatively objective measure—that is, the taking of too much or too little time—the members of the group could not agree and, thus, could never be unanimously satisfied.) How does one tolerate the discomfort of not pleasing all people? Ellen participated in this discussion, since it was an issue with which she had long struggled. Part of her "unselfishness" stemmed from the wish to please everyone; and, in so doing, she lost sight of her own wishes and needs.

Peter's statement also opened up the whole question of time sharing in the group—an exceptionally "hot" issue for any therapy group, but an issue that is only rarely discussed even in the most advanced of groups. With the help of the leaders, the group forthrightly discussed several difficult questions: Which members were getting enough time in the group and which members were not? How were decisions made about who got time in this group? And the people who weren't getting enough time: was that a common state of affairs for them?

By this time Ellen had recovered from her crying, and the group helped her explore why she had reacted so strongly: Why all the tears? Why was she so highly sensitive to the accusation of selfishness? The exploration led Ellen into the issue of greediness and sharing—always an issue of vital concern for an anorexic or bulemic patient. Ellen revealed a great deal about her feelings regarding food, eating, greediness, her desire sometimes to eat everything at the table, her gulping other people's leftovers, and so on. By the end of the meeting, Ellen had done more work and opened up more issues of central importance for herself than she had in all of her previous group meetings, either on this current admission or on a previous one.

The therapist, of course, did not fail to emphasize to Peter that his risk taking was the impetus for this intensive and successful meeting. By the end of the meeting, the original intention of the therapist was realized: Peter had ventured in the group and had his fears about risk taking disconfirmed!

"Gentling" Anger

There are several other methods of "gentling" anger. Consider the following situation: Ann, a young woman in the group, wept copiously throughout the first part of a session. When she had finally composed herself and was able to speak, she related an incident that most of the members of the group already knew about. She had been romantically involved with Rick, another member of the group, for a few days. He had decided, rather abruptly, to terminate their relationship. Ann was pained by the break-up and by seeing Rick on the ward every day. Her pain was intensified by Rick's decision not to talk to her about their relationship for seven days; he said he needed that time to collect his thoughts. On this particular day Ann, extremely upset, had approached Rick and asked to talk to him about what had happened. Rick rebuked her, saying that it had been only six days, and he had told her that he wanted to wait seven days.

It was no secret, therefore, to the group that Ann was feeling very angry toward Rick. Moreover, the therapist was confident that Rick, a well-defended substance abuser, could well tolerate some expression of anger toward him. What options were available to the therapist? How could he help Ann, who was terrified of expressing anger, directly express her feelings toward Rick?

One recourse was to ask her to express her anger "once

removed." It always gentles anger to express it in the subjunctive tense. Thus, the therapist could say to Ann, *"If* you were going to express your anger at Rick, what might you say?" This simple linguistic gimmick is a useful tool for the therapist in a number of different situations.

Another way the therapist can "once remove" anger is to ask other people in the group to role-play for a moment or two, to pretend they are the angry person and to express the anger that they think he or she might be feeling. In this case, after a number of people have expressed what they thought Ann was feeling, she might be asked which of the various comments fit her own feelings most closely.

Still another option—the one the therapist successfully employed in this situation—is to make the expression of anger safe by carefully circumscribing it. The therapist suggested that Ann express some of her feelings toward Rick, but that she do so with an arbitrary time limit—for example, sixty seconds.

Therapist Modeling

Another way that the leader can help members explore, in a safe way, their responses to their anger is for the leader to offer a model of dealing with anger that may permit the members to work vicariously. On occasion it is useful for co-therapists to disagree with one another. If they disagree but still continue to respect one another and continue working together with one another, they provide excellent modeling for patients. In chapter 5, I shall describe a technique in which observers and therapists discuss the meeting in front of the patients. This format provides an excellent opportunity for therapists to model healthy disagreement.

There are times when the leader has to take a particularly assertive stand. If, for example, you have set up explicit rules in the group, you will at times have to enforce them. Thus, if the group has rules about not admitting late-comers, it will be necessary for you to deny entrance to patients arriving late. It is good modeling if the therapist is relatively transparent in such situations. You may ask for members' reactions to your actions, but you do well also to reveal your own discomfort at your own act. You may reveal your mixed feelings: on the one hand, you feel it is the correct procedure and is best for the group because it will result, ultimately, in group members being there on time and in the group meeting having fewer disruptions; simultaneously, however, you feel a bit guilty and concerned that you may have wounded the patient who was seeking admission. You may also point out that you will respond to these concerns by making certain that you meet with the excluded patient after the group.

Even the most tranquil, well-balanced therapist will, from time to time, be subjected in inpatient group therapy to events that will cause him or her to get angry. This is an event of considerable impact for patients and should be carefully handled.

Consider this clinical illustration: During the middle of one group meeting, a psychiatrist opened the door of the group room and beckoned to one of his patients who stood up and left the room to meet him for an individual therapy session. The group therapist felt exceedingly annoyed at this disruption to the group. For one thing, the ward policy had been clearly stated to all admitting psychiatrists that patients were not to be removed from the therapy group meeting; second, that particular patient had been one of the central figures of the meeting, and her exit was particularly disruptive for the group. For a minute or two, the group therapist smoldered and then decided to act promptly on his feelings. He went out into the hallway and confronted the offending psychiatrist.

The group therapist and the psychiatrist had a brief argument that was sufficiently loud to be overheard by the group members. Three or four minutes later, the group therapist re-entered the group, followed a few minutes later by the patient. This was obviously an event of considerable importance to the members, and the group therapist urged them to discuss their reactions. Several members talked about feeling frightened to see two therapists in such open disagreement. They were reminded of old feelings at seeing their parents fight. Still other patients felt it was refreshing and expressed admiration for the way that the two therapists could express their disagreement to one another but nonetheless keep communicating.

The therapist modeled transparency to the group. He commented that he had been irritated for the first couple of minutes after the patient left, and decided that, although it was uncomfortable for him, it would be best for him to deal with those feelings by confronting the psychiatrist. He mentioned also, however, that in the brief hallway discussion he could clearly understand the psychiatrist's position: the latter had had several emergencies that day and had no other time when he could see that patient. He had called the ward and asked the nursing staff to keep the patient from the group meeting, but the message had not been relayed to the patient. Thus, even though both points of view—the group therapist's and the admitting psychiatrist's—were entirely reasonable, it still did not negate the fact that strong feelings could be evoked and expressed. It was a valuable exercise in modeling, and several patients referred to it later in the course of their hospitalization as having been important to them.

Conflict Resolution

No matter how hard one tries to avoid it, some open conflict between patients is unavoidable. Thus the therapist must be adept at conflict resolution, not only finding ways to terminate the conflict but, if possible, making constructive use of emergent anger.

Psychotherapy consists, in general, of an alternating sequence of content and process, of affect evocation and understanding of the evoked affect: in other words, a phase of heightened emotional arousal is followed by an attempt (by the individual patient or the group) to understand the meaning of that emotional experience. When anger is the affect in question, the therapist needs to guide the group quickly into the phase of understanding and clarification. Thus, at the first signs of conflict, the therapist may simply act decisively and change the flow of the group by commenting to this effect: "Let's stop for a few minutes now, take a step or two back, and try to make some sense out of what's just happened here in the group. Who has some ideas about it?" The therapist may comment simply that anger is very problematic in our lives, and it is important that we try to understand the anger in this group as much as we can.

The task is to pull the members quickly out of the conflict and into a more objective posture from which they view their therapy from a longer perspective. Thus, the therapist makes statements like, "John, obviously it's not your anger or your relationship with Joe that needs to be solved here in the group. It's unlikely that you and he will be seeing one another outside the group; thus, in a sense it's irrelevant about who's right and who's wrong and who will win and who will lose. What's really important is what the two of you can learn about yourselves from this conflict so that you can apply that to yourselves in your outside lives."

There are many ways of transforming a conflict between group members into something constructive. One important concept to keep in mind is mirroring: one may respond negatively to another because one sees parts of oneself in that other. Often the attributes in question exist at an unconscious level: that is, one disowns or splits off hated parts of oneself and externalizes them onto another individual to whom one responds very negatively. Sometimes the term *projective identification* is used to describe this mental operation in which one projects parts of oneself onto another person with whom one subsequently develops a close and unusual identification. Consequently, if two people are in conflict, it is often useful to inquire if each sees some part of himself or herself in the other. Such a question, if properly timed, can result not only in conflict resolution but in useful personal exploration on the part of the protagonists. If there is a *double mirror reaction*—that is, each of the individuals sees disowned parts of himself or herself in the other—then there is likely to be a strong mutual antagonism. Frequently it's useful to inquire about positive feelings that antagonists may have toward one another. It may be particularly helpful to examine aspects of the other that one envies. Keep in mind, too, that if two people are in conflict with one another, it also implies that they take one another very seriously. Not infrequently when patients finish a group or leave the hospital ward, they will, in retrospect, comment that their chief antagonist was particularly useful to them. It has been said that one's friends (especially spouses) are one's worst enemies, since they often discourage personal change and growth. Being angry at another person means that one takes the other seriously, that one allows the other to matter to one. If a patient in the hospital has an absolutely empty or neutral relationship to another person, hardly exchanging a word or a gesture and certainly not exchanging powerful feelings, then it's inevitable that the other person is going to be of no real help to the individual in acquiring self-knowledge.

Sometimes *role reversal* is a useful technique of conflict resolution. When individuals are locked in conflict, a predictable sequence occurs. Antagonists develop the belief that they are right and the others are wrong, that they are good and the others bad. Characteristically these beliefs are held with equal conviction and certitude by each of the two opposing parties. A breakdown in communication ensues. The two parties cease to listen to each other with any degree of understanding. Not only do they stop listening but they may unwittingly distort their perceptions of one another. Perceptions are filtered through a screen of stereotype; the other's words are shaped to fit one's preconceived view of the other. To counteract this mutual distortion, patients must learn to understand the other and to enter the other's experiential world. If patients who are in disagreement are instructed to switch roles and to present the point of view, the feelings, and the arguments of the other person, they are often able to have an entirely new perspective on themselves and their conflict.

If two people in conflict have been in the hospital for a few days, and the therapist has evidence that the two of them have also had positive feelings toward one another, then there may be more leverage. For example, in one group meeting two patients who had previously spent a lot of time with one another, Matt and Ruth, were in considerable conflict. Ruth had been angry at Matt for two days and refused to speak to him.

In the group meeting Matt said that he wanted to work on their conflict, but Ruth declined, saying that she was not in a "place" where she could talk to him. Her reasons were that Matt had blown up angrily on three or four occasions on the ward recently, and she had grown very frightened of him. His rudeness to her two days ago was the final straw. She concluded that it was simply best not to interact with him any longer.

The therapist felt that she was "writing off" Matt, and asked whether she was and how long a sentence she was going to give him. Ruth answered that it was probably a life sentence and, responding to questions from other members, began discussing her judgmentalism and the fact that it was common for her to "write people off" permanently.

Was there anything Matt could do to receive a shorter sentence? Nothing, it seemed! Matt wondered if there was anything else about himself that led to her decision to close herself up to him. Ruth said that she was needy but that she saw Matt as even more needy and she felt reluctant to give to anyone who had nothing to give to her. Matt commented that, the day before, he had seen Ruth doubled over in pain on the terrace and had desperately wanted to give her something. He had been tempted to play his guitar to her to make her feel better (he was

159

an excellent musician). He didn't do it, nor could he even make the offer, because he knew that Ruth would shut him out. Other members of the group then commented that there were times when they, too, wanted to help Ruth but were afraid their offer would be received as intrusion rather than as help. This meeting began with conflict but ended with an important exploration of key issues for both Matt and Ruth. Matt learned something very important about the consequences of his anger on other people, especially people who were important to him. Ruth obtained some important feedback about her irrevocable judgments and her modes of discouraging potential help for herself.

Another means of conflict resolution is to help the members avoid global accusations, judgments, or condemnations. When two individuals are in conflict and make sweeping condemnations of each other, the conflict is invariably unsettling and unconstructive. It is important to steer patients away from global statements of dislike for another individual—that is, for the other individual as a person—and to attempt to help the members state what traits or what behavior of the other person they dislike. Criticism, thus formulated, is far more likely to be constructive: to hear some aspect of one's behavior or of oneself being criticized is far less painful than to hear one's whole person being criticized and rejected; furthermore, there is the additional message that behavior is changeable, and that one can do something to redeem oneself.

Often the therapist can help the accused engage in some self-dissection. In other words, if someone is very critical of another person, the therapist may help the former investigate what part of himself or herself dislikes that behavior in the other: "Whose voice is inside of you taking that position?" "Are there other parts of you who like that behavior or who like other aspects of that person that we haven't mentioned?"

Therapist Transparency

The *transparency* (that is, the self-disclosure) of the therapist has a curvilinear relationship to outcome: too much and too little therapist transparency are *negatively* related to good outcome. The rule of the golden mean prevails: there is an optimal level of therapist transparency. Most inpatient group therapists, especially those whose primary training is in long-term outpatient psychotherapy, err in the direction of too little self-disclosure. I have emphasized that inpatient group therapists, in comparison to therapists leading long-term outpatient groups, must be more structured, more supportive, and more active. They must be more self-disclosing as well.

Therapist Self-Disclosure: Why Not?

The major ideological barrier to the self-disclosure of the group therapist is a belief that a "blank screen" therapist enhances the therapeutic process. This belief is based on the traditional psychoanalytic legend that the paramount curative factor is the resolution of the patient's transference to the therapist. The analytic therapeutic assumption is that the patient will relate in a transferential mode to the therapist who remains opaque; and, that through the resolution of this transference, therapeutic understanding and change will ensue. But, as I have argued elsewhere,[23] there is little evidence to support this hypothesis. First, transference is a hardy organism! The patient will perceive the therapist in a unrealistic, transferential manner regardless of the therapist's presentation of self. Second, and far more important, the therapist, by maintaining an aloof, impersonal persona, sacrifices many potentially powerful therapeutic options. I believe that the tradition of therapist opacity serves the end of therapist comfort rather than that of therapeutic effectiveness.

In the acute inpatient therapy group, the argument that the inpatient group therapist must remain opaque so as not to contaminate the transference, makes no sense whatsoever. The overriding principle is that the therapist must operate in such a way as to facilitate the group's attaining its goals for the members. None of the goals of the inpatient therapy group (encouragement of participation in after-care psychotherapy, learning that talking helps, problem spotting, engagement in the ward psychotherapy program, alleviation of iatrogenic anxiety) are facilitated by therapist opacity. On the contrary, the therapist's self-disclosure greatly accelerates the work of the inpatient group.

Types Of Therapist Self-Disclosure

The rationale behind therapist self-disclosure is not that disclosure *per se* is to be embraced as a primary principle of therapy; instead, therapist self-disclosure must be instrumental: it must facilitate the attainment of primary therapy goals. This general principal provides guidelines for the nature and the extent of self-disclosure.

"Total" therapist transparency is neither possible nor desirable. Therapists must disclose in a manner that provides patients with support, acceptance, and encouragement, and can do so through selective self-disclosure. It is your task not to manufacture positive feelings but to locate and express your positive feelings and your recognition of the patient's strengths.

It is not possible to work with psychotic patients without experiencing powerful personal reactions, including fear, bewilderment, deep discouragement, pity, anger, and, at times, even hatred. To disclose these strong feelings in a group when you are attempting to implant a sense of safety and acceptance is obviously contraindicated. Self-disclosure must be *in the service* of the primary goals of therapy. A patient who is desperately in need of support will not be benefitted by hearing the therapist describe personal feelings of dislike for, or distrust of, him or her.

Patients who are demoralized will not benefit from hearing therapists discuss their personal demoralization or their discouragement in working with patients. Patients who desperately need a sense of structure will not benefit from hearing therapists discuss their deep sense of puzzlement or confusion. Elsewhere I have described an outpatient group formed and led by two group therapists who were dedicated to the idea of therapist transparency.[24] From the very beginning of the group, they indulged in unflinching honesty. In the very first meetings they openly expressed their uncertainty about group therapy, their self-doubts, their personal anxiety. In so doing, however, they sabotaged important therapeutic tasks: that is, maintenance of the group, development of trust in the therapeutic process, and development of group cohesion. The majority of the members of this outpatient group dropped out of it in the first few sessions.

Another of the primary tasks of the therapist is to build a group that focuses on here-and-now interpersonal interaction. (I shall shortly discuss in detail the therapist's strategies in this domain.) This task dictates another guideline to self-disclosure: the therapist who discloses here-and-now feelings, rather than events of his or her personal historical past or current personal life, facilitates the movement of the group far more effectively. Many of these general statements about self-disclosure will become more apparent in the clinical examples to follow.

Advantages of Therapist Self-Disclosure

Modeling

Judicious therapist self-disclosure provides excellent modeling for patients—modeling in openness, in self-disclosure, and in risk taking. For example, consider a group session in which the group could not get started. An attempted suicide on the ward the previous evening had been so deeply unsettling to everyone that there was enormous resistance to all the therapeutic activities of the day. After a few minutes of silence and a couple of anxious false starts, the group therapist disclosed his personal feelings to the group. He stated that he felt unsettled by Joan's suicide attempt the night before, and that he wondered whether he might have done something to prevent it. He felt, even though he knew it was not rational, that somehow he might have picked up some clues from Joan had he listened more intently. He mentioned, too, that he couldn't help feeling angry at Joan—angry at her for not allowing others to help her; angry, too, because he felt that in some ways the suicide attempt seemed almost a spiteful act. The therapist's disclosure in this instance plunged the group members quickly and helpfully into a trusting, cohesive session in which they shared their own reactions to the suicide attempt with great candor.

At the beginning of another session, the therapist picked up Dudley, the ward cat, and carried it outside the group room. He explained to the group that he had been saddened by the death of his own cat the week before, and that the presence of Dudley in the room augmented that sadness and would constitute a distraction to him during the meeting. This simple act had enormous consequences. Not only did the group work with unusual trust and effectiveness during that meeting, but the patients referred back to it in subsequent meetings on numerous occasions. At that time there was in process a research project in which patients were asked, among other things, about critical incidents in psychotherapy. It was remarkable how many patients referred back to this disclosure on the part of the therapist as having been highly significant to them.

Therapist self-disclosure also provides good modeling of social skills which patients may then consider and possibly try on for size. For example, a common technique that you may use, when interacting with a patient who appears reluctant to speak,

Strategies and Techniques of Leadership

is to express aloud your dilemma. For example, you might say, "Chris, I have a couple of feelings as I'm talking to you. On the one hand, I'd like very much to hear more from you and keep inviting you to participate more in the group. At the same time, I'm feeling uneasy that I may be pressuring you too much or nagging you or intruding on your privacy, and it's important for me to let you know that." Such a comment models much that may be valuable in social interaction: honesty, caring, consideration for the other.

Increasing a Patient's Trust in the Therapeutic Procedure

Patients will have more trust in a therapeutic procedure if they see that the therapist is willing to engage in the same procedure. For example, in one meeting the therapist was interacting with a new group member in an effort to help her enter and interact in the group. But the interaction between the two became very sticky. The patient balked; the therapist tried harder and became mildly irritated. Soon therapist and patient were at an uncomfortable impasse. The therapist then turned to the rest of the group, acknowledged the impasse, and wondered if the group would help him and Edna understand what was happening between the two of them. He especially asked for some feedback about his role in creating the impasse.

Among the comments that were made was that the therapist was pushing too hard. After all, Edna had been sick in bed with the flu for a couple of days, it was her first meeting, she was ill and scared. The therapist seemed not to have been sensitive to her situation but, instead, was wholly insistent on her doing what he wanted her to do. The therapist acknowledged the feedback; he checked it out with Edna who agreed that that was precisely how she felt. The therapist commented that that was valuable for him to hear, that often he did become too aggressive and enthusiastic and tended to lose sight of where a patient was.

The therapist's behavior facilitated the work of the group. The patients felt validated. The therapist listened to them and respected their feedback. Moreover, he demonstrated his trust in the procedure of therapy—a trust that encourages patients to try the water themselves.

Increasing a Patient's Understanding Of, and Trust in, the Therapist

Debriefing interviews with patients corroborate that judicious therapist self-disclosure helps patients feel more trusting and comfortable with their group therapists and other authority figures; it will also have positive repercussions for their work with future therapists in their lives.

Consider this clinical illustration: A therapist began a meeting with this statement: "I'd like to start the meeting today by talking about something that has been concerning me. I feel uncomfortable in the group today because of yesterday's meeting. I'm aware that both Linda and Nancy came to the meeting yesterday wanting to work, and I helped them explore some important issues, but both of them ended the meeting feeling highly distressed and much worse than they felt when they entered. I guess I want to check that out with them and to see what we might have done differently yesterday and how we can work in such a way today that the group doesn't end up making people feel worse about themselves."

The response of the group to this initial comment by the therapist was very positive. Linda responded that she had felt awful at the end of the meeting the day before but hoped she could do something about that today. She felt awful yesterday because she had related so many "despicable" things about herself in the session and left it convinced that other people felt she was so repulsive they wouldn't even want to associate with her. She decided, with the help of one of the nurses, that what she really needed to do in the group today was to find out from others if that were true.

Nancy stated that she, too, felt upset after the meeting yesterday—but in an important and constructive way. She got in touch with feelings that she had been reluctant to explore in the past, and she had a particularly helpful session with her individual therapist following the group. The rest of the group expressed some appreciation for the therapist's concern, and the ensuing meeting proved to be unusually trusting and constructive.

And another example: Karen was a patient who was very frightened of the therapist but also very angry at him. She began one meeting in a petulant, quasi-confused state. With the therapist's help, she declared she wanted to work on her irritability. The therapist spent approximately twenty minutes trying to help her explore her feelings of anger, especially toward him or toward other people who might represent authority. The work was highly unproductive because of Karen's fear and her passive aggressivity. Ultimately the therapist shifted the group focus to other members in the group. In the final few minutes Karen expressed anger at the therapist for having interrupted her and commented that his choosing to work on other issues was proof to her of her own unimportance and worthlessness.

The therapist responded: "I appreciate your saying that, Karen. I know how hard it is for you to express critical feelings to me. But maybe it would help if you could only know what it was like being me in the group today. First, I was under some pressure because there were nine people in the group, three of whom will be leaving the hospital today. I had a sense of wanting to do as much as possible for as many people as I could. I tried my best to help you explore some of your feelings but, at the same time, I felt that it was highly uncomfortable for you and that I was not only not being helpful but was pushing you in directions where you didn't want to go. After about twenty minutes I began to feel that it was really necessary for me to look at the other members in the group, and thus I switched off.

But my switching off is by no means reflective of any lack of interest in or dislike of you."

The following day Karen said that the therapist's comments had been helpful; he seemed more human, and she, for the first time, thought about what it was like being a therapist.

Earlier I stated that it is important that the therapist convey a sense of confidence and competence to patients. One of the modes of creating structure is for you to have a clear sense of your personal therapeutic strategy and be clear and concise in statements and actions. This does *not* mean that a therapist should attempt to appear infallible to patients. One of the principles of good modeling is that you are able to admit errors and encourage patients to discuss openly their criticisms of you.

Consider this clinical illustration: A therapist led a therapy group that was frequently observed by other therapists or students. The patients were aware of this observation and had been assured that no one who knew them personally would be permitted to observe the group without their permission. In speaking with the observers after one meeting, the therapist learned that a woman who had come to observe that one session had, in fact, known Alma, one of the patients. A year ago Alma had enrolled in an adult education course in assertiveness training led by this observer, and subsequently they had had a very brief social relationship.

Since there was great tumult on the ward at that time, because of a couple of severely disturbed patients and because Alma herself had been in considerable crisis, the therapist (unwisely) decided simply to "deep-six," or bury, the incident and not discuss it with the group or with Alma. The observer in question had not planned to observe the group again; her relationship with Alma had not really been personal; the therapist concluded that there was too much unrest in the group already to add this extraneous issue. Furthermore, he felt embarrassed at his laxity in not having instructed the observer to leave if she knew any of the patients in some other capacity.

As luck would have it, one of the nurses, who did not know of the therapist's decision, mentioned in passing to Alma that her old teacher had been in the observation room. The following day Alma caught the therapist just before the beginning of the group and requested a few minutes with him after the group meeting to talk about the incident.

The group session that day happened to be characterized by considerable evasiveness and disengagement on the part of the members. The therapist decided that he was colluding in that disengagement by his own evasiveness, and decided to deal with the issue openly in the group. He invited Alma to tell the group about the situation and her reactions to it. Following that, he discussed his part in it with extreme candor: he stated that he felt he had made an error, and decided to try to bury it in the hope it would go unnoticed. In retrospect, he knew now it would have been far better to discuss the issue openly with Alma rather than simply hoping that it would go away.

The therapist helped to take things even further than the patients were inclined to go, and labeled the situation as a real crisis of trust in him and helped them to talk about that distrust. Once again, the therapist stated, he had learned that every time he had attempted to withhold something, it had backfired; the incident had increased his resolve to remain open with patients.

As a result of this disclosure, the patients' trust in him increased rather than decreased; his admission of his fallibility and his willingness to discuss his feelings enhanced their willingness to take risks in the group. A patient who had been in the group for five days revealed that a friend of hers happened to be a personal friend of the therapist, and that she had been afraid to talk in the group lest he would repeat to the friend things she had said there. The therapist's openness in dealing with Alma allowed her to discuss this fear and to be reassured that he would maintain confidentiality.

Therapist Transparency and Feedback

The therapist's personal reactions to patients constitute an invaluable pool of data, which the therapist should judiciously share with them. The therapist's feedback is always powerful information to patients and should be delivered against a background of support.

A clinical illustration: Esther was a distant, cold, intelligent, and highly materialistic businesswoman. She spoke incessantly about her business affairs, her various real estate deals, how much money her depression was costing her, how her husband was attempting to rob her in their divorce proceedings, et cetera. The staff members were very frustrated in working with her, because any comment they made to her was answered in some way having to do with the *idée fixe* of material possessions.

In one group session the therapist penetrated her armor with the following comment: "Esther, I've been thinking a lot about you, and I'd like to share a fantasy that I've had. Whenever I think about getting to know you or getting close to you, I immediately have the visual image of all sorts of material possessions getting between us—houses, cars, furniture, et cetera. Whenever you talk here in the group about your material goods, I always feel like you're putting some barrier up between me and you. I can't say whether others have this reaction, but it's a very strong feeling of mine."

This same general strategy may permit the therapist to give feedback in a wide array of situations. Take, for example, the obsessive patient who ruminates interminably about a fixed set of concerns: the most effective leverage the therapist can bring to bear is to persist in pointing out how the patient's comments make the listener feel.

Consider this comment: "John, I have some feedback for you. Several times during this session today I tried to make some type of personal approach to you and engage you in some type of discussion with me. But each time I've done that, somehow in the next couple of minutes you are back discussing your business failures and all the various problems related to that. I know those issues are important to you, but nevertheless when you refuse to engage me in any manner but talk about business, I end up feeling shut out of your life entirely. I can only imagine that if I were a friend of yours outside the hospital, I would sooner or later feel so rebuffed by you that I would give up trying to make a connection with you. I wonder whether that doesn't happen to you outside and whether that results in your being pretty isolated in your life?"

Or consider this comment that the therapist made to another patient: "Henry, you have a marvelous gift of language. You use words beautifully, and I really like listening to you talk. But if I just went on listening to you, I have a feeling that I wouldn't be of much help to you, and there's something important I want to say to you. Often—for example, just over the last three to four minutes—I've had the very strong feeling that your words and your sentences and your paragraphs get in the way of my trying to relate to you. My experience is that I try to approach you, then you start speaking, and I find myself very entertained by what you've said but, rather than feeling closer to you, I end up feeling further away; it's as though your words and paragraphs constitute some sort of lattice work—a wall gets erected between us. Did you know this? Is this the way you want to affect me?"

In each of these examples, the strategy is the same. The therapist implies that he wishes to get close to the patient, but the patient's verbal behavior is such that the therapist feels distanced by him. By focusing on each patient's wish for closeness, the therapist is able to give each some important feedback —feedback that, if presented in other ways, might be perceived as attacking or rejecting.

Note, too, that these two statements follow another important principle in the presentation of feedback. It is important that the person who delivers feedback comment primarily upon his or her personal feelings rather than make some type of guess about the other's motivations. In other words, it is far preferable to say, "When you speak like that, I feel shut out," rather than, "You're shutting me out." The last statement frequently evokes defensiveness and closes the other down. The first statement cannot be denied or attacked because, after all, the speaker is merely commenting upon the personal feelings and reactions to which each of us is entitled.

In summary, there is a great deal to be gained and nothing to be lost by judicious therapist transparency: the therapist models adaptive group and social behavior for the patients; the patient's trust in therapy and in therapists is increased; the patient feels valued; the therapist is able to support the patient more humanly and to give the patient valuable feedback.

Conclusion

Therapists leading inpatient groups have very different strategic considerations from group therapists in other settings. Their time frame must be radically altered: their therapy group has a life span of only a single session. Hence inpatient group therapists must be more active and quickly efficient in their work. The brief duration of therapy and the severity of pathology both demand that inpatient group therapists adopt an approach that is structured and highly supportive. They facilitate the work of the group by being active, efficient, structured, supportive, and judiciously transparent.

There is one remaining major principle of inpatient group therapy technique, to which I shall now turn: the inpatient group therapist must be able to work effectively in the here-and-now.

Chapter 4

Strategies and Techniques of Leadership: The Here-and-Now

In chapter 2, I discussed some of the basic principles underlying the use of the here-and-now in traditional outpatient group therapy. In this chapter, I shall discuss how the inpatient group leader can work effectively in the here-and-now.

First, recall that the here-and-now in psychotherapy refers to a focus upon the events of the immediate therapy session—that is, upon what is happening *here* in this therapy room *at the present time.* A here-and-now focus de-emphasizes consideration of the patient's past historical life and of his or her current life situation. *Nota bene,* I use the term *de-emphasize.* A here-and-now focus does not state that either the past history or the current life situation is irrelevant or unimportant. Every individual is shaped to a great degree by the historical events of his or her personal life; every individual has to live in the outside world; and obviously, effective therapy must help one adapt more comfortably to one's real life situation. The important point is that a therapy group cannot help the patient by focusing on past history or upon "outside" life problems. A focus on the here-and-now maximizes the efficiency of the therapy group; the here-and-now is the power cell of the small therapy group.

Rationale for the Here-and-Now

Facilitation of Interpersonal Learning

Why all this emphasis on the here-and-now? How does focusing on it contribute to therapeutic change? To answer these questions, I first have to present two basic assumptions—assumptions with which few clinicians would disagree.* The first assumption is that psychopathology is to some degree, probably a very great degree, interpersonally based. Even though individuals present for therapy with a wide array of different types of symptom, therapists make the assumption that there is an interpersonal component in all symptomatology. This is the core assumption of the interpersonal theory of psychopathology, and it leads to the corollary that therapists treat not the manifesting symptom but, instead, the underlying interpersonal pathology.

The second assumption is that the patient's interpersonal

---

*See my text *The Theory and Practice of Group Psychotherapy* for a full discussion of these assumptions.[1]

pathology is recapitulated in the small therapy group. No matter what the patient's interpersonal difficulty—be it arrogance or aggressiveness or dependency or greed or narcissism or any of the infinite number of maladaptive ways individuals have of relating to one another—it will be manifested in his or her behavior in the therapy group. Thus, the group becomes a "biopsy" of the patient's interpersonal behavior, a social microcosm of each of the patients in the group.

If these two assumptions are true, then the rationale for the emphasis on the here-and-now becomes evident. To discover the nature of an individual's basic pathology, the therapist need not obtain from the patient a detailed historical account of that pathology. All the data that the therapist really requires for the assessment of the patient's basic difficulties is evident in the process of the group. Each patient re-enacts maladaptive interpersonal patterns in the course of the therapy group sessions. Moreover, there are many observers of this behavior, each with a slightly different perspective. There is, thus, an extremely rich lode of data, and the therapist's task is to mine that data and to make it available to the patient. By helping individual patients to see themselves as others see them and to understand their maladaptive ways of relating to others in the group, the therapist will help patients understand what has gone wrong in their individual social worlds at large.

The here and now focus provides not only an invaluable source of information for each patient, but also a safe arena in which patients may experiment with new types of behavior. One of the reasons that behavior becomes fixed is that individuals develop tenacious, calamitous fantasies: that is, they believe that some extremely unpleasant event would occur were they to behave differently. For example, an obsequious, passive man is likely to harbor a fantasy that if he were to act more assertively (for example, disagree with someone, interrupt, ask for more time for himself, or express anger) he would suffer extremely unpleasant consequences (for example, rejection, massive aggressive retaliation, ridicule). If change is to occur, these calamitous fantasies must be disconfirmed. But the disconfirmation must be based on experience; the calamitous fantasies are not based on reason, and no amount of intellectual insight will dispel them.

The effective therapeutic mechanism consists of one's trying these dreaded types of behavior and discovering that one's calamitous fantasies are not fulfilled. It is a powerful therapeutic moment when, for the first time, an individual acts assertively and finds acceptance, increased respect, and greater liking by others, rather than anger or rejection.

But it is extremely difficult to try out new behavior in one's ordinary social surroundings. The risks are high: valuable relationships may be fractured; people upon whom one is dependent may go away; one has no assurance of receiving honest, "game-free" responses from others. The here-and-now of the therapy group is an infinitely safer place to experiment with new behavior. The relationships are real but, at the same time, "not for real"; the other group members are important to one at the moment but will play no major role in one's future life. Moreover, a fundamental rule of the therapy group is that, no matter what, members keep communicating with one another. The presence of the therapist further reduces the risk; the patient is assured of a supportive presence who will monitor the responses to his or her changed behavior.

Successes in the therapy group soon generalize to "out-group" behavior. The group therapist generally assumes that this transfer of learning occurs automatically: after patients have successfully tried out new behavior in the group, they gradually make analogous alterations in their behavior elsewhere. Some patients fail to make this shift, and the therapist must pay more deliberate attention to the process of transfer of learning from the in-group situation to such a patient's outside life.

Facilitation of Other Curative Factors

Not only does the here-and now focus facilitate interpersonal learning but it also provides an avenue to the filling of other curative factors in group therapy.

Cohesiveness

If cohesiveness is to develop in a small therapy group, two criteria must be satisfied:

1. The members must experience the group's activities as intrinsically rewarding.

2. The members must experience the group task as personally relevant and must perceive the group to be effectively locomoting toward accomplishing that task.

The here-and-now focus satisfies these criteria. An interactionally based group is invariably alive, its intrinsic task is stimulating; members are deeply engaged in the process: the great majority are involved in any given interaction, and no one is far from center stage at any given time. Furthermore, if the therapist adequately prepares patients for the group, the relevance of the here-and-now focus is readily apparent. The major assumptions are not difficult to comprehend: patients have significant interpersonal problems, and these problems may be understood and corrected by examining the patients' in-group behavior. Even if one argues that one has come into the hospital for other reasons which are more biologically or socially based (such as hallucinations, depression, or loss of job), one is generally able to acknowledge that, in addition to these major problems, there are aspects of one's interpersonal relationships that one would like to improve, and that it makes sense to use the group for what it does best—that is, correct maladaptive interpersonal behavior.

A "then-and-there" group will not satisfy these criteria. Groups led in this fashion rarely develop much cohesiveness. Generally a then-and-there format focuses on the patients' outside problems that were responsible for hospitalization. The group attempts to problem-solve—an attempt that is always unsuccessful because the data is presented to the group by a demoralized, biased observer. Time does not permit an intense focus on the problems of more than two or three members. Hence many members remain uninterested and unengaged. Ultimately, such a group is perceived by the majority of members as irrelevant and unsuccessful.

Cohesiveness has another payoff for the inpatient group situation. As the result of feeling accepted and supported by one another in the small therapy session, members are likely to continue relating with one another in a supportive fashion during the rest of the day. Hence they will feel less isolated, derive more help from one another, and are more likely to participate in other aspects of the ward therapy program.

Altruism

Members are helped in therapy groups as the result of their being helpful to others. There are numerous ways in which patients can be useful to one another. In a then-and-there group, they can provide support to one another and occasionally offer solutions to the situational problems plaguing one another. A here-and-now focus provides far more opportunities for patients to be useful to one another: in particular they may offer one another invaluable feedback about interpersonal presentation of self. Feedback is the very heart of the interactional process, and I shall discuss the therapist's contribution to feedback shortly.

Existential Factors

A here-and-now focus is particularly effective in helping members assume personal responsibility. One of the most fascinating aspects of the small therapy group is that everyone is "born together." Each person enters the group without any historical connections or ingrained patterns of behavior with the other members. Each person then carves out his or her interpersonal space in the group. The therapist who is adept can help each patient understand that one is responsible for the niche that one has carved for oneself, and that therefore one is responsible for the way that others regard and treat one. Everything that happens to a patient in the group happens as the result of his or her own behavior.

The therapist attempts to take patients through a discernible sequence of learning:

1. How am I seen by others? (the feedback process).
2. How does my behavior make other people feel?
3. How does that behavior affect other people's opinions or impressions of me?
4. And, finally, How do all of these steps culminate in my feelings of self-worth?

Note that all of these steps have their source in the patients' behavior. This learning sequence has the potential of helping the patients understand that they are personally responsible for others' reactions and behavior toward them, and responsible as well for their own self-regard.

The Two Stages of the Here-and-Now

The here-and-now focus, if it is to be effective, must consist of two steps—two symbiotic tiers—neither of which have therapeutic power without the other. In the first *experiencing* step, the group members must live in the here-and-now: they must focus their attention on their feelings toward the other group members, the therapist, and the group. But the here-and-now focus, although stimulating and often exciting, is not therapeutic without the second *understanding* step. In this step the group must be helped to make sense out of the here-and-now "experiencing." The group must examine itself, it must study its own transactions, it must become self-reflective and examine what has just occurred in the group. Thus, the therapeutic use of the here-and-now is dualistic: *the group experiences itself in the here-and-now and then doubles back on itself: that is, it performs a self-reflective loop* and examines what has just occurred.

The dualistic nature of the here-and-now has important implications for therapist technique: one set of techniques is required for the experiencing stage, and another, for the "self-reflective" stage. In the first stage, the therapist must know how to activate the group, how to guide it into here-and-now experiencing. In the second stage, the therapist must know techniques that facilitate the act of self-reflection. Often we refer to the second-stage techniques as "explanation," "clarification," "interpretation," or "process commentary." (The word *process* is used in many different ways in psychotherapy. I use it to refer to this second step of the here-and-now focus. "Process" must be differentiated from "content." When individuals interact, the content of their interaction is self-evident: it consists of the explicit words exchanged between the participants. But when we inquire about the process of the interaction, we ask this question: What do these words [that is, this content] tell us about the *nature of the relationship of the people involved in the interaction?* Thus, "process" is always a statement about relationships.) The therapist's task in the second stage of the here-and-now is invariably to clarify or illuminate some aspect of process —some aspect of the relationships between the group members.

Throughout this text I have described innumerable examples of working in the here-and-now. In fact, every single therapist intervention or comment that I have described is a here-and-now intervention. Not once have I presented a comment by the therapist that focuses on outside, non-here-and-now material. In chapter 5, I shall describe a model of a therapy group meeting that explicitly guides the members into a here-and-now approach. For now, I shall briefly recapitulate basic therapeutic strategies.

Stage 1: Activating the Here-and-Now

The most important advice I can give to help a therapist guide a group into the here-and-now is to "think" here-and-now. In other words, whenever the group is engaged in any discussion, you must be silently pondering, "How can I move this into the here-and-now?" You must be like a shepherd who is continually heading off strays—strays into "outside" material, into discussions of past events of their lives, into abstract intellectual discussions.

The therapist must help the members be personal to one another, look at one another, direct comments to one another, use each other's names. Your task is to channel outside to inside, abstract to specific, impersonal to personal. Thus, if a member starts off with an abstract complaint (such as, "I would like to be more assertive," or "I am too easily intimidated"), you must find a way to transform that abstract comment into something specific and into something involving another member of the group. For example, you might say, "Please look around the room today. By whom do you feel intimidated?" Or if a member talks about being lonely and isolated, you might, in analogous fashion, bring the patient into the here-and-now by asking such questions as "How have you cut yourself off from the people in this group? To whom have you tried to get close? Whom have you been reluctant to approach?" et cetera. The same general strategy pertains to the entire array of interpersonal complaints.

Stage 2: Illumination of Process

If group members merely "experience" the here-and-now—that is, engage solely in expression of feeling toward one another—they will view the group as intense, exciting, or powerful but learn very little from it that they can transfer to other situations. Substantial research evidence demonstrates that, to profit substantially from a group experience, members require some cognitive framework that will allow them to make sense out of the here-and-now experiencing.[2] The specific ideological school in which the explanation is couched (that is, psychoanalytic, interpersonal, transactional analysis, or gestalt, for example) is less important than the fact that some explanation be given.

Many examples of process illumination were presented in the last chapter. Consider, for example, the incident between Matt and Ruth. The therapist "activated" the here-and-now by urging these two patients to express and air their feelings toward one another. Ruth had refused to talk to Matt, and only with some considerable encouragement from the therapist was she willing to pursue her feelings toward him in the group. She stated that she had "written off" Matt, and refused to interact with him any longer. Matt discussed his hurt and anger at Ruth's treatment of him.

The revelation of these feelings was the first stage of the here-and-now. In the second stage, the illumination of process, the therapist helped Ruth look at her unforgivingness, her practice of "writing off" people, and then he encouraged her to examine the consequences of her behavior. She learned that Matt and other members as well were often reluctant to approach her for fear of being rebuffed. Consequently, her judgmentalism prevented her from obtaining the support and nurturance she wanted from others. Matt, on the other hand, was helped to look at the consequences of his behavior, especially how his outbursts of anger frightened others and caused them to avoid him.

Or, consider the example of Peter and Ellen: The here-and-now experiencing consisted of Peter (encouraged by the therapist) saying one negative thing in the meeting. He mildly criticized Ellen for taking too much time in the group. Ellen was distressed by his criticism, and Peter felt profoundly guilty as a result of Ellen's reaction.

The rest of the work was process illumination. The therapist helped both Ellen and Peter examine their behavior. Ellen examined some of the reasons for her extreme reaction—her need to be loved by everyone, her fearfulness of her own greed, her difficulties in asking for things for herself, and so on. Peter, too, considered some of the reasons for his reluctance to assert himself and gradually explored the irrational nature of some of his calamitous fantasies.

Here-and-now activation and process illumination are symbiotic: they must coexist if the here-and-now group is to be therapeutic. There is a delicate balance between the two stages; and, depending upon the needs of a group, the therapist can emphasize one or the other. For example, in an outpatient group of engineers, who may use highly intellectualized defenses, the therapist may focus more on attempting to help the group experience the here-and-now—to express feelings toward one another, to give feedback to one another, to let others matter to them. In a group where too much emotion is being expressed, the therapist will "slow down" the group and, by emphasizing the stage of process illumination, prevent its members from feeling overwhelmed. For example, in chapter 3, I described how the therapist can limit conflict in inpatient groups by immediately moving into process illumination with a statement like, "Let's stop now for a few minutes and take a few steps back and see if we can understand what's happening between Mary and John."

Special Considerations of the Here-and-Now for the Inpatient Group

Although the basic strategy for the therapist working in the here-and-now is similar in inpatient and in long-term outpatient group therapy, there are, nonetheless, important differences. One obvious difference that I have emphasized previously is a function of the duration of therapy: inpatient therapy is so brief that there can be no working through of interpersonal pathology; the therapist must be content with interpersonal problem spotting, brief process illumination, and encouraging patients to pursue and solidify, in their aftercare therapy, what they have learned.

Another important difference in strategy is dictated by the severity of illness of hospitalized patients. The members of an inpatient group may feel too fragile, too needy, or too stressed to engage one another in the here-and-now and to integrate the data that emerges from their interaction. Inpatients are so acutely uncomfortable that they demand some direct and immediate relief to their pain. Consequently, they are often baffled by, and resistant to, a here-and-now approach in the therapy group: it seems indirect, off target, irrelevant to their personal distress. Furthermore, their anxiety is often so intense that they have difficulty tolerating the anxiety that is often inherent in face-to-face interaction or in assimilating interpretations offered by the therapist.

Demonstrating the Relevance of the Here-and-Now

Accordingly, the inpatient group therapist must alter his or her technique to address this degree of stress. Considerable attention must be paid to the issue of relevance of the group work to each patient's personal distress in life. In the previous chapter, I described how the therapist provides an explicit description of the rationale of group therapy in the opening stage of the group. But it does not end there. Repeatedly, throughout the session, the therapist must continue to demonstrate to patients how the group procedure has relevance to their "outside" problems. The therapists can do this effectively by making each patient aware of parallels between patterns that emerge in the group and problems that exist in his or her life situation.

Consider this clinical episode: A woman patient informed Sarah that it was difficult to relate to her because she (Sarah) always seemed so distant and aloof. Other members agreed and commented that they, too, had tried to approach Sarah but that somehow she fenced herself off from them. Sarah commented, "That's just the way I am. I know I've often been accused of being a snob, but frankly I'm simply not interested in having close relationships. Furthermore, I don't think I have anything in common with the members of the group here that could possibly result in a longer-lasting relationship."

Sarah's response was provocative and could lead either to an impasse in the group or to an angry response from the other members who had just been informed that they simply weren't important enough to matter to her. Furthermore, Sarah evidenced little motivation to pursue the issue because, as she explained to the group, she was in the hospital because she was depressed. If others had difficulty relating to her, that was *their* problem, not hers.

The therapist obtained some leverage by helping Sarah understand the relevance of the group interaction to her dissatisfaction in life. He raised the question of whether her posture (that is, being a snob, being uninterested in having close relationships) had any disadvantages for her in her life. Did she pay a price for it? Was there anything about the way she related to others that she would like to change? At the same time, the therapist reduced both the pressure on Sarah and her defensiveness by observing that many people in the group were interested in her; obviously people found her attractive and desirable and regretted that they were unable to get close to her.

Sarah softened at this point. She stated that she'd always been this way and didn't think she could change but that, indeed, she did pay a price for her attitudes toward others. Her depression was precipitated by her recent divorce, and she had been desperately isolated and immobilized at the impossible prospect of trying to form a new set of friends and acquaintances.

One option available to the therapist at this point was to help Sarah explore how her interpersonal style may have played a role in the breakup of her marriage. Was it possible that the behavior she exhibited in the group—her aloofness, judgmentalism, and unwillingness to be touched—had driven her husband from her? This line of inquiry is tempting but must be avoided: it is a common tactical error. It would have focused Sarah and the group on an outside issue—a husband who was not present in the group and whom the group members did not know. It would have led to a hasty, superficial, and probably unsatisfactory exploration of Sarah's marital failure and left most of the other members feeling unengaged and frustrated.

Instead, the therapist chose to continue focusing on the here-and-now. He emphasized to Sarah that the feedback by the members in the group might be very useful in helping her to develop a new set of friends and to deepen her relationships with others. Might there not be, he wondered, people in her life who feel the same way the group members feel toward her—that is, who are attracted to her, who want to get close to her but sense her aloofness and misinterpret her fear of closeness as snobbism or supreme self-sufficiency? Sarah was in the hospital for only three days but learned something very important: that unbeknownst to herself, she sent out messages that prevented her from getting what she really wanted from people.

Patient Fragility

Demonstrating the relevance of the here-and-now to the major life problems of each of the members increases the willingness of each to engage in the group task. Having established an optimal motivational set, the therapist must address the fragility of the group members. In the discussion of therapist support in chapter 3, I emphasized the most important guiding principle in this regard: a here-and-now approach is *not* synonymous with confrontation, with conflict, with pointing out others' weaknesses, with getting gut feelings out, with a destructive "Who's afraid of Virginia Woolf?" approach to human relationships. On the contrary, through the therapeutic use of the here-and-now, members establish trust in one another; emphasize strengths, support and help one another; and gently provide mutual information about how each is perceived and affected by the others.

Feedback

The very heart of the interactional approach is the process of feedback (the sharing of one's perceptions of the other). The therapist must direct considerable attention to teaching members how to give constructive feedback and how to make use of the feedback that is offered to them. Group members do not engage in the process of feedback naturally and spontaneously. Feedback is not a commonplace transaction. As a matter of fact, there are very few situations in life where one feels free to comment directly upon the immediate behavior of another person. Generally such direct feedback is taboo; virtually the only place it is permissible is the parent/child relationship and, occasionally, an exceedingly intimate (or exceedingly conflicted) relationship.

Generally the therapist must initiate the feedback process. Once, however, he or she has established appropriate norms in a group, patients may take the initiative in requesting feedback. For example, they may begin a meeting by stating as their agenda (see the following chapter) that they would like to know how others see them or what they do that puts people off or that intimidates others.

The therapist must then help members give helpful feedback. Often the first task is to assist members to be more discriminating in their feedback. The first round of comments is often "pablum" feedback: such statements as: "I think you're a nice guy," or "I think you're O.K.," or "I like you a lot," or "I find you very pleasant." The leader can provide more helpful and discriminating feedback by inquiring what the recipient of the feedback has learned from it, or how helpful that round of feedback was, or which of the comments he or she has found most useful.

Generally this inquiry helps the feedback givers become more discriminating. One learns that although it is pleasant to hear oneself being considered a "nice guy" or "O.K.," it is at the same time not particularly useful. The therapist may provide assistance by discussing the concept of *blind spots:* that is, there are things about oneself that others (in this instance, the other members of the group) can see that one cannot see oneself. Thus, an important way that members can be mutually helpful is by making one another more aware of blind spots. Members, then, are encouraged to offer to the individual who requests feedback something that that person does not already know or perceive about himself or herself.

The therapist can facilitate this process by phrasing instructions to patients in a supportive manner. One particularly effective mode of eliciting feedback is this question: "Let's suppose that, after you leave the hospital, you and John were going to be roommates [or working together closely, or shipwrecked together on an island, and so on]. What aspect of John's behavior would get in the way of your developing an ideal relationship with him?"

The wording of this question also illustrates another rule of feedback delivery. The therapist must help members provide feedback on particular traits or behavior of one another rather than make sweeping comments about another person's essence —comments that are rarely helpful and generally lower self-esteem and evoke defensiveness. One does not profit from hearing another say, "I just don't find you attractive," or "I just don't like to be around you," or "I don't find you very interesting." It is infinitely more helpful to hear about some specific aspect of one's behavior that puts people off or causes them to avoid one. Individuals cannot help but profit from such comments as: "I get very uncomfortable talking with you, Joe, because you never look at me. The way you avoid my glance causes me to feel that you're not interested in what I have to say or that you're trying to avoid me"; or "I'm not entirely comfortable with you because you never disagree with me. Consequently I don't know your opinion on anything. I have the sense you're only telling me what you think I want to hear from you"; or "I don't like the way you keep knocking yourself all the time."

Note, too, that all these examples of feedback focus on something that is clearly within the patient's power to change. Comments about unchangeable aspects of an individual (for example, physical appearance) are often, especially in short-term hospital work, not constructive. In long-term therapy groups there is often time to work through feedback about physical appearance. In such groups one may learn important information about the impact of one's physical appearance on others and thus gain a clearer vision of one's interpersonal presentation. Furthermore, those who respond to someone's physical appearance may learn a great deal about themselves. One person's physical appearance will almost invariably have a very different impact on, and a very different meaning for, the various members of a group. This phenomenon encourages each member to explore why he or she responds to a particular person in a particular way. In an acute inpatient group, however, there is no time for such working through, and feedback on negative aspects of physical appearance almost invariably result in defensiveness and closing down rather than in opening up and learning.

Therapists become so used to the process of feedback that they may, at times, forget that, for the great majority of group members, it is an entirely novel process and elicits considerable anxiety. Often group members are so sensitive to feedback that they freeze and do not listen well. They may distort what they have heard, but are so anxious they do not ask for clarification.

For example, in one group, Carl stated that he thought Don was "too absorbed" all the time. Don's reaction was quick and vehement; within minutes he was sobbing while lamenting that people did not appreciate that he really did care deeply for others. Why is it, he continued, that though he persistently put out to other people, he was always rewarded with ingratitude and accusations?

The therapist at this point called a halt to the experiencing stage of the here-and-now and moved Don into the stage of process illumination. The therapist noted that Don did not give himself a break in this transaction and seemed to grasp immediately onto the worst possible interpretation of Carl's feedback. What alternatives were available to him? Don, with the help of the rest of the group, explored a couple of other options. For one thing, he might have asked Carl some questions about what he meant by "too absorbed" just to make certain that he, Don, fully understood Carl. Another option would have been to get some feedback from the remaining members. Did they all agree with Carl's observation? Was it idiosyncratic of Carl?

Don pursued the first option and asked Carl exactly what he meant by "absorbed." Don, of course, thought that Carl had meant that he, Don, was selfish and only thought about himself; but, as it turned out, Carl's meaning was entirely different: he meant that Don was eternally psychologizing, always absorbed in problems—either his own or in other people's. Carl observed that Don never gave himself a break: he was never on the volleyball court, he was never out for exercise, he never played games with other people, he never let go and had fun.

The whole incident had profound implications for Don, opening his eyes to the possibility that his jumping to the wrong conclusion about Carl's feedback might have been not an isolated incident but a reflection of an ongoing pattern of his own.

Keep in mind that negative feedback always hurts. The therapist must be responsive to this fact and help relieve the patient's pain even though the patient denies it.

Consider this clinical example: Herb, highly attractive and schizoid, discussed his great difficulty in establishing and maintaining intimate relationships, especially ones with women. He asked the other group members for feedback that might help him understand why things never worked for him with women. Lorraine, an attractive young schizophrenic, gave him this piquant feedback: "If I eat an abalone, I am really interested in the meat and not in the shell. Even if the abalone has a nice shell, it's really what's inside that counts."

Herb smiled, formally thanked her, acknowledged his interest in what she had to say, and commented that he would consider it carefully. As the group continued, however, it seemed clear that Herb was preoccupied with Lorraine's comment. He did not listen well to other comments made to him and disengaged himself from the other members.

The therapist, despite Herb's disavowals, operated on the assumption that he was hurt by this feedback, and asked him to go back in time seven or eight minutes and share with the group exactly what he felt when Lorraine spoke to him. Herb merely continued to repeat his previous declaration. Pressing him harder, the therapist commented that he could see a lot of pain reflected in Herb's face at that moment.

Finally Herb said, "O.K., here's what I was feeling. Look who's talking! Lorraine, I don't see you any better off than me."

The therapist acknowledged Herb's anger but asked him to go down another layer. What was beneath the anger? Herb denied any other feelings, and the therapist expressed them for Herb, commenting, "If I were you, I would have felt some pain when Lorraine said that to me." Herb nodded, and tears filled his eyes. The therapist said, "Could you give those tears a voice?" Herb then turned to Lorraine and said, "Lorraine, what you said makes me feel bad, it makes me feel that I'm nothing inside, and that hurts a whole lot." Lorraine's immediate response was, "Now I like the meat and the shell."

This processing of feedback was a very important interaction for Herb. His ability to express pain and hurt was, much to his surprise, the very thing that made Lorraine feel closer and more attracted to him. He had learned something important. What he had asked from the group was help in understanding why his relationships with women always failed. He learned that, in the service of keeping his outer shell sparkling, he had squelched the more human, more vulnerable parts of himself.

Feedback begets feedback. The individual who gives feedback will ultimately learn something about himself or herself during the process. For example, Jerry had been in several group meetings, and invariably his feedback was labeled as pleasant or comforting but generally unhelpful by the person to whom he directed it. The members of the group then proceeded to give Jerry feedback about his reluctance to take a radical stand on almost any issue. Jerry was helped then to discuss his fear of offending anyone and his great wish to be loved and respected by everyone. The result of Jerry's behavior was that he had become an exceptionally bland figure. Although he offended no one, he also interested no one. Diplomacy and neutrality are wonderfully important in international relations but may make for devastatingly dull interpersonal ones.

Another clinical incident: Jeff and Michael were trying to relate to one another but encountering much difficulty doing so. Michael was always laughing even though he said he was depressed, and other members in the group told him that his laughter confused them. Jeff commented that he wasn't confused; instead, he could "see right through" Michael. Michael responded very negatively to this, and their ensuing interaction became abrasive and defensive.

At this point the leader intervened, suggesting that Michael repeat what he thought Jeff had told him. Michael's interpretation was that Jeff had said that he, Jeff, was much cleverer and could see right through Michael, the poor simple-minded soul. Moreover, other members of the group agreed with Michael's interpretation, even though they stated that this interpretation did not entirely fit Jeff's demeanor. Jeff was astonished at this interpretation but could understand why his words were interpreted in that way. What he had really meant to tell Michael was that he, Jeff, felt close to him, and that the two of them were on the same wavelength. The group then helped Jeff explore why he had not been able to say this more straightforwardly to Michael. Soon Jeff began exploring his difficulties in saying something unequivocally positive to any man.

Feedback becomes more constructive if the one providing it describes his or her feelings—feelings evoked by the other person's behavior. Therapy is facilitated when one says how one felt when X said something to one, not what one thinks about X or about X's statement. As with all of these techniques, the therapist may provide explicit instruction or model this feedback procedure for the others.

Consider this example: A meeting began with ten members sitting in a circle on sofas or chairs. One woman, despite empty chairs, sat or occasionally stretched supine on the floor in front of one of the chairs. At the beginning of the meeting, this patient had stated that she wanted to work on developing closer relationships with other people.

Later in the meeting the therapist gave her this feedback as a method of helping her work on her agenda:

"Rita, I want to share a feeling I've been having about you

today, because I think it fits in closely with your agenda. I've been trying to think of how it would feel for me if I were one of your friends on the outside, and I'm aware that it's hard for me today to relate to you, in the same way that I relate to the other members of the group, simply because of your sitting on the floor. It's got nothing to do with formality or informality, because I like to sit on the floor myself. But what is important is that I find myself sitting up very high looking down upon you; you're sitting very low looking up at me. That creates a kind of disequilibrium or big gulf between the two of us, as though you're young or small or little and I'm bigger and older. Does that have any use or meaning for you? Does it click with other things that others have told you about yourself or that you know about yourself?''

Bizarre, Disruptive Incidents: Grist for the Interpersonal Mill

Another major difference between the use of the here-and-now in inpatient and in outpatient groups is that the former frequently are punctuated with dramatic, unpredictable events. In contrast to the typical outpatient group, members of an inpatient group are so severely ill, so often suffering from a thought disorder that irrational, inexplicable events are not uncommon: a member may suddenly blurt out inappropriate or psychotic comments; one may make bizarre accusations; one may bolt out of the room; one may express unaccountably powerful negative and positive feelings; one may fall asleep and snore; one may respond to hallucinations. Such a range of unexpected, often unavoidable events may leave the group therapist's head reeling and prompt him or her to enter the next group meeting grim-visaged and white-knuckled.

But there is a basic principle that may inoculate the therapist against disequilibrium—a principle that enables him or her to transform the most convulsive events into useful therapeutic work. That principle is simply: *all events of the group are to be used as grist for the interpersonal mill.*

Recall the basic assumption underlying the use of the here-and-now: each patient's in-group behavior is reflective of that patient's out-group interpersonal behavior. In other words, the part is reflective of the whole. Thus all events of the group are ultimately informative; and if the therapist can keep his head and sustain the group in a work phase, all group events constitute important data which can enrich therapy. If an event is dramatic and extreme, it may be that the protagonist is too stressed to make use of the learning available at the time (but may indeed be able to integrate the material at some later date); but certainly the strong reactions of the other members to the event can be harnessed for therapeutic work.

No new principle is required here. I have already made the point that interpersonal events in the group are the data of therapy. An infinite variety of events occur; and the therapist, by focusing the group's attention upon an event, can help the members analyze and learn from it. The major issue here is the degree of affect involved. There is a wide range of group events —some that appear to the group trivial or innocuous, some that appear cataclysmic. Whatever the event may be, the therapist's task is to apprehend its therapeutic potential and to make it available to the group. Some clinical vignettes are illustrative. I will begin with less dramatic, every-day incidents and then gradually escalate to more cataclysmic events.

No Room on the Sofa

Paul and another patient were sitting on a two-person sofa at the beginning of the meeting; and Eleanor, a very obese woman, strolled over and asked whether she could sit between them. Paul said, "Sure," and Eleanor squeezed in. A few minutes later, Paul, with some effort, extricated himself and, muttering something about needing a little more room, moved over to one of the many empty chairs in the circle.

The therapist, after a few minutes, focused upon the process of that incident. What was Paul feeling when Eleanor asked whether she could join him on the couch? What might he have said to her? Paul volunteered that he could have said, "Eleanor, there's not quite enough room. I prefer that you sit in one of the other chairs."

"But," Paul countered, "that would be devastating for Eleanor." Eleanor commented, "Maybe that's just the kind of thing I need to hear." The therapist called Paul's attention to the fact that he had given Eleanor the same message a few minutes later by getting up and moving somewhere else. Only it was an indirect message and left Eleanor in an ambiguous situation and himself feeling much self-contempt.

The discussion of this incident had considerable "outside" relevance to Paul. He had learned the previous day that he was going to be fired from his job because of his suicide attempt and his current psychiatric hospitalization. He was dealing with the issue of whether he should simply allow that to happen or whether he should seek legal counsel and defend himself against an illegal firing. His work with Eleanor and the couch was, in essence, work upon this key issue.

Passive Control

Chuck attended a group session for the first time. The therapist greeted him and oriented him to the group but got no response of any kind, not even a nod, and felt uncomfortable, left hanging, and uncertain whether to continue or wait for Chuck to respond to him. Later in the group the therapist returned to this incident and shared his feelings with Chuck. Other members of the group then commented that during mealtime they had tried to talk to him, and he had moved to the end of the table to be alone. Their responses varied: some felt hurt, some insulted and angry, some puzzled. Chuck was astonished; he had been unaware of his impact on others. He was especially struck by the therapist's discomfort. That he, Chuck, could have this influence over the therapist was surprising, since he felt extremely small and frightened: his reticence with people was prompted by his sense that others were all bigger, quicker, and stronger than he was.

The Therapist Gets Angry: Betty Gets a Stomachache

A group is always significantly affected when its leader gets angry. Such an incident occurred when Jack, a very psychotic patient, attended a meeting of an optional higher-level group. Jack had been abusive to other patients and threatened several of them with physical violence; and earlier that day, it had been necessary to obtain a fourteen-day legal "hold" on him. The group leader had been one of the two psychiatrists to sign this hold.

After only a few minutes of the session, it was obvious that Jack had come not to work in the group but instead to harangue and threaten the therapist for signing the hold. After a few minutes of this, the therapist became visibly irritated at Jack not only for attacking him personally but also because Jack was obviously scuttling any work the group could do that day. The therapist expressed some of this anger and told him that he, the therapist, would talk with him later, but that now he was out of line and had to leave the group. Jack escalated briefly and then, with several parting verbal shots, finally left the group. This incident, which lasted about five minutes, was unsettling to several of the members, especially to Betty, who asked to leave the group because of severe abdominal pains. (She was a somatizer who had had repeated hospital admissions for severe, undiagnosable abdominal pain.)

The therapist tried to use the incident as grist for the mill and tried every means of influence at his disposal to persuade Betty to stay in the meeting and to talk about, rather than give in to, her pain. She agreed to stay five more minutes and to try to talk about what she was feeling. The group asked Betty to track down the onset of the pain, and it seemed clear that it began during the heated exchange between the therapist and Jack. Betty grew defensive, withholding, and categorically denied that the two were connected in any way. The therapist, who had a good supportive relationship with her, confronted her in a gentle manner and said he simply couldn't buy that. He expressed several thoughts to her: "Betty, I know you have expressed some positive feelings about me. I also know that you see me as a gentle person since you said in yesterday's meeting that that was one of the things you like about me. How could you not be shocked, therefore, at my losing my cool and being angry at a patient? And why are you refusing to even look at this possibility? You come faithfully to this group. I know you want to change. Why are you not willing to look at yourself?"

With such intense persuasion—all done in a supportive manner, not in one to humiliate her—Betty began to acknowledge that her pain had indeed begun during the interchange between the therapist and the patient, and that she was extremely frightened at the therapist's anger. To the therapist's "Why?" Betty answered that if he lost his temper at Jack, then it was entirely possible that ultimately the therapist would lose his temper at her as well.

The therapist escorted her farther: "What then? What if that happened? What can you imagine happening between you and me?" Betty then ventured into some important areas, including her wish to be taken care of and her great dread of disapproval from the therapist and from other men, especially men whom she respected.

By this time the whole group was involved in a fairly animated discussion; several other members had strong reactions to the therapist losing his temper. Some, like Betty, felt frightened; others felt empathy for the therapist and grateful that he had gotten Jack out rather than allow the group's time to be entirely consumed; others felt closer to the therapist since he appeared more human.

The therapist, in the midst of this discussion, gently asked Betty whether she could say something about the extent of abdominal pain she was having now, and Betty was "herself surprised." Her pain was gone; she had completely forgotten about her abdomen for the past twenty minutes. The therapist did not miss this opportunity to help her learn from this incident. Several times in the meeting, and in the final "wrap-up" as well, he suggested that this was indeed a decisive meeting for Betty. It was the first time that she really had "taken charge" of her pain; during the session she had been able to pinpoint its origin and, even more important, had been willing to work on the pain rather than to be defeated by it by leaving the room. The therapist emphasized to Betty that the meeting could be a prototype for dealing with pain in the future: that is, she could be sensitive to the events surrounding the onset of pain and take the risk of discussing with another person her feelings associated with those events. Pain is a signal that one is experiencing psychic stress; the pain is not the significant psychic event; it is the cue that may lead one to identify that event.

Pandemonium: Sweeping Up after the Storm

A meeting of a higher-level group began with one member, Jill, alternately sitting and lying on the floor because of back pain—the chief reason she was in the hospital. She had been on the ward for a few days, but this was her first group meeting in this optional group. When the therapist urged her to participate in the session, she stated that she simply wanted to watch others work in the group that day. The therapist persevered and encouraged Jill to formulate an agenda (see chapter 5). She was a well-defended, somatizing patient without evidence of high levels of anxiety, and the therapist confronted her more than he might have a more psychologically vulnerable patient. Finally, Jill stated that she had been hurt often and had to learn to trust people more; perhaps she could work on that in the group. The therapist (in accordance with the principles of agenda formulation presented in the next chapter) guided her into formulating the agenda in here-and-now terms. He asked Jill to identify those members who made her feel least vulnerable and those who made her feel somewhat more vulnerable. Jill resisted answering the question by commenting that she felt vulnerable to exactly the same degree to everybody in the group. (This claim to equality of feeling is a common "front-line" resistance to working in the here-and-now. It is never true! The therapist must persevere and help a member differentiate the others in the group.) Accordingly, the therapist opined that such neutrality seemed improbable. Jill, finally, acquiesced and said, "O.K., the people that I feel most vulnerable about are Bill and Marilyn and Kate." (All three, as it happened, were homosexual.)

Bill, an effeminent, flamboyant homosexual with a hysterical character disorder, became extremely upset at Jill's naming him as one of the people who might make her feel more vulnerable. He demanded to know her reasons and reminded her, "I'm your friend, I try to be nice to you, we talk together all the time. Why choose me? How could you do that to me?"

Jill responded, "It's not you, Bill! It's just that I have some mixed feelings about homosexuals. When I was a child, my uncle was murdered by someone who was involved with him homosexually, and this created a scandal for my whole family. Furthermore, homosexual men in San Francisco often date me to use me as a 'cover' for them."

Jill's explanation seemed to distress Bill even more, and he began pouting, sulking, and then weeping loudly. He had been sitting next to Jill, but moved to a chair on the opposite corner of the room, while wondering aloud, amidst his tears, if he would ever get over this insult. He stated that he had come to the hospital for help, and that this group meeting had set him back at least two or three weeks.

At this point Jill's back pain became very intense and was not alleviated by any sitting or reclining position; she began pacing around the room, stating that it was only by walking that she could get any relief for her pain. Needless to say, this was extremely distracting, and the group members became overtly angry at Jill for so disrupting the group.

At this point, things were not going well in the meeting!

But the therapist, an experienced group leader, kept his head and used these unhappy events as grist for the mill. He urged Bill and Jill to work on the data that had been generated. First, the therapist helped Bill recognize and express his feelings more directly. As Bill was too distraught to speak for a while, the therapist used a technique that is often helpful at such times: he asked other members to speak for Bill—that is, to speak as though they were Bill. With their help, Bill gradually abandoned his self-destructive, indirect mode of expressing his feelings to Jill (that is, by weeping, hysterics, tormenting himself, and exaggerating his distress in order to instill guilt in her) and much more simply and directly commented that his feelings were hurt, that he liked Jill very much and was dismayed to realize that she had no respect for him. He also stated that the pain he was feeling in his chest and abdomen was very intense, and he wished that Jill could somehow soothe him or make it go away.

To express his pain directly was important work for Bill, highly relevant to his major reasons for being in the hospital. On several occasions, after a loss, or a threatened loss of love by a lover, he had responded with self-destructive behavior, generally some suicidal attempt. Indeed, his current hospitalization was occasioned by wrist slashing, following a domestic quarrel with his lover. Thus, it was very helpful to Bill to be enabled to express his pain and craving for love directly, rather than to resort to self-destructive behavior (as he had earlier in the meeting).

The leader encouraged Bill to examine another aspect of the

incident: his obvious overreaction to Jill's comments. The other two members Jill had named had evinced little distress, even though one was Jill's roommate. It was readily apparent that Bill had overpersonalized the situation; after all, Jill had been careful to point out that her choice of the three people in the group was not on a personal basis but had a great deal more to do with her idiosyncratic responses to homosexuality *per se*.

The leader then turned to the pacing Jill and asked, "Jill, could you go back in time to approximately eight minutes ago? I think it would be very important if you could talk about precisely what you were feeling just before you started pacing around the room."

Not unexpectedly, Jill resisted this suggestion and commented that she couldn't remember and that her back was hurting her too much to think. The therapist persisted and spoke for her; "You know, Jill, I have a very strong hunch that you might have been a little pissed at me for pressing you so much in this meeting." Jill picked this up quickly and said, "Right! You got me into this! I just wanted to observe the group today, and you pushed me into saying some things I didn't want to say! And then what did you do? You just abandoned me to the lions."

Although Jill expressed these feelings with a great deal of heat, they were nonetheless exceedingly welcomed by the group. The therapist responded quickly and warmly to them by letting Jill know that he felt bad at having caused her so much pain and uncomfortable at her being angry at him; but he also stated that, for the first time in the meeting, he felt really in touch with her and that he and she were communicating directly. He liked that and felt closer to her. He asked for feedback from other members, and the others all reinforced her direct expression of feelings. Some agreed that the therapist had nagged her too much. They felt more engaged with her because they knew where she stood. They respected her for speaking her mind; in so doing, she was communicating far better than by expressing her feelings through pain and pacing.

In addition to rewarding and reinforcing Jill's behavior, the therapist tried to take her a bit farther by going back to when things went off target in the group, and asking her if she could once again respond to his question about who might make her feel somewhat vulnerable there. She had responded impersonally by naming people who were only symbols of an uncomfortable issue; she had not really addressed anyone personally. By this time Jill understood the therapist entirely and stated that she felt threatened by Steve, a university professor who made her feel ignorant and bumbling. The meeting continued from that point in a fruitful vein; others had a similar response to Steve and proceeded to investigate their reactions.

By staying with these dramatic events and putting them to therapeutic use for several members of the group, the therapist transformed a potentially disastrous meeting into an exceedingly productive one: Bill learned a great deal about more adaptive modes of expressing his psychological pain and about his overreaction to others' comments about him; Jill learned some invaluable lessons about the genesis and the alleviation of her somatic pain.

Group Terror and Its Aftermath

The last vignette illustrates one final point about the "grist for the mill" principle: if a protagonist is too acutely disturbed to be able to benefit from an incident, the therapist may help other members derive something of therapeutic benefit from it. There are two major technical approaches, either or both of which may be available to the therapist:

1. Members will respond differently to the same incident, and an exploration of these different responses often facilitates self-exploration. If several witnesses to the same event respond very differently, only one explanation is possible: *the responses reflect*

very different inner worlds. Differing responses to the same stimulus is the group therapy *via regia* to self-exploration.

2. A crisis in the group is an opportunity to explore modes of coping with crisis and offers as well a therapeutic entry into the realm of responsibility assumption.

The following vignette illustrates both of these strategies: Ten members were present in a meeting. The group had had hard-working and intensive meetings over the previous few days. In the meeting that day, there were two new patients. One of them, a large, menacing individual named Harrison, gave evidence in the very first minutes of the meeting that he would not be able to use the group. He took a seat outside of the circle and sat listening to a portable stereo with headphones. The therapist, in retrospect, would have done well to ask him to leave at this point but remembered that Harrison, during an admission the year before, had worked well in the therapy group.

The therapist invited Harrison to join the circle. Harrison conformed but, a few minutes later, changed his seat and moved once again to a chair outside the group circle. When the therapist urged him again to join the circle, Harrison became defensive, stating that he was feeling great and didn't want people to get on his case. Some of the other members of the group wondered why Harrison was in the group if he felt good and didn't want to work on anything. But that inquiry made matters worse, and Harrison grew more resistant. The group then attempted to focus on some other members, but Harrison's looming, angry presence bound up the energy in the group and prevented any productive work with others.

As it turned out, the other new patient in the group was also exceedingly psychotic. The cacophony of that patient's scrambled speech with Harrison's impulsive disruptive commands made for a note of real craziness in the group. By the halfway point in the meeting, all the members of the group were visibly jangled; some talked about wanting to scream or bolt out of the room, and some really looked as though they were on the verge of leaving.

Harrison became extremely angry at anyone in the group who made comments to the other psychotic patient, with whom he obviously identified. He finally stood up and shouted at one of the women for having been unfair to this other patient. The therapist intervened and told Harrison to sit down, calm down, and try to talk out his feelings in the group. Harrison turned threateningly toward the therapist and assumed a posture of attack. He finally turned on his heels, sent some chairs spinning, and stomped out of the room, leaving behind a stunned, frightened group of individuals.

The first tack that the therapist took was to introduce calmness and order into the group by gently reminding the members that there were approximately thirty minutes left of the meeting, and that it would be a good idea to decide about the most useful way to spend those thirty minutes. The therapist opined that, since there were several very upset people in the meeting that day, perhaps the group ought to devote itself to helping as many members as possible to feel better in the next thirty minutes.

Some members stated that the best way for them to feel better would be to leave the room, and asked permission to do so. The therapist said that he, of course, could not bar the door but that, in his opinion, leaving the site was the most unhelpful thing they could do for themselves. After all, in the past, many of them, he pointed out, had characteristically responded to stress by withdrawal, and one of the purposes of hospitalization was to help them find more successful ways of handling stress. Some members suggested that they try to support one another. Others proposed that they get things off their chest by airing the feelings they had about Harrison.

The group members proceeded to express their feelings, and their great anxiety gave way to astonishment at the wide array of feelings emanating from them all. Some were angry at Harrison for having wrecked the meeting: they felt deprived of time to work on their own issues. Others felt angry at the therapist for not having had the foresight to keep Harrison out of the group: the therapist had allowed Harrison to scuttle the group in the same way that the rest of the ward staff had allowed him to scuttle the other therapeutic ward activities that day. Other members felt very threatened at what had happened. Two of the men talked about their fears of physical confrontation with another man. One of the women talked about her terror of irrational men and the type of physical abuse she had endured as a child from a psychotic father. During this discussion, which lasted approximately fifteen minutes, the group was much more animated and relaxed and experienced a sense of mastery.

In the final several minutes of the meeting, the group's attention turned to the member who had the most extreme reaction to Harrison's onslaught. Judy, a nineteen-year-old girl, huddled in a chair, her teeth chattering and her facial expression one of terror. Gently the group helped her talk about her great fear of Harrison and of what might have happened in the group. The therapist took a matter-of-fact tone and wondered what might have happened. "He might have attacked you," Judy said. The therapist said, "So what, so he would have punched me in the nose. There were ten people here in this group and some ward staff in the observation room and plenty of others on the ward who would have helped. So what if I got a punch in the nose? Worse things have happened to people, and they've recovered."

Judy's excessive reaction emanated from what Harrison symbolized to her; and, with much effort, she shared with the group an experience of hers. She had been raped a year previously and had never fully discussed with anyone the rape or her reactions to it. During this meeting she got in touch not only with her fear of Harrison and of the man who had sexually assaulted her but with her rage as well. What terrified her most was not her fear of Harrison but her rage and her almost uncontrollable desire to lacerate him. Judy received enormous support in the group, especially from three women members who also had been sexually assaulted and shared many of her feelings.

In the last five minutes of the meeting, the therapist "checked in" with each of the members: it was clear that the dust had settled and the intensive dysphoria present thirty minutes previously had dissipated. The therapist summarized the process: there had been a catastrophe, the group members had felt extraordinarily uncomfortable, they had taken the responsibility of doing something about their discomfort, they had chosen to share their distress with one another and to attempt to understand the nature of their reactions. Moreover, they had been highly successful: they had converted a potentially catastrophic event into a highly therapeutic meeting.

Conclusion

The focus on here-and-now interaction is as important in inpatient group work as in other forms of group therapy. An interactional focus permits patients to alter maladaptive, self-destructive interpersonal patterns; it also creates a group in which the members are supported, stimulated, mutually helpful, and engaged in a task they perceive as relevant to their lives. If the here-and-now focus is to be therapeutic, it must consist of both an experiencing and an understanding phase.

The clinical exigencies of inpatient group therapy require special technical considerations in the use of the here-and-now:

1. The brief duration of therapy dictates that the interaction be used primarily for reinforcement of strengths and for interpersonal problem spotting rather than for "working through" problems.

2. The great severity of distress dictates that special attention be given to the demonstration of relevance.

3. High patient fragility makes it mandatory that feedback (and, indeed, all aspects of the interactional process) be exclusively supportive and constructive.

4. Lastly, all unpredictable, potentially unsettling group events can be considered grist for the interpersonal mill and can, with proper technique, be used to therapeutic advantage.

Chapter 5

The Higher-Level Inpatient Therapy Group: A Working Model

I suggest that an optional group for higher-level patients (see chapter 2 for a discussion of composition) be held daily for approximately seventy-five minutes. Higher-level groups are the most complex of the inpatient groups to lead and require that the leader be trained in basic group therapy techniques. In this chapter I will describe one possible structure for a higher-level group. Keep in mind that this structure augments, but is not a replacement for, fundamental training in group therapy. The group may be led either by a single therapist or by co-therapists. The co-therapy format makes the group less demanding for the therapists, provides an excellent medium for training neophyte therapists by pairing one with an experienced therapist, and often is more fun for therapists. By no means, however, is the co-therapy model a requirement; the group can be led effectively by a single competent therapist.

One basic blueprint of a seventy-five-minute session is:

1.	Orientation and preparation	3 to 5 minutes
2.	Agenda go-round (each member formulates a personal agenda for that meeting)	20 to 30 minutes
3.	Work on the agendas (the group attempts to "fill" as many agendas as possible)	20 to 35 minutes
4.	Therapists' and observers' discussion of the meetings. (If there are observers behind a one-way mirror, they enter the room and, together with the therapist, discuss the group in front of the patients.)	10 minutes
5.	The patients' response to the summary discussion	10 minutes

Orientation and Preparation

In chapter 3, I presented a detailed illustrative example of the initial statement that the therapist makes for each session (see pages 115–117). If there are new patients present, as there usually are, the orientation must be more detailed than if one is simply reminding the more experienced members of the basic structure and purpose of the group.

The Higher-Level Inpatient Therapy Group

The basic plan of the opening statement is to provide a basic orientation to the members, then to describe the purpose of the group, and, finally, to clarify the procedure that the group will follow.

In the *basic orientation statement*, the therapist reminds the patient about the time of the meeting, about its length, and about the presence of observers, if any, and may review some basic ground rules of the group (for example, the necessity of arriving punctually or rules about smoking).

The *purpose of the group* must be presented to each patient in extremely lucid terms. New members are always anxious and often confused, and the therapist cannot err in the direction of being too coherent and too explicit. As the sample introduction in chapter 2 indicates, the therapist makes a short statement about the importance of working on relationships with other people and asserts that the investigation and improvement of interpersonal relationships is what groups can do best and will be the focus of this group. Furthermore, the therapist lets it be known that the group will be able to be most effective by helping people understand as much as they can about the relationships they have toward one another in the room.

The therapist then outlines the *basic procedure* of the group, describing briefly the five phases of the group I have just described and being especially careful to inform new members of the presence of observers in the room or behind the mirror who, toward the end of the session, will discuss the meeting with the leader(s). The therapist then sets the stage for the next step by commenting that each session begins with a *go-round*, in which the therapist touches base with each person, asking what he or she would like to work on in the group that day. The work must be appropriate and able to be achieved in the therapy group time.

This short statement about the agenda leaves new patients very perplexed and often anxious. The therapist does well simply to reassure them and to let them know it is the therapist's job to help each person formulate an agenda and that the group will begin by letting the new patients participate last.

The Agenda Go-Round

It is important to launch a meeting with some structured vehicle that permits the therapist to make some contact, however brief, with each member in the group. In groups with a stable composition—for example, long-term outpatient groups—the therapist has considerable information at his or her disposal about each of the members of the group and generally requires only a short time to determine the point of urgency for a particular group session. In the rapid change of the inpatient group, the therapist is often confronted with individuals about whom he or she has little information. A structured "go-round" allows the therapist to scan the group quickly, to make contact with each person in the room, and to obtain a bird's-eye view of the work possible for the group that day.

Furthermore, a structured exercise at the onset of a meeting conveys a clear message to each patient that activity and participation by each is expected. If the therapist allows the group to start on its own, there will almost invariably be a period of silence, confusion, ice-breaking ritualistic comments, and casting about for some useful or convenient topic for conversation. In a long-term stable group, the situation is different: experienced culture-bearing members will take responsibility for launching the meeting. Or if not, if the group silently refuses to begin the session, there will always be time to analyze the meaning of this resistance. But the inpatient group has neither the luxury of culture bearers nor the time to investigate resistance. The life of the group is, as I have said, but a single session;

and without a launching task, the minutes will click by, and invaluable time will be lost, with no offsetting advantage.

What type of initial structured go-round is preferable? Many options exist. The most obvious one, used by many group leaders, is to ask each patient to describe briefly why he or she is in the hospital. It may be argued that this form of go-round is a "no-nonsense" approach, since it focuses directly upon the life crisis and the ensuing decompensation that brought the patient into the hospital.

But there are many disadvantages of such an opening gambit. For one thing, a patient's perceived reasons for entering the hospital are often several steps removed from the work one can do in a therapy group. Patients may be in the hospital because of substance abuse or because of some external event (for example, the loss of a job, the malfeasance of another, the loss of a lover) or because of some other externalized complaint (for example, a psychosomatic ailment, ideas of reference, or hallucinations) or because of some primary biological disturbance (such as major affective disturbances). To concentrate on these reasons for admission emphasizes the then-and-there and makes it more difficult for patients to use the resources of the group. Often the reasons for hospitalization are complex, and not infrequently most of a session may be consumed in an investigation of the admission stories of the new members. Furthermore, it becomes repetitious for older members to continue to restate their reasons for entering.

Another commonly used initial go-round is for the therapist simply to ask each patient to state something about the way he or she is feeling that day. This tack accomplishes the task of touching base with each patient and obtaining a sense of the overall emotional state of the members of the group, but it often steers the group into a *cul de sac:* it neither provides a blueprint for the remainder of the meeting nor orients patients toward the changing of dysphoric feelings.

In my opinion, a highly effective way of beginning a meeting is to ask each patient to formulate a brief personal agenda for the meeting. The agenda identifies some area in which the patient desires change. The agenda is most effective if it is both realistic and "do-able" in the group meeting that day. I urge the members to formulate an agenda that focuses on interpersonal issues and, if possible, on those that in some way relate to one or more members of the group meeting in that session.

The very best agendas are those that reflect some issue that is of core importance to the individual's functioning, which is interpersonal in nature and may be worked on in the here-and-now of the group. Some examples of agendas that lead to useful, effective work in the group:

1. "My problem is trust. I feel if I open up and be honest about myself, other people, especially men, will ridicule me. I feel that way, for example, about Mike and John [two other members of the group that day]."

2. "I feel like other people consider me a nuisance. I think I talk too much and want to find out if that's true."

3. "I put up a wall around myself. I want to approach others and make friends, but I'm shy. Consequently, I stay alone in my room all day. I feel I have some common interest with Joe and Helen [two other members], but I'm scared to death to talk to them."

Later in the chapter I will give many other examples of agendas; but, for the moment, consider these three. Each deals with a concern that is central to the individual speaking. (Note, however, that in none of these three instances was the problem stated in the agenda the actual precipitating cause for hospitalization. The first patient was an anorexic; the second, a young alcoholic; and the third had made a serious suicide attempt.) Furthermore, each of these three agendas expressed an interpersonal concern. Lastly, each had a here-and-now component: that is, each concern could be examined in the context of that patient's relationship with others in the group that day.

The Advantages of the Agenda Go-Round

The major advantage of the agenda exercise is that it offers the therapist an ideal solution to the dilemma of having either too much structure or too little. The exercise provides a structure for the meeting but simultaneously encourages patients to assume autonomous behavior. Each patient is urged to say, in effect, "Here is what I want to change about myself. Here is what I choose to work on today."

The agenda provides the leader with a wide-angle–lens view of the group work that can be done that day. He or she quickly makes an appraisal of which patient wants to do what type of work and which goals intersect with the goals of others. Furthermore, the agenda serves the function of initiating interaction between members.

The agenda encourages patients to assume a more active posture in psychotherapy. Often the agenda exercise is exceptionally useful in their ongoing therapy once they leave the hospital. Patients are encouraged to state their needs explicitly and straightforwardly—a particularly therapeutic exercise for those patients who habitually ask for help in indirect and self-destructive ways—for example, through self-mutilation or other self-destructive acts. (As I shall emphasize later, not all agendas can or will be filled or even addressed during the meeting; but for many patients, the formulation—not the completion—of the agenda is the key therapeutic task.) The agenda task teaches patients to ask explicitly for something for themselves. It helps them understand what therapy can do and their responsibility for using or not using therapy. They realize very clearly—and this is a point I shall discuss at length—that if they formulate an inadequate agenda, they are unlikely to profit from the meeting.

The agenda often requires homework. Patients know that it is expected of them, and many patients plan their agenda early in the day. Again, this is often a useful form of education about how to use the therapy process. Several patients have commented that the agenda exercise helped them to organize themselves early in their hospitalization: the process of thinking ahead about their problems in an overt, systematic manner was clarifying and relieving. Furthermore, several patients reported a sense of mastery or even exhilaration at being able to formulate some concrete task and have the sense of completing that task for themselves during the therapy hour. Some patients, especially those with "examination anxiety" patterns or concerns about failure, may be excessively concerned about constructing a daily agenda. Often the therapist must relieve this pressure by acknowledging the difficulty of the task and by reassuring the patient that part of the therapist's task is to help the members formulate an agenda.

Helping Patients to Formulate Their Agendas

The formulation of an agenda is not an effortless, automatic task. Patients do not do it easily, and the therapist must devote considerable effort to help them in this task.

For one thing, the great majority of patients have considerable difficulty understanding precisely *what* the therapist wants and *why*. The task must be explained to patients simply and lucidly. The therapist may give examples of possible agendas and painstakingly help each member shape his or her own. The therapist must also explain to patients *why* he or she wants an agenda by stating the advantages of the agenda format.

Agenda formation requires three steps and the therapist must escort most patients, especially in their first meeting, through each of the three steps:

1. The patient must identify some important personal aspect that he wishes to change. Moreover, the task must be realistic: that is, the aspect must be amenable to change and appropriate for a therapy group approach.

2. The patient must attempt to shape his or her complaint into interpersonal terms.

3. The patient must transform that interpersonal complaint into one that has here-and-now ramifications.

These remarks about agenda shaping may be made clearer by clinical illustrations.

Consider a meeting in which a new woman member offers as her agenda item: "I'm depressed and what I want to work on in this group is getting over my depression." This agenda will lead to no useful work in the group. First of all, it is unrealistic. The time frame for the agenda must be *a single meeting:* that is, the agenda must refer to a task that can be accomplished in one session. This particular patient had been depressed for years; how could a single therapy group meeting possibly alleviate that depression? Furthermore, the agenda is too vague, it is not specific and not consonant with the explicit activities of the group. Groups cannot work on "depression": there is no toehold; it is interpersonal problems, not symptoms, that constitute the currency of dynamic psychotherapy.

When helping a patient transform an unrealistic agenda, such as this one, into an appropriate working agenda, it is important to acknowledge the importance of the patient's agenda. After all, in this patient's experience it *is* her depression that is the key reason for her being in the hospital. But the therapist must help the patient to obtain a more realistic perspective on the therapy of the depression. For example, one might say, "Being depressed is the pits, and of course you want to feel better. That's *the* goal, and a very appropriate goal, for your entire course of therapy. To alleviate your depression, however, weeks, even months, of therapy will be required. The important task for today is, How to begin? What can you work on in this group now? What groups can do best is to help people understand what goes wrong in their relationships with one another. What would you like to change in the way that you live with or relate to other people? Your relationships to people, in a way that may not yet be clear to you, are closely related to your depression. If you will begin to work on your ways of relating to others, I feel strongly that ultimately, not in a day, you will begin to experience much less pain in your life."

Or, consider another example: A male patient offers this agenda: "I've lost my job, I have no future, I don't know what to do with my life." The group that attempts to work on this agenda will, without doubt, embark on an unrewarding campaign destined ultimately to fail. The members will focus on the outside problem of one individual. They will attempt, on the basis of inaccurate information, to determine why he lost his job and make some determination of his skills and ability to find another. The majority of the members of the group will be bored and impatient. They may never have seen this member before yesterday, and they may know he will depart tomorrow. Hence, there is not time for true concern about him to have developed; nor is there any foundation for hope of reciprocity: that is, that the time and attention given to solving the outside problems of another person will be "returned" to the giver. The rapid turnover of patients vitiates the possibility of just returns.

Just as he did in the previous example, the therapist must acknowledge the patient's distress but try to place it in the perspective of the work of the group. Thus, the therapist might say, "This must feel devastating to you. I can see how the pain of what has happened must dwarf everything else in your mind now and make it hard to pay attention to other things. But distressing as your loss of job and the problems of finding another must be, I do not see how the group can specifically help you with that. It sounds like an issue you could best work on in your individual therapy or in your work with a vocational counselor or an occupational therapist. Let's see how *this* group could help you. What could you work on here that might be helpful to you?"

Most likely the patient will persevere about wanting to work on the job loss or might conclude that there is nothing the group can offer him. The therapist's task at this time is to search for some interpersonal component of the patient's problems. In such a situation I begin to sift silently through a number of interpersonal hunches: "Does this man's interpersonal style have anything to do with his losing his job? Or, perhaps his obsequious, self-denigrating manner creates obstacles in applying for and obtaining another job. He doesn't seem to acknowledge his pain. I wonder what he does to get help for his feelings of distress. Does he ever get any support from others? Can he ask for help? Who helps him? He seems very down on himself. I wonder what it feels like for him to tell us about his failure. I wonder if there's someone in the group he feels especially ashamed to tell," etcetera.

By investigating some of these interpersonal leads, the therapist can generally help a patient relinquish an unrealistic agenda and arrive at one appropriate to the group.

In this clinical example, Harvey, a paranoid schizophrenic crop duster, was admitted to the hospital because of his bizarre, self-destructive behavior. He claimed that his only problem was vertigo (not a good thing for a crop duster to have!), and declined to participate in the agenda task. His admission to the psychiatric ward was a mistake, Harvey claimed; he belonged on a medical ward.

The therapist responded, "It's unfortunate that you were admitted to the wrong ward. But as long as you're here, why not take advantage of what we've got to offer? You know, I often consider this ward a postgraduate course in self-discovery. There are dozens of expensive courses in the community in self-exploration or personal growth. You can never learn too much about yourself. All of us keep learning and growing. We've got expert instructors in this group. You're paying for it anyway, it's all gravy. Why not take advantage of the opportunity?"

Harvey was disarmed by this approach. He opined that it made good sense, and stated that he guessed he could work on why people so often accused him of lecturing to them.

By using such strategic approaches, the therapist is able,

without too much difficulty, to help shape each patient's agenda into interpersonal language. The interpersonal agendas vary widely, but the great majority are expressed in one of the following formulations:

1. I'm lonely; there is no one in my life.
2. I want to communicate better with people.
3. I want to be able to express my feelings and not hold everything inside.
4. I want to be able to assert myself, to say No, and not to feel overpowered by others.
5. I want to be able to get closer to others and to make friends.
6. I want to be able to trust others, I've been hurt so often in my life.
7. I want some feedback about how I come across to others.
8. I want to be able to express my anger.

Transforming the Interpersonal Agenda into a Here-and-Now Agenda

Recall that the agenda task consists of three steps: (1) identification of a personal area that the patient wishes to change; (2) transformation of the complaint into interpersonal terms; (3) statement of the agenda in here-and-now terms.

The list of agendas I have just cited satisfied the first two criteria. The therapist has one remaining task: *to help members transform these general interpersonal agendas into specific agendas involving other members of the group.*

Once this basic principle is grasped, the technical work is straightforward. Let us reconsider each of the eight agendas I have listed and examine some approaches the therapist may take to shape them into here-and-now agendas.

1. *I'm lonely; there is no one in my life.*

"Can you think and talk about the way you are lonely here in the hospital? From whom have you cut yourself off in this group? Perhaps a good agenda might be to try to find out how and why you've made yourself lonely here."

2. *I want to communicate better with people.*

"With whom in this room is your communication good? With whom is it not entirely satisfactory? With whom here in this room would you like to improve your communication? Is there some "unfinished business" between yourself and anyone else in this group?"

3. *I want to be able to express my feelings and not hold everything inside.*

"Would you be willing to express the feelings you have here in the group today as they occur? For example, I wonder if you'd be willing to describe some feelings you've had toward an issue or some person so far today as we've been going around the room doing these agenda go-rounds?"

4. *I want to try to assert myself, to say No, and not to feel overpowered by others.*

"Would you be willing to try that today? Would you try to say one thing that you'd ordinarily suppress? Would you select the people in the group today that most overwhelm you, and see if you might be able to explore some of your feelings about that? Would you like to ask something for yourself? How much time would you like for yourself later in the group today?

5. *I want to be able to get closer to others and to make friends.*

"With whom here in this room would you like to get closer? I wonder whether a useful agenda might not be to try and explore what keeps you away from trying to get close to these people. Would you try some different way of approaching them today? Would you like feedback from them on how you create distance?"

6. *I want to be able to trust others, I've been hurt so often in the past.*

"Would you try to explore that with members of this group? Who in this room do you particularly trust? Why? What is there about them? Which people in the room might seem somewhat difficult for you to trust? Why? What is there about them? What do you have to fear from anyone here in this group? In which ways do I threaten you? What do you have to fear from me?"

7. *I want some feedback about how I come across to others.*

"Why do you want the feedback? [Try to tie it in with some important aspect of the patient's problems with living.] What aspect of yourself would you like some feedback about? From whom here in the room do you especially want some feedback today?"

8. *I want to be able to express my anger.*

Work on this particular agenda is delicate, and I discussed it at length in chapter 4. To summarize, it is advisable to steer clear, so far as possible, of overt conflict in the group. One approach to such an agenda is as follows: "Expressing anger is scary to an awful lot of people and it may be too much to try and express a lot of anger here in the group. However, one problem that many people have with anger is that they let it build up inside of them until the sheer amount of it gets to be very frightening. Perhaps one way you might be able to work on it here is to try and let some of the negative feelings out while they're still in a stage of slight irritation or annoyance, before they build up to real anger. I wonder, then, if you would try in the group today to express slighter feelings of annoyance or irritation just as you first perceive them to be forming. For example, would you be willing to talk about some annoyance that you've had with me or with the way I've been leading the group thus far today? Would it be all right with you if I were to check back with you at other points during the group today to see what annoyance you've experienced?"

The therapist's responses to each of these agendas are designed to guide the patient into here-and-now exploration. Each response represents, of course, only one of many possible interventions; and each therapist must construct a repertoire of interventions that are consonant with his or her personal style. Let us consider general strategies upon which specific techniques must rest.

The Higher-Level Inpatient Therapy Group

Help Guide Patients from the General to the Specific

Help the members be exceedingly specific with their complaints and with their feelings toward other people. Interact with others. Address others explicitly and by name. Once a member is specific and names someone else (for example, "I want to get closer to Mary, but I feel put off by her"), then the stage is well set for the next phase of the meeting because almost certainly Mary's interest will be kindled, and she will inquire of that patient at some point in the meeting, "What do I do that puts you off?"

Be Gentle But Persistent

Nag the patients. Encourage, cajole, persuade them to formulate a workable agenda. This may be mildly irritating to them, but in the long run it has a high yield. Repeatedly, in debriefing research interviews, patients commented that, though they may have been annoyed during a meeting, they ultimately appreciated the persistence of the therapist. It is necessary to be gentle with patients who are having a difficult time understanding the task. Supply agendas for them, if necessary, in their first meeting or two. Avoid any comments that might injure sensitive feelings.

One useful technique to decrease a patient's irritation is to allow him or her to monitor the procedure. Check in with the patient and ask, on more than one occasion, "Am I nagging you too much?" Or, "Am I pressing you too hard?" Thus you allow the patient to have a sense of controlling the interaction and of being able to terminate it when he or she really wishes to.

Help Patients Differentiate One Another

One of the most common modes of resistance to interacting with others is the reluctance to differentiate one person from

223

another. Thus, a woman patient may say she feels isolated in
life and yet will decline to differentiate the group members
sufficiently to say that she feels slightly closer to one person
than to another. As true interpersonal exploration and all the
ensuing interpersonal learning cannot really begin until individuals start to differentiate one from the other, it is important to stress this task. The therapist may underscore the problem and comment that the failure to differentiate between
people is another way of staying distant and unengaged—precisely the patterns patients are trying to change.

Strive for Some Commitment

Even a very small commitment in the agenda statement provides important therapeutic leverage. For example, if one comments that one is intimidated by others, obtain a commitment
from this patient to name some of the people who most and
least intimidate him or her in the group. Or, if one states an
agenda of wanting to learn to express feelings, then attempt to
extract a commitment from that patient to express in this meeting at least one or two feelings that he or she usually suppresses.
Or, if one frames an agenda of wanting to learn how to ask for
things for oneself, then attempt to extract a commitment that
that patient will ask for some specified amount of time (even
three or four minutes) for himself or herself in the group that
day. Or, if one says that one wants to reveal more of oneself,
obtain a commitment to disclose some personal data that the
group has not known before. Each of these commitments represents "credit" in the bank upon which the therapist can draw
later in the session.

Be Positive and Constructive

Do not foment conflict in the group. In the agenda go-round,
therapists help to avoid conflict and facilitate the development
of a trusting, constructive atmosphere by starting with positive
feelings. If, for example, one states that one's problem centers

on being unable to feel close to others, then the therapist best facilitates investigation of this area by beginning the exploration of the positive side of the spectrum. Ask, for example, "With whom do you feel most close in the group?" or, "With whom is your communication good?" et cetera. Once safety has been established, you can gently move to the more problematic areas, with such questions as: "With whom do you experience some blocks in communication?" The general strategy consists of starting on the far side of anger and cautiously inching up on it until you find an optimal area for therapeutic work.

Transform Resistance into Agenda Work

Not infrequently patients will seem unalterably resistant to the agenda task. They may be too depressed, too demoralized, or too convinced that they cannot change and would be better off dead. In such instances, it is always important to locate and ally oneself with the healthy part of the patient, the part that wants to live. One of the advantages of making the higher-level group optional is that the therapist can always assume that the part of the patient that decided to come to the group that day is striving for growth.

The agenda go-round may be construed as an exercise in helping individuals to get their needs met. By accentuating that aspect of the agenda, the therapist circumvents resistance and forges a therapeutic alliance. Exhortations to "ask for something for yourself," "get your own needs met," "be more selfish," or "learn to value yourself and take care of yourself more," are basically highly supportive to the patient. They all suggest that the therapist feels strongly that the patient is worthwhile and deserving of care and attention. Therefore, agenda pressure by the therapist need not evoke defensiveness. Rarely will someone object to being considered too selfless, too unselfish, or too giving. Nor will one ever take umbrage at a therapist who exhorts one to ask for more for oneself.

Occasionally the resistance stems from problems in the therapeutic relationship. For example, a patient may resist the agenda task as part of his or her overall struggle to defeat the therapist. Such trends are relatively easy to determine and generally will be reflected in the patient's posture toward many therapeutic activities in the ward. If the conflict is considerable, you may first have to clarify the patient-therapist relationship. The therapist is, you may point out, easy to defeat, but the patient's is a Pyrrhic victory: its losses far outweigh its gains. Why be an adversary? After all, you, the therapist, are there to help. Why and whence the conflict?

"Final Product" Agendas: Clinical Examples

Fully formed agendas vary widely in detail, general content, and form; and it is neither possible nor necessary to present an exhaustive list of them. Representative agendas drawn from group meetings may, however, illustrate the texture of a workable agenda:

1. "Rick talked about being gay in the group yesterday, and I have a lot of feelings about that which I didn't share."

2. "Would you [addressing the men in the group] still talk to me and care about me if I didn't have my eye makeup on?"

3. "I've been annoyed about Steve's [another member of the group] "hyper" behavior. I'm afraid that I hurt his feelings when I mentioned it this morning."

4. "I want to know how my rocking affects everyone in the group."

5. "I've been told I'm not real. Yesterday you two [pointing out two members of the group] said you could take me for one of the staff. I want to find out what that's all about."

6. "I've got to find out why I'm so scared to talk in groups, especially in front of people [designating three members] my own age."

7. "In a group this morning someone told me that I blend into the woodwork. Is that the way you see me, too? If so, I want to work on that."

8. "I want to be able to deal with my anger toward the men in the group."

9. "I need to learn how to talk about my sexual feelings in front of other people."

10. "People think I'm weird because I'm phobic about touching anything. I felt really bad about being laughed at yesterday for playing cards with gloves on. I want to explain to everyone what it's like to have these kinds of fears."

11. "I said some crazy things in the community meeting this morning and I'm very upset about having talked like that. What do you all here feel about me after this morning?"

12. "I want to know whether there's something about me or the way I behave that would make a man want to rape me?"

These are "final product" agendas. They have been fully processed and shaped by the therapist and are far different from what patients started out with. For example, the last three agendas were offered by patients who had each been in the group for over twelve meetings. Each agenda is the product of considerable therapeutic evolution. The last agenda was formulated by a patient who, during her first several meetings, declined to talk at all about the fact that she had been raped. Finally, after learning to trust the group and hearing other patients talk about having been sexually assaulted, she was willing to discuss that and, only with much therapeutic work, was able finally in this agenda item, to confront the possibility that she, *unlike most rape victims,* may unwittingly have played some significant role in what had happened to her.

Resistance to the Agenda Task: Responsibility Assumption

Earlier in this discussion of the agenda, I remarked that forming an agenda is difficult for patients simply on a cognitive level.

Many patients have difficulty comprehending the relevance and the mechanics of the task, and thus far I have concentrated on methods the therapist can use to help overcome these cognitive difficulties. But there is a second reason that patients find the agenda task troublesome; this reason has deeper roots and offers a more obstinate impediment to therapy. The very nature of the agenda task reaches deep into many patients' psychopathology and evokes fierce resistance. Thus, despite the most lucid instructions, some patients may be unable to comprehend the task, refuse to engage in it, develop considerable anxiety during it, or, for reasons that are unclear to them, be angry at the entire exercise.

In order to formulate a coherent strategy to overcome this resistance, the therapist requires some understanding of its source. At both a conscious and an unconscious level patients' balk at the agenda because the task confronts them with "responsibility." The therapist who is to understand fully the nature of the resistance, must understand the concept of responsibility—the subtext of the agenda task.

Responsibility refers to "authorship." To be aware of one's responsibility means to be aware of creating one's own self, destiny, life predicament, feelings and, if such be the case, one's own suffering. The existential frame of reference in psychotherapy posits that there are certain "ultimate concerns" that individuals must face (either consciously or unconsciously) in their lives. In my *Existential Therapy*, I describe these ultimate concerns as death, isolation, meaninglessness, and freedom.[1]

Of these four ultimate concerns, freedom is most germane to the resistance evoked by the agenda task. Freedom has two major components: responsibility and willing. We shrink away from a confrontation with freedom (and from each of the other ultimate concerns as well) because such a confrontation results in great anxiety. The individual avoids facing responsibility because awareness of one's responsibility is deeply frightening. Consider its implications. If it is true that it is we, ourselves, who give the world significance, who create, through our own choices, our lives and our destinies, if it is true that there are no external references whatsoever and that there is no grand design in the universe, then it is also true that the world is not always as it had seemed to us. Instead of a world design around us and solid ground beneath us, we have to face the utter loneliness of self-creation and the terror of groundlessness.

There are many clinical modes that patients use to avoid knowledge of responsibility: one may displace responsibility for one's life upon others through externalization, placing the blame for what has gone wrong upon some external figure or force; one may deny responsibility by considering oneself as an "innocent victim" of events that one has oneself (unwittingly) set into motion; one may deny responsibility by being temporarily "out of one's mind"; one may avoid autonomous behavior and choice in different ways; one may behave in a way that elicits "taking over" behavior from others; one may develop a compulsive disorder in which one experiences one's actions as out of one's control.

An important initial step in the therapy of patients with all of these clinical disorders is to help one appreciate one's role in creating one's own distress. In fact, if a patient will not accept such responsibility and persists in blaming others, either other individuals or other forces, for his or her dysphoria, no effective therapy is possible. Consequently, responsibility assumption is a crucial first step in therapy, but it is a step that meets much resistance: at an unconscious level, the patient resists responsibility awareness because of anxiety about groundlessness that invariably accompanies full awareness of responsibility.

There is another source of anxiety in responsibility assumption. If patients become aware that they are responsible for their current life predicaments they also veer close to appreciating the extent to which they have been responsible for the course of their past lives as well. For many patients that awareness incurs considerable pain: as one looks back upon the wreckage of one's life, upon all one's unfulfilled potential, all of the possibilities never examined or taken, then one becomes flooded with guilt—not guilt in its traditional sense, which is related to what one has done to others, but guilt from an existential sense, which refers to what one has done to one's own life.

Thus, the simple act of forming an agenda is not so simple after all; it confronts patients with issues that have roots steeped in anxiety, roots reaching down to the very foundations of their existence. Consider the steps a patient must take in the proper formation of the agenda.

Realizing That There Is Something about Oneself One Must Change

It is an extraordinarily important step for a patient to realize that there is something about himself or herself that he or she must change. Indeed, for some patients who externalize to an extensive degree, it is an entirely sufficient goal of the acute inpatient psychotherapy group. Patients who regard their problems as "out there"—that is, unfair treatment by employers, abandonment by a treacherous mate, or victimization by fate—cannot begin the change process until they come to terms with their own personal role in their life predicament. Otherwise, why change? It would make more sense for therapy to be directed toward changing not oneself but the offending other party. As long as patients remain in an externalizing mode, the psychological help that they can accept is limited to such modes as commiseration, support, problem solving, advice, and suggestions.

Hospitalized patients who externalize considerably constitute a relatively large percentage of the inpatient population. They include such diverse clinical entities as psychophysiological disorders, paranoid disorders, patients who are involuntarily hospitalized, and most patients who are substance abusers.

The Higher-Level Inpatient Therapy Group

Identifying Some Specific Aspect of Oneself One Would Like to Change

The identification of some specific piece of work is an important focusing task for each patient. Many patients are so demoralized and so overwhelmed by the shambles of their lives that they despair of change. To force oneself to identify a starting point, to commit oneself to a discrete task, often inspires hope and combats confusion.

Communicating One's Wishes to Others

It is an exceedingly important step for patients to learn to communicate their wishes to others, and one that addresses a very important facet of many patients' psychopathology. It brings home to one that others cannot read one's mind; that others cannot know one's wishes automatically; that one has to state one's wishes aloud or they will never be known, much less gratified.

The awareness that one must communicate one's wishes is important because it leads to the insight (distasteful though it may be) that we are truly alone, that there is no omniscient servant looking over us, that we will not change unless we change ourselves. The agenda format brings this insight home via another route as well: patients, after attending many meetings, gradually comprehend that, if they do not formulate an agenda, they will derive little benefit from the meeting. After even a couple of meetings, patients know perfectly well what type of agenda gets attention and results in effective work. At some level of awareness, the agenda initiates an internal dialogue in which patients are forced to come to grips with their unwillingness to change.

Agenda work with a depressed woman patient illustrates some of these issues. She felt defeated and self-contemptuous and stated the following agenda: "I feel like an absolute failure.

Today what I want from the group is simply support. I need lots of strokes from people."

The therapist urged her to stretch farther: "What kind of strokes would you like? What would you like to hear them say to you?"

Now, of course, this line of questioning is highly irritating. It's annoying to be required to state what positive things one wants people to say to one spontaneously. The patient's reply reflected exasperation. She snapped, "If I have to tell them what to say, then it doesn't count!"

Yet at another level it counts very much that the patient not only expressed her pain but identified precisely what would make her feel better. This is a giant stride on the road to learning how to become her own mother and father—and, for this patient as for a substantial number of others, that is the major goal of psychotherapy.

Learning How to Take Care of Oneself

One of the most common problematic situations the therapist encounters in the agenda go-round is the presence of a patient who declares himself or herself too upset to perform the task.

Consider the following clinical illustration: One of the members of an inpatient group, a young woman, Diane, sat crumpled up on the sofa, head in hands, and, a couple of minutes after the onset of the meeting, began sobbing loudly. When asked about her agenda, she replied in a tremulous voice that she had been in bed crying all morning, that she was unable to function and highly suicidal. "I'm just too overwhelmed to give an agenda. I just want to be here in the group today. That's all I can say."

First, let me consider the most likely scenario if the therapist allowed the meeting to run its natural course. The group members would undoubtedly come to her rescue. It is difficult to ignore someone in extremis. They would try to nurture her, but most likely (as the therapist knew from other sessions) Diane would find ways ("yes, but") to deflect nurturing efforts. Eventually the group would become annoyed with her monopolization of the meeting and discouraged and irritated at their inability to be helpful to her.

Even if the group were successful in nurturing Diane, even if they were to cradle and to nurture her, by no means was it clear that such a meeting would constitute good treatment for her. Each time she had been thus supported in the past, she felt better for a while; but her relief was evanescent and evaporated, leaving no crystals of self-knowledge that might be useful to her in some future crisis. The task of the therapist was to work with Diane in such a way as to provide her with tools that might be useful to her in her next episode of great distress.

To accomplish this task, and to avoid the anticipated countertherapeutic scenario for both Diane and the group, the therapist had to help Diane assume responsibility for her own therapy. The most appropriate starting place was to help her commit herself to trying to use the group to help herself feel less upset. The therapist had to proceed by gently pressing her to formulate such an agenda. He could begin with "Diane, what could you do today so that seventy-five minutes from now, when you leave this room, you might feel better?" If she were unable or unwilling to respond to this inquiry, the therapist could search for other ways to help the patient draw upon her own resources. He could ask, "Diane, you've felt like this before. What has helped you feel better in the past?" Or, "Diane, I know that there have been times here when you felt the group was useful to you. I've seen you walk out of the group feeling better than when you walked in. What helped you in those meetings?"

The therapist used all of these approaches to lead Diane gently toward responsibility assumption. She balked at the therapist's first couple of inquiries but eventually said that she had been helped in the past by sharing intimate things with the group. One thing that really upset her now was that she had no one close to her to speak with. She lamented not having some intimacy in her life.

The therapist responded, "Then, Diane, you do know one way to help yourself feel better, and that's to be intimate with someone else." When Diane agreed, the therapist had established some therapeutic leverage which permitted him to proceed. He asked, "Diane, how can you go about making yourself feel more intimate with other people?" Diane, who had at this point stopped sobbing, said she knew that she could feel more intimate if she would be her real self, stop wearing a mask, and tell people something real about herself.

By now Diane had accomplished two thirds of the agenda task: she had identified some changeable aspect of her behavior and had couched it in interpersonal language. What remained was only to bring the agenda into the here-and-now. The therapist asked, "Diane, could you look around the room and select someone here with whom you'd like to do that, to be closer and to tell something real about yourself?" Diane selected Lisa, a young woman close to her own age. The therapist asked whether Diane would rather do that now in the group or after the group meeting. She felt she would prefer to do it after the meeting; and with the therapist's urging, she and Lisa set up a thirty-minute appointment after the group session. Diane also made a commitment to share some of the things she and Lisa discussed with the group the next day. (The following day we learned that Diane had told Lisa in great detail about her binge eating—an aspect of herself that constituted an important source of her self-loathing and was a secret she had rarely shared with anyone.)

At the end of the meeting, the therapist commented that Diane looked a lot better and checked out with her whether in fact she felt better. When she agreed, he reinforced the learning by asking what she thought had helped her to feel better. She was able without difficulty to comment that it had been her reaching out to other people in the group.

It is important that the patients store such knowledge so that they can build up a repertoire of behavior that helps them take care of themselves in the future. Therapists wish to dislodge patients from the belief that improvement as well as decompensation are out of their control and simply fall, like rain, into their lives. It is common for therapists to investigate, in great detail, events responsible for a patient's decompensation; but it is equally important to explore the events responsible for a patient's doing better. Whenever a distressed patient improves, it is important for the therapist to pose the question of what happened to bring about the improvement. If, for example, one comments that one's improvement followed a conversation with a nurse, another patient, or a doctor, then explore what happened in that conversation that seemed to make that patient feel better. Underscore the helpful components of the conversation, so that he or she can "own" them and invoke them again at some future time.

Some therapists are reluctant to analyze improvement. They cite the old story of the centipede who, when asked about how he could walk so well with all of those legs, took to inspecting his pace so carefully that his spontaneous rhythm broke down, and he was no longer able to walk. Some fear the same thing might happen in therapy: that is, that improvement represents a precarious balance, and the therapist might tip the scales by vitiating its spontaneity or by exposing the "magical" aspects of improvement. To my mind, this is not a significant problem; if improvement has such a fragile foundation that it disintegrates with the slightest scrutiny, it is unlikely that it will serve the patient very well in the future.

Agenda Resistance: A Guide to Psychopathology

When the agenda task evokes anxiety because it thrusts deep into core areas of pathology, the therapist's task is not merely to help the patient formulate an agenda but to use the resistance as a guide to help the patient identify, appreciate, and initiate work on some of these key pathological areas. Some clinical examples may illuminate this point:

Fear of Isolation: Margot

Margot was a thirty-five-year-old psychiatric nurse who was admitted for the fourth time to an inpatient unit following a suicide attempt. Although often considered a model patient in most of the ward therapeutic activities, she was extraordinarily resistive to the agenda process. She found herself unaccountably angry at the agenda task as well as unable to formulate an agenda, an inability that made her feel stupid and incompetent in the group. This was a disconcerting and unusual situation for her, since she had excellent verbal skills and much psychological sophistication.

Margot had considerable curiosity about herself and was quick to acknowledge that her blocking and her anger at the agenda task seemed to have irrational roots. Soon her agenda in the therapy group began to be: "I want to find out why it's so hard for me to form an agenda."

Her first level of insight was that she had always been a giver. In her profession as a psychiatric nurse she gave continuously. It was against her grain to ask for help. She was quick to understand the importance of this difficulty in asking for help, since her multiple self-mutilating acts and suicidal gestures were, she was quite certain, implicit requests for help.

What other reasons, the therapist asked, made it hard for her to ask for help in an explicit fashion? After the therapist reiterated the question over several meetings, Margot became aware of her strong wish that the therapist know what she wanted without her having to ask for it. There was something exceedingly uncomfortable at the thought of there being no one "out there" for her, no ultimate rescuer who silently guarded her.

She soon discussed parallel situations in life. For many years she had experienced great panic whenever she was alone. She had been divorced for several years, and although she knew that she was not psychologically or financially equipped to care for her daughter, she was unwilling to give her up, even though her husband had remarried and was anxious to take custody of the child. She recognized that she kept her child with her, not for the child's sake but for her own: she used her daughter as a buffer against isolation. At a deep but murky level, she had always known this and had experienced corresponding guilt and self-contempt.

Margot's panic when alone was far in excess of the typical feelings of loneliness, social rejection, or the fear of being unprotected against an intruder which many divorced individuals experience. Instead, she had a pervasive sense of not existing and, like many borderline patients, felt real only by virtue of another person's perception and affirmation of her.

Margot's dependency on others for her sense of realness had pervasive implications both for therapy and for her social relationships. One of her great fears was that her therapist would forget her, and she described with great anger and dread an incident in which a therapist, who had treated her for about a year several years previously, had met her on the street and required "almost forty-five seconds" to remember her name.

Her discomfort at formulating an agenda helped her understand how her fear of isolation dominated her life. For example, in each of her previous hospitalizations, she had fallen in love with exceedingly unsuitable and often highly disturbed male patients; she could now apprehend that she so feared isolation that she chose to bond quickly with a man, any man, rather than to confront her loneliness.

Need for Dependency: Hal

Hal, fifty years old and depressed, was admitted to the hospital for the third time. Each of his hospitalizations had been precipitated by his wife's threats to divorce him. During the group meetings he found himself hopelessly unable to comprehend or to formulate a reasonable agenda. He grew increasingly annoyed and responded irritably, "If I knew what was wrong with me, I wouldn't be here." This attitude seemed particularly puzzling, since on his previous hospitalizations he had used the group effectively.

Finally, with continued urging by the therapist, Hal stated an agenda: "This morning in a 'metaphor' group several of the patients described me as a 'Greyhound bus with a flat tire and no driver.' I want to know from those of you who were in that group exactly what you meant!"

When the leader asked Hal what hunches he had about the meaning of the metaphor, he balked and, despite his high intelligence, pleaded utter puzzlement. His passive and helpless stance toward the agenda task paralleled his entire approach to therapy. For example, he stated that he entered the hospital because his wife had decided to get a divorce for reasons totally unknown to him. Bafflement, passivity, and what appeared to be feigned ignorance blocked every step of therapy.

The group leader persisted in helping Hal form an agenda by reminding him that he had attended other group meetings that had appeared useful to him. "If so, how had the group helped?" Hal acknowledged that the group had been useful in the past, and stated, almost sheepishly, that he had benefited by revealing himself and being accepted by others.

The therapist and the other group members could then underscore a central problem for Hal: he was in considerable distress; he had many resources at his disposal to help himself, but he persisted in wishing to believe that he knew nothing and could do nothing. The metaphor of the bus with no driver was very apt: Hal was hiding inside, under the seat, feigning ignorance, waiting to be driven. Eventually the group pinpointed the problem by confronting Hal: "Why do you pretend not to know how to help yourself? What's the payoff? What's in it for you?"

This was an effective exercise in "problem spotting." The agenda exercise helped identify a problem that Hal could address in all of his therapies—both group, individual, and marital-couple. We learned later, from a discussion with his marital therapist, that the problem that had been spotted in the therapy group articulated closely with the work in couples therapy. Hal's wife had left him because of his passivity and dependency, and he had responded by becoming even more passive and helpless—just as he had done in the therapy group. His unconscious wish was that his extreme helplessness would deter his wife from leaving him—just as in therapy he wished that his extreme dependency would result in all of his needs being anticipated and filled by the therapist and the group. Had the therapist corroborated his helplessness, Hal's maladaptive behavior would only have been reinforced. By confronting Hal with his inner duplicity ("Why do you pretend not to know?"), the therapist helped him identify one of his basic characterological problems.

With such patients as Margot and Hal, who have extreme problems in the spheres of passivity and dependency, the major part of the therapeutic work is the process of formulating an agenda (and not agenda filling, which transpires later in the meeting). In other words, to be able to identify, to state, and to take responsibility for change constitutes change for such individuals. Therefore, the formulation of an agenda may come very slowly. The therapist must not make the error of assuming that it is the prelude for therapeutic work: this formulation often *is* the therapeutic work.

Being Afraid to Grow Up: Junior

"Junior" was a twenty-three-year-old depressed woman who was admitted to the hospital immediately following her decision to give up for adoption her five-month-old illegitimate child. During her first group meeting, she, unlike everyone else in the group, sat on the floor nervously twirling her hair. She was the last one in the group to be asked for an agenda, and her only reply was a whispered, weeping, "Guilt." When pressed, she blocked completely, only managing to sob, "I can't do it, I don't know why I can't do the agenda."

The therapist, sensing that further pressure would not be productive, tried a different tack. He stated, "Junior, I think I know why you can't form an agenda." Junior, her interest piqued, looked up expectantly. The therapist said, "You've been taking care of a baby for several months, and now you want to be taken care of yourself." Junior whispered, "Yes." One of the members of the group asked then, "Is that why you speak in such a whisper all the time?" Junior once again whispered, "Yes." The therapist asked her, "How old do you feel right now in comparison to the others in the group?" (A question, incidentally, that is often productive.) Junior responded, "I feel very, very, very young."

At this point the way was open for the establishment of an agenda and a contract. The therapist posed the leverage-producing question: "Are you satisfied with that?" Junior responded in a rather loud voice, "No." "Then," said the therapist, "perhaps a useful agenda might be to try and learn how to be more grown-up here in this group." Junior agreed, and later the therapist continued to work on the agenda by asking other people to do some role playing and to state how they would, in a grown-up way, formulate an agenda if they were in Junior's position. Three patients immediately responded. One woman commented that she would want to do some work on her feelings of shame over having to give up her baby. Another said that she would want to talk about her rage at the baby's father, who deserted Junior, and at all men. Another stated that she would say, "I'm exhausted. I've done all that I can and I want to be taken care of right now."

This was an significant meeting for Junior. Although she stayed on the ward another three weeks, she commented, in a debriefing discharge interview, that getting in touch with how young she felt and how much she wanted to be taken care of was the most significant thing she had learned throughout her whole hospitalization.

Agenda Formation: The Completion of the Task

There is tremendous variation in the types of agenda formulated by members. The agendas are a function of many factors, including the composition of the group that day, its stability, and its size. If the group is relatively stable, and all the members present have formulated agendas in previous meetings, the agenda go-round may be completed quickly. By no means does this indicate that the members will use the same agenda every day. Occasionally an individual will work on the same agenda for several days in a row, but generally agendas will change to some degree: an individual may change focus because of the presence of different members in the group or because the previous day's work opened up different vistas. If there are many new members in a meeting, the agenda go-round will consume much more time. If the group is large, less time will have to be spent on each agenda.

A well-conducted agenda go-round results in a banquet of clinical material which should launch the group into productive use of the remaining time. Consider the following meeting of nine patients:

In approximately twenty-five minutes, an energetic, supportive therapist helped the members formulate these "finished" agendas:

1. "I was a battered child. I've got a lot of feelings about that I haven't worked out. I've never talked about that with other people, and I would like the group to try and help me talk about it."

2. "I have some unfinished business with you [the group leader] left over from yesterday's meeting, and I'd like to talk about that today."

3. "I've got to learn how to identify my feelings. I think I've

got to do it alone, but I want to try to talk about feelings that come up during the meeting."

4. "I've got to learn how to take more risks with others and assert myself more, especially with the other men here."

5. "I'm feeling very vulnerable and hurt, and I want to work on that in the group. I'd like to be able to tell all the people in the group about all the various ways I hurt."

6. "I've got some strong feelings about a conversation I had earlier with Mike [another patient in the group] this morning, and I'd like to try to work on those."

7. "I don't have the energy to state an agenda today." The therapist pressed her by asking a question that is usually effective: "If you were to have the energy to state an agenda, what do you think it would be?" The patient went on to say, "I think I'd like to ask for feedback from the other people in the group, especially from the men, since I usually seem to antagonize men for some reason."

8. "I want to talk about the feelings I have about my physical appearance. It's got to do with my size. I'm so big and tall that everyone seems to feel they can lean on me for help."

9. A new patient: "I'm in the hospital because my psychiatrist [a woman] left town for a few weeks. I'm in love with her and I want to marry her, and I'd like to work on that in the group." The therapist inquired about how the group could help him, because, after all, his psychiatrist wasn't present in the group. "Was it possible to work on something more relevant to the group?" The patient then stated that he was developing somewhat similar feelings toward one of the women in the group and perhaps he could talk about those feelings.

Agenda Filling

The completion of the agenda go-round signals a clear juncture in the meeting. The therapist may use this juncture as another opportunity to confront the group with the theme of responsibility assumption. For example, the therapist may state: "Well, we finished the go-round, and it is clear that people have stated some really important agendas. How shall we proceed now? How would you like to start working on them?" If the therapist catches someone's eye at this point, it is tantamount to an invitation to that person to proceed talking about his or her agenda; thus, the therapist may choose to stare at the floor for a couple of minutes.

This strategy encourages someone in the group to take the responsibility of saying, "Well, I'll begin," or "I think we ought to start with Joe's agenda." This initial act is often highly symbolic and may be an important phase of work for the members (and there are many) whose agendas lie in one of the following areas: asking for time for oneself, learning to ask for help, asserting oneself, taking risks, or tuning in to the needs of others.

That minute or two of silence, during which the members deal with the issue of how they should begin the meeting, is a pregnant phase. Sometimes the therapist can, with profit, process this period later in the meeting. You may inquire about the feelings both of the people who spoke and of those who didn't but wished they had. Was there relief or disappointment when someone did take the responsibility of asking for time for himself or herself?

General Strategic Guidelines

The agenda filling phase of the group will in many ways resemble any interactionally based therapy group meeting in which the therapist helps members explore and alter maladaptive interpersonal behavior and attempts to facilitate the development of as many of the therapeutic factors as possible. The therapist must attempt to build as much cohesiveness as possible, to encourage altruistic behavior, to make it possible for patients to experience universality, to help them develop socializing techniques, to develop hope. And as in any therapy group, the therapist will facilitate interpersonal change by helping members not only to request, receive, and provide feedback but also to trust and to support one another and to disclose themselves.

But there is one important difference. Since therapists have at their disposal working agendas for each patient in the group, they are able to direct the work of the meeting in a "customized" and efficient manner. The time span of the inpatient group is a single session, and the information that the therapist harvests from the agenda go-round allows him or her to operate at maximum efficiency during that session. The therapist knows which patients need to learn to give feedback and which need to learn to receive it, which patients need to learn to be more active and which need to learn to listen and be sensitive to the needs of others. In short, the therapist has a blueprint of action that should ensure effective and highly relevant group work.

The Greatest Good for the Greatest Number

If there are, let us say, ten members in a meeting, all of whom have tendered workable agendas, and there are thirty minutes remaining, it is obvious that not all the agendas can be explicitly dealt with during the remainder of the group session. The ther-

The Higher-Level Inpatient Therapy Group

apist must, therefore, state explicitly at the beginning of the meeting that the agenda go-round is part of the work of the group, not a prelude to work, and that there is no certainty that all agendas will be met. Instead, the agendas constitute *what members would like to work on if time permits.* If this point is not explicit, some patients will feel that the therapist has failed to keep a commitment to them. Indeed, some patients, because of transferential tendencies, are particularly inclined to experience the meeting in this manner; they require several explicit repetitions of the fact that there is no promise to meet every agenda and that, in fact, time limitations generally make it impossible to do so.

Nevertheless, given these restrictions, it is important that the therapist deal with as many agendas as possible; it is generally feasible to do some therapeutic work on the great majority of agendas in each session.

The achievement of this goal requires, first of all, great attentiveness on the part of the therapist. At the end of the agenda go-round, you should, regardless of the size of the group, be able to recall each person's agenda. With practice you can easily keep in mind the agendas of as many as twelve to fourteen patients. It is far easier to recall agendas if you are particularly active in helping patients shape their agendas. You can train your memory for agenda recall by going over each person's agenda in a discussion with a co-therapist or an observer after the meeting.

Work on Several Agendas Simultaneously

It is highly advisable and almost always possible to work on several agendas at once. Avoid, if you can, working on a single agenda at a time, and avoid, as much as possible, one-to-one work in group sessions. Instead, attempt to fit the agendas together. The effective group leader resembles an orchestra leader who blends each member's contribution.

For example, The agendas of three members of an eight-person group were as follows:

Barth stated that he wanted to learn how to make friends. "I've never had any real close friends, and I don't think I know how to go about making friends."

Yvonne stated, "I want some feedback. I want to learn more about the way that I relate to people so I can make a go out of a reconciliation with my husband. I'm told I do something to turn people off, but I'm not sure what it is."

Stuart stated, "My doctor says, and I agree, I've got to learn how to share more of myself. I keep everything stuffed down, and sometimes I feel I'm going to burst."

Stuart began the meeting by saying, "I'll take a risk." And indeed he did! He revealed some self-destructive fantasies about burning himself to death and shared a psychotic belief that his lust for a young teenage girl had in some way been responsible for a fire in his house that had almost killed his family.

After this high-level disclosure, the therapist had a wide variety of options available to him. But, using the principle of trying to blend as many agendas as possible, the therapist deliberately turned to Barth (whose agenda was that he wanted to learn how to go about making friends) and asked him how he felt about what Stuart had said. Barth responded to Stuart in a very impersonal fashion suggesting, "I think whenever you have fantasies like that you should phone your therapist!"

At this point a marvelous opportunity was available to do some active work on Barth's agenda. The therapist turned to Stuart and asked how he felt about Barth's comment? Did it make him feel friendly toward Barth? Did it make him want to know Barth better, or did it make him want to move away from Barth? Stuart stated, in effect, that he'd felt distanced and untouched by Barth. The therapist then could, with Barth's help, ascertain that this had not been Barth's intention, that he had wanted to reach out to Stuart and say something warm or supportive to him.

The group then discussed what types of statement Barth might have made that would have helped Stuart feel closer to him. The therapist commented that one key ingredient for the formation of friendship is mutual self-disclosure. When one, in this case Stuart, reveals something about oneself to another, the former, the revealer, is at risk and is most effectively comforted and reassured by the other person's reciprocally disclosing something of himself. Barth was invited to try again and ultimately shared something of his sexual feelings toward a sister-in-law, which evoked much guilt. Stuart then confirmed that at this point he felt closer to Barth.

The therapist asked Yvonne how she felt about Stuart's comment. (Recall that her agenda had been to learn how she turned people off, so that she might have a better chance of a successful reconciliation with her husband.) As was her wont, she launched into a longwinded, convoluted story with considerable irrelevant detail about her first and second husbands and a number of neighbors as well, calling them all by their first names. After a few minutes everyone in the group felt confused and irritated. The leader then interrupted Yvonne and said that he felt this was an important time for her to stop and to get the feedback she had requested. Yvonne pleaded for only another minute and, to everyone's astonishment, got immediately to the point and shared her belief that some of her bad thoughts were responsible for her son's mental retardation.

The group at that point gave Yvonne considerable feedback. They told her that they had learned, in the last minute, that she had, in fact, something very important and highly relevant to say to Stuart, but *en route* she had confused and irritated them: she had used first names of people whom the group did not know, she brought in much irrelevant material, she didn't build bridges that enabled the group to understand the relationship between her story and Stuart's disclosure. Stuart stated that initially he had tried to listen attentively to Yvonne, but after a few minutes he had grown dizzy, had given up any hope of her saying anything relevant to him, and had long since tuned her out.

Thus, in a space of approximately ten minutes, three agendas were addressed and worked on effectively.

Put the Agendas to Work

The therapist should let the agendas do as much of his or her work as possible. It is important to remember all outstanding assignments or commitments that were made in the agenda go-round and to "call in these debts" at appropriate points throughout the meeting.

Suppose, for example, a patient becomes extremely tangential and speaks for a very long time about some obscure, "outside," impersonal issue. Since inpatient group therapy requires a single-session time frame, you must regard time as too valuable to waste large chunks of it in unproductive ways. It serves no purpose to allow the speaker to continue: not only will the speaker not profit from the monologue but ultimately he or she will incur the anger of the other members who will feel cheated of their time in the group.

But why should you stop the speaker when you can let other agendas work for you? For example, Fred, another patient in the group, may have this agenda: "I want to be able to get my needs met, to be able to ask for time in the group." The presence of a monopolizing patient presents a marvelous opportunity to work on such an agenda, and the therapist's task is then to find a way to help Fred intervene. Simply an opportune glance at him may be a sufficient cue. Or, the therapist may have to interrupt the monopolist and ask, "Fred, I wonder what you're feeling right now." Given the proper atmosphere, Fred will express some of his chagrin at having no time for himself in the group. Such a course of events is excellent therapy for Fred who begins to fill his own agenda, and it is also good for the monopolist who needs very much to hear about the repercussions of his or her behavior on the other members. Note here that the emphasis is *not* on helping the group to express anger at the monopolist but, instead, on guiding the group down a gentler channel which provides the monopolist with information about how his or her behavior prevents others from getting their needs met.

Take another clinical example: Suppose there is in the group, Gail, a profoundly distressed patient who is weeping copiously and obviously needs comforting. Why should the therapist comfort her when there are patients in the meeting with one of these agendas: "I want to learn how to get closer to others," or "I want to learn how to get in touch with my feelings," or "I want to learn how to open myself up and express my feelings." By encouraging one of these patients—Sylvia say—to respond to the distressed patient, the therapist multiplies his or her effectiveness.

The therapist can use the same procedure as in the previous example: a visual cue to Sylvia or, that failing, a direct summons. Sylvia's first response may be that she wanted to comfort Gail but didn't know what to do. At this juncture the therapist has a number of effective options: to inquire, for example, into Sylvia's first impulse. What did she wish to do? What passed through her mind when she saw Gail crying? If she were to try to comfort Gail, what might she do? Once she expressed some of these inclinations, the therapist might turn to Gail and ask her to respond to Sylvia's inclinations. "How would that have felt?" "Would that have helped?" "What might have helped the most?" "Was there anything else that Sylvia could do that she would find comforting right now?"

At this stage the whole sequence will generally evolve into a highly therapeutic one for both parties. For one thing, Gail is, to some degree, required to comfort herself by commenting on what would have helped. Sylvia, the would-be comforter, learns either that she had the knowledge in the first place of how to comfort Gail, or that she could have easily obtained it through a simple question.

If time and circumstances permit, the therapist could pursue the issue in a couple of other ways. By attempting to comfort Gail verbally or physically, you can encourage Sylvia to act out what she has learned. Sylvia could, for example, change her seat and, sitting next to Gail, hold her hand, put her arm around her, and so on. The sheer act of doing what one was previously afraid to do is made even more therapeutic if it is coupled with cognitive understanding of the obstacle that heretofore has blocked such behavior. Thus, you can urge Sylvia to discuss what had stopped her from having acted this way earlier in the meeting. What was her fantasy of how Gail might respond or of what other members of the group or the therapist might have thought of her?

Take one further example: Suppose a patient, Irene, has formulated an agenda that included a commitment to take some risks in the group and to reveal something important about herself that day. The therapist notes that the end of the group is rapidly approaching and Irene has revealed nothing of herself so far.

The therapist can easily enough "call in the debt" by explicitly reminding Irene of her commitment, or by inquiring about how she's feeling at the moment, or by asking her to imagine for a moment that the meeting has already ended, and to discuss what disappointment she might have had about the session that day.

But, on the principle of putting other agendas to work, the therapist can call upon a patient whose agenda was "to learn how to tune into other people," and ask him or her to guess how other people in the group may be feeling right now, or to identify some of the unmet needs he or she senses in the group, or—more pointedly—"What do you think Irene is feeling right now?"

The Higher-Level Inpatient Therapy Group

Be Active in the Agenda-Filling Task

As I have noted many times previously, the inpatient group is no place for an inactive, nondirective therapist. The therapist must be as active in filling the agenda as in formulating it. On those rare occasions when a group is highly self-sufficient and self-propelled, the therapist may be less active: it is not advisable for the therapist to take over work the group is able to perform for itself. Generally, however, the therapist must guide the discussion, actively call on patients, and act as a "matchmaker," fitting agendas together with one another.

The therapist also "calls in" a patient's commitments. If, for example, an agenda has included expressing some critical feelings one might have about the meeting or about the way the therapist is leading it, then it is the task of the therapist to remind that patient, often more than once during the session, of that commitment. It is rare that patients, especially new ones, will gratuitously initiate such comments. Critiques by patients on the process of a meeting almost invariably quicken its pace and deepen the engagement of the members. Thus, it aids the group as well as the particular patient to call in meeting-critique commitments.

Agendas May Be Filled Both Directly and Indirectly

I have focused thus far primarily on the direct, explicit filling of such concrete agendas as: "I want to learn to express feelings," "I want to communicate better with John," "I want to feel less intimidated by Jane," "I want feedback about the way I come across," "I want to know how I turn men off," "I want to learn how to make friends."

Frequently, however, agendas are filled in an indirect fashion. Consider this clinical example: Donna was an abject, despondent patient who was unable to formulate an agenda and persevered in saying that she felt like a total "nerd"—small, inept, and insignificant. Her inability to formulate a here-and-now agenda made her feel even more stupid and ineffective. Eventually she agreed to an agenda of "I want to feel more significant and valued by the other group members." The therapist addressed her agenda by enlisting her assistance during the session. For example, during pauses he asked Donna, "Where do you think we should go now?" When Donna responded, "Let's look into some other agendas," the therapist asked her, "Which ones?" She chose one and was successful in helping that patient to work, as well as other patients later in the session. By providing Donna with a task that she performed effectively, the therapist helped her to feel less insignificant and less stupid. She received some real-life (albeit "once removed," as the therapy group always is) disconfirmation of her self-derogatory feelings.

A similar agenda was offered by Frank, a depressed, silent, macho, proud young man. In the second week of therapy, Frank said he wanted to use the group to talk about his feelings of worthlessness. He said he didn't know how we could help him, but thought it might help simply to share his despair. He shared a great deal about himself with the group, especially about feeling stupid, about his envy for his wife because of her education, about being simply a dumb jock who operated heavy machinery, et cetera. The women had especially been turned off by Frank's tough, macho stance; but the more he revealed about himself, the more they appreciated his sensitivity. The men in the group followed suit: they like him more; and, in addition, several expressed their envy at his ability to operate many different types of complex heavy machinery. Thus, in several unanticipated ways, Frank ended the meeting feeling far less worthless than when he had begun.

Beyond the Agenda

The agenda is a structure-providing device; it should not be allowed to become a limiting one. Frequently the agenda serves as a springboard to propel the group into rich clinical domains that could not have been anticipated in the agenda go-round. On such occasions the therapist must flow with the current of the group and attend to the "point of urgency" in the session.

A portion of a therapy group meeting is illustrative. In the meeting with eleven members, three agendas were particularly relevant and dominated much of the last part of the meeting. Bob had informed the group at the end of the previous session that he was gay, and his agenda now was to share with the group some of his feelings about that disclosure.

Carol said that she felt withdrawn and isolated, and that it had a lot to do with her distrust of men; she had often taken risks and then gotten hurt as a result of her risk taking. The therapist asked whether such an incident had occurred in this group, and she said, yes, one had occurred with him (the therapist), and that perhaps it might be a good thing to work on that.

Edward, a paranoid, psychotic young man said that his agenda was to tell the group something about his world as he experienced it so that people would understand his comments better.

Bob began the meeting by saying that yesterday was difficult for him, but that he was glad that the fact of his being gay was out in the open. The therapist asked whom especially had he been afraid to tell. Bob said he worried yesterday that Jim might be intolerant, but that Jim's subsequent openness and acceptance of him had been tremendously supportive, and he (Bob) was very grateful to Jim. The therapist commented that others of his patients who were gay feared that heterosexual men in the group would feel threatened by them. Looking gratefully at the therapist at that point, Bob stated that that was precisely his fear, and that he wanted to let the other men in the group know that he was not about to make a sexual pass at any of them.

Was there anyone else in the group whom Bob had some concern about telling? Bob admitted that he had some trepidation about telling Edward, who had been judgmental and verbally abusive to several of the patients on the ward. Edward, in a surprisngly open manner, denied that the disclosure changed his feeling about Bob. In fact, Edward commented that he, too, had a great deal of sexual confusion and wondered whether he also wasn't gay. This was an astonishing revelation from Edward, who had been extremely paranoid and secretive. Several of the patients at this point expressed their admiration and liking of both Edward and Bob for being willing to trust the group and take such risks.

Carol then took the floor and said that her agenda the day before had been to learn to take risks; she had been prepared to tell the group important things about herself, but the therapist had not helped her. His neglect had stirred up a lot of feelings she had about being exploited by men who then betrayed or discarded her; perhaps it didn't make sense, but she felt the therapist had seduced her a bit by asking her for an agenda and then dumped her by not helping her work on it later in the meeting.

Taking an active approach, the therapist asked Carol whether there was something that she would be willing to tell the group today about herself, something that seemed important and would feel helpful to share? Carol proceeded then to talk for approximately fifteen minutes, relating poignantly how she had been sexually abused by an older male relative throughout her adolescence—an experience she could not share with her parents who, she knew, would have either blamed or disbelieved her. On a couple of occasions, when she took a chance and shared the information with some man, he (including a former therapist) had sexually exploited her. Today, after years of silence, she thought that she would try again.

The response of the group was overwhelmingly supportive. Carol was tremulous and weeping during her account and received much physical and emotional support from the other members who supplied Kleenex, hands to hold, and hugs. Three of the women shared similar personal accounts of sexual abuse. Everyone in the group, except Edward, offered Carol something. When he was asked how he felt about what Carol had said, he stated that first he wanted to do his agenda: that is, he wanted to tell the group something about the way he experienced the world; he wanted the group to know where he was coming from before he answered Carol.

In just a few brief minutes Edward gave an extraordinarily graphic view of his inner psychotic world, sharing with the group his belief that throughout his life he'd been manipulated by people, by the press, by the arrangements of books in the library, by motion pictures, by thought control, by brain waves from other people that made him move in ways he didn't want to move. For a couple of years now Edward had been convinced that the world was not really as it seemed but was all arranged in such a way as to manipulate him.

At that point in his story, he turned to Carol and said, "And now if you want to know what I feel about what you've said, here it is! It's all bullshit! I don't believe it even happened." He turned to Bob and said, "I don't believe you're gay"; and turning to another member of the group, he said, "I don't believe you were a heroin addict"; to another, "I don't believe you were an alcoholic"; and to the therapist, "I'm not sure you're a therapist." Edward turned back to Carol and said, "I don't believe that you were ever sexually abused, you made up the whole story in order to have some kind of effect on me, God knows what, probably sympathy." At this point Carol burst into tears and bolted from the room and from the ward as well. (The police brought her back two hours later.)

Since there were only a couple of minutes remaining in the session, this material had to be dealt with by the ward staff during the remainder of the day and in the small group on the subsequent day. Edward was shaken by the strength of Carol's reaction to him. He was further impressed at the marked difference between his reaction to Carol and that of everyone else in the group. Carol was deeply wounded by his remark, but in the following meeting she allowed the group to help her examine an important theme. One of her important belief systems was that men did not really listen to her and were not sensitive to her needs and her pain. But the group confronted her with the fact that she had treated Edward in precisely the same way. After all, he had been careful to preface his comments to Carol by saying he first wanted to let the group know what a crazy world he lived in. The material he presented to the group, as everyone (including Carol) knew very well, was obviously psychotic. Yet Carol insisted that this incident merely reconfirmed the fact that she could not trust men. Nor did she allow her belief system to be influenced by the fact that eleven of the twelve people in the room (half of whom were male) had been deeply supportive of her.

Bob commented that he often supported Carol, but that she did not seem sensitive to his pain. She had not been one of the members who had supported him earlier in the meeting when he had talked about his feelings about being gay. Nor had she been one of the members who had supported Edward when he had done some heavy risk taking and talked about his concern about his own homosexuality.

It seemed evident that Carol clung to her belief in the untrustworthiness of men by distorting some events and selectively not attending to others. The therapist helped her explore this theme by focusing on his own relationship to Carol. He responded to her perception of him as basically uncaring for her because of his failure to help her self-disclose in a previous session. He shared with her his concern that in that session she seemed so labile he decided it would be best not to expose her to more pain. He thought that, in a large meeting with many other pressing agendas, she might not have received the time and attention she required.

All of these complex issues constituted important therapeutic work. They were all introduced by the agenda task but went far beyond the original agenda formulation.

The Higher-Level Inpatient Therapy Group

The Agenda Procedure: Problematic Aspects

No therapy procedure is without its drawbacks; and although the agenda format increases the group therapist's efficiency, there will always be patients who are deeply critical of the procedure. Some data is available from the Stanford group therapy research project that investigated the attitudes of fifty-one patients toward their hospital group therapy experience.[2] Thirty-three of these patients had attended at least one meeting of a higher-level optional group that used the agenda format I have presented here.

Of these thirty-three patients, twenty-one (63 percent) commented that the agenda was an extremely valuable procedure. (I have incorporated, in the preceding text, their descriptions of the advantages of the agenda.) Eight patients (24 percent) felt positively about the agenda but described problems connected with it. Four patients (12 percent) felt negatively about the agenda.

Several types of problem were described. The most common complaint was that the agenda procedure evoked severe examination anxiety. Patients feared that if they produced a poor agenda, they would be criticized and their stupidity or inferiority would be exposed. Many of these patients spent considerable time during the day prior to the group thinking about their agenda.

Now anxiety is not necessarily a bad thing in psychotherapy. Therapy almost invariably requires some degree of stretching on the part of the patient, and stretching always implies tension. (It has been said, "If the shoe fits, you're probably not allowing for growth.") But the benefits of anxiety in psychotherapy are curvilinear in nature: that is, there is an optimal amount of anxiety; either too much or too little anxiety impedes the therapeutic work. If anxiety is so intense that patients fail to show up for therapy, then the strategic approach is incorrect: no therapy can be done on an absent patient. The therapist must be sensitive to this issue and reduce anxiety for the vulnerable patient as much as possible.

If patients perceive the therapist to be continually supportive and protective, the threat is lessened. A particularly active therapist, who energetically participates with the patient in shaping the agenda task, also reduces anxiety. I recommend that the therapist actively reassure members, especially new ones, that, of course, it will be difficult to formulate an agenda but that it is the job of the therapist(s) in the group to help in that task.

That, prior to the meeting, some patients spent much time planning an agenda is, of course, not in itself a drawback. On the contrary, such planning prompts patients to take therapy more seriously, to think about it more frequently, and to play a more active, responsible role in the procedure.

Other complaints from patients in this study seemed less substantial. One patient took umbrage at the word *agenda* as being reminiscent of a corporation board meeting, and suggested *goals* in its stead. Some patients commented that the agenda procedure was restrictive and prevented them from working on the major life issue with which they were grappling. For example, one woman complained that her chief problem was that her son was a drug addict, and that the group never permitted her to discuss him and to obtain guidance on how she might cope with him.

The other complaint was that some patients felt let down because they formulated an agenda that was never "filled" or, at times, even addressed later in the meeting.

The therapist best addresses these two complaints (that an agenda feels restrictive or that is unfilled) by explicitly discussing and predicting these issues in the orientation to the group in the first few minutes of the session. The therapist must explicitly delineate the goals and the procedure of the group and explain clearly why groups focus on interpersonal issues and why, for example, it would be unproductive to focus at length upon a problematic relationship with a child who was a substance abuser. If the therapist is careful not to invalidate the patient's need but refers the patient to another, more appropriate setting to deal with that issue (that is, individual or family therapy) and suggests that the group is more effective with another type of focus, then the patient is less likely to feel cheated or discounted.

An explicit statement that all agendas can often not be addressed will help to decrease the sense of betrayal. If the therapist emphasizes that it is, to a large extent, the patient's responsibility to see to it that agendas are filled, and also that the formulation of the agenda in itself constitutes therapy, then fewer patients are likely to feel unacknowledged.

The Final Phase

The final phase of the group meeting consists of an analysis, or "wrap-up," of the first hour of the meeting. There are many models one might employ for this purpose. I prefer to divide this final twenty minutes into two equal segments: (1) a discussion of the meeting by the therapist(s) and any observer(s) (either in the room or behind a one-way mirror), and (2) the group members' response to this discussion.

In the first segment, the co-therapists and observers form a small circle outside of, or in the middle of, the patients' circle and conduct an open analysis of the meeting just as though there were no patients listening and watching.

(If there happen to be no observers of the group on a particular day, the co-therapists can hold their own discussion; or if they feel they have contributed all that they can during the meeting, they may invite the patients to analyze it themselves. Or, a solo group therapist can process the meeting together with the members.)

In their discussion the leaders review the course of the meeting with particular focus upon their own leadership. They may wonder what they missed, what else they might have done in the group, whether they left out certain members, whether there would have been better ways to handle a particular situation in the group.

The observers are encouraged to participate actively in this discussion. The only instructions are that they attempt to make all their comments constructive; that if they are going to be critical, they confine criticism to the leaders; and that they attempt, if possible, to say something about each member of the group. Observers are also advised to avoid describing a group as "boring"—a comment that is never constructive and invariably evokes defensiveness and resentment on the part of the patients. (As a general rule, observers of a psychotherapeutic process who feel bored do so out of inexperience or a lack of knowledge about the dynamics of the patients. The more one knows about therapy, the more interesting does each therapy session become.)

The therapists make an attempt to discuss, even briefly, their view of each patient's experience—the type of agenda, the degree of activity or involvement, the work done on the agenda —and their estimation of each patient's degree of satisfaction. They discuss the entire course of the meeting, the general group climate, degree of engagement, irritation, or dissatisfaction; review the choices that they made in the meeting; and raise the question of others they might have exercised or of important issues they may have overlooked.

In the final ten minutes the meeting is once again thrown open to the patients. They generally spend most of this time responding to the observer(s)'s comments, exploring issues suggested in the therapists' discussion, processing the meeting themselves or, occasionally, working on unfinished business of the session.

The Higher-Level Inpatient Therapy Group

Format of the Final Phase: Evolution and Justification

As the "wrap-up" format I recommend is not traditional, I consider it necessary to describe its development and justification.

Evolution

Since I lead groups in a university hospital, I often have students (generally two to four) observing my groups, generally through a two-way mirror. For a period of many months, I used a traditional format for observation: the students observed the group, and afterward we (co-therapists and observers) met privately to analyze the meeting. Patients never respond favorably to such an observational format. Although they appreciate the necessity for on-site training for young clinicians, patients nevertheless feel "used" and intruded upon. The patients on my ward expressed much disgruntlement: they did not like to be "guinea pigs"; they raised the question of whether they were the "main act" or whether the group was primarily for the students (as one patient put it, "Which side of the mirror are the therapists on?"). Other patients commented that observers robbed the group of a sense of intimacy or dignity.

Other patients feared the observers would not respect the confidentiality of the therapy meeting. Some patients, especially those with paranoid ideation, were so threatened by the observational procedure that they removed themselves, either physically or psychologically, from the group. All attempts to reassure the group members about confidentiality, to introduce them to the observers, to remind the members that the patient is the primary concern in good teaching, failed to dispel the patients' discontent at being observed.

Later, in an effort to reduce the adverse affects of observation and to make the process useful to patients, I employed another format: at the end of the group, patients and observers switched places, the former entering the observation room and observing the student-observers and the therapists as they discussed the meeting. Finally, in an effort to save time, the observers simply entered the group room after the meeting and, forming a small circle with the therapists, spent ten to fifteen minutes in discussion, to which the patients silently listened.

Patients were intensively interested in the observer-therapist discussion. Over and over they commented on the many feelings and thoughts it evoked, and regretted having to end the meeting without the opportunity to air them. Furthermore, many patients wished to interact with the observers, either to obtain clarification of a comment one had made or to respond to a question one had posed.

The final step evolved naturally: ten minutes were added to the meeting to provide patients with an opportunity to express their reactions to the observer-therapist discussion, to pose questions, and to pursue work that had been stimulated by observer or therapist comments.

The response of the overwhelming majority of patients to this format has been unequivocally positive. With one stroke the observational process was transformed from a negative experience into a valuable component of the group therapeutic procedure. The input of the observers was so valuable that patients were invariably disappointed if none were present on a particular day. In fact, one patient felt so strongly about the positive value of hearing the observers discuss the group that each day, before deciding to attend a session, she checked the observation room to make sure there were observers present.

The Stanford group therapy research project specifically inquired into patients' reactions to this format, and there was strong consensus that the final twenty minutes was an integral, vital part of the therapy group session. When patients were asked what percentage of the value of the group stemmed from the last twenty minutes, they placed on it a value that far exceeded the actual time involved. Some patients, in fact, ascribed to the final twenty minutes a value of as high as 75 percent of the total group value.

Rationale

Though this procedure may seem unconventional and threatening to many therapists, it is based on fundamental group therapy principles. Earlier I emphasized that, to be therapeutic, the here-and-now approach must include two stages: the *experiencing* component, which is followed by *reflection upon* (or processing of) that experience. Interpersonally based psychotherapy consists of an alternating sequence: first, affect is evoked, and then that affect must be analyzed and integrated. The final phase represents the second, the self-reflective, phase of the here-and-now.

This phase does not constitute the entire processing or understanding of the experiencing phase of the here-and-now. I have provided many examples of the therapist's explaining or clarifying some important experience in the group. The therapist might, for example, "stop the action" and suggest to the group, "Let's try to make some sense of what has just been happening"; or, in a variety of ways, offer clarifications or interpretations based on here-and-now events.

But the final phase is a highly concentrated period of process commentary in which the therapists and any observers review all the key events of a meeting in an attempt to provide the patients with a cognitive framework for the events of the session.

Antecedents of the "wrap-up" Format

Though the self-disclosure required of the therapist in this format may seem considerable, the procedure of patients observing group leaders and observers is not without precedent. In fact, the origins of the sensitivity-training group date back to such a procedure.[3] In 1946, in a summer institute for community leaders, a group of observers met each night to discuss the process of the discussion group they had observed during the day. When the members of the group learned about these nightly sessions, they asked to observe the discussion. The laboratory leader, with some trepidation, agreed; and for several evenings, the group members sat in an outer concentric circle listening to the observers discuss them. This proved to be a compelling experience and generated enormous interest and interaction. The leaders of the laboratory realized that they had stumbled onto a powerful tool of education—that is, experiential learning; and from this insight developed the sensitivity group with built-in mechanisms for feedback both from members and from leaders.

A regular component of early sensitivity-training groups (or T-groups) in summer laboratories was the "fishbowling" exercise. In this format one group sat in a circle around another group; and periodically chairs were switched so that the outer group became the inner and discussed the process of the inner group they had just observed.

There are two reports in the literature of a "fishbowling" format being used in inpatient groups.[4] In these groups the patients met in an inner circle without a leader, while the staff observed from the outer circle. In the final fifteen minutes, the groups exchanged places, and the patients heard the staff discuss their leaderless session.

There is precedent for this format in outpatient practice. I have, for many years, invited members of my long-term outpatient groups to observe my student-observers discuss them after a session; and Eric Berne has reported a similar procedure.[5] Over a period of fifteen years I have used a related technique —a shared, written group summary.[6] At the end of outpatient group sessions I write a detailed group summary (an editorialized narrative summary, including detailed process analysis and considerable disclosure of my strategic therapeutic plan) and mail it to the members before the next week's session.

The Higher-Level Inpatient Therapy Group

"Multiple therapy" is yet another example of a procedure in which patients observe their therapists discuss the treatment process.[7] In this procedure, used for the teaching of psychotherapy, several therapists (usually one or two teachers and four to five trainees) meet together with one patient for a series of sessions. During these meetings the therapists interact individually or jointly with the patient but often may engage in a discussion among themselves analyzing some particular aspect of the interaction of the entire group. The therapists may disagree with one another or question one another about the reasons for a particular statement or question. Obviously this format has no economic future, but it has proven an excellent teaching vehicle and is invariably regarded as beneficial by patients.

Each of these formats—the observed inpatient group "wrap-up," the observed outpatient observer discussion, the group summary technique, multiple therapy, T-group "fishbowling"—entail considerable therapist (or observer) disclosure—especially disclosure about the "innards" of the therapeutic process. Each of these formats emphasizes analysis of process, and each provides patients with some cognitive framework by which one is able to make sense of the here-and-now interaction and transfer what one has learned in therapy into other situations in life.

None of the many possible objections to this procedure (for example, that patients who know too much about the therapeutic strategic procedure, or are aware of the therapist's uncertainty or lack of conviction about certain areas, will cease to have faith in therapists) have materialized. In each of these formats, patients are intrigued by the discussion, feel validated that the therapist treats them with respect by involving them in the discussion of their own therapy, have more respect rather than less for the therapist as a result of his or her sharing of uncertainty, and invariably profit from the cognitive framework with which they have been provided. One of the major results of such a procedure is that therapy becomes demystified. Patients begin to understand that there is nothing mysterious or magical about the therapist or the therapeutic procedure. As a result, they are less likely to be dependent upon the therapist or to be infantalized by the therapeutic procedure.

Other Advantages of the "Wrap-up" Format

Patients have a wide array of reactions while observing the final discussion, but one strong reaction is shared by all patients: they find it a compelling experience to hear themselves being discussed by others. Whatever the reason (I have always regarded it as analagous to the child listening outside his parents' bedroom door as they talk about him), the interest in this phase of the meeting is heightened and consequently becomes heightened for *all* phases. The greater the interest and engagement of the members, the more important does the group become to each. The greater grasp that members have upon the cognitive framework of the group therapy procedure, the more relevant and valued does the work of the group become. This enhancement of cohesiveness facilitates a host of other therapeutic activities: patients trust one another more, they self-disclose more, they feel closer to one another, they develop more trust in the therapist and the therapeutic procedure.

The final phase is an excellent opportunity for therapists to do some invaluable modeling. For example, co-therapists may discuss some of the dilemmas and concerns that they have experienced during the meeting. They may express their puzzlement about what they might have done differently to help a negativistic patient; they may ask the observers for feedback about their (the therapists') behavior. Were they, for example, too intrusive? Or, did they put too much pressure on a particular patient?

It is advisable for therapists to share some of the dilemmas they have faced in a meeting. For example, you might state in the final discussion that you very much wanted to help a patient who is in a particularly bad spot that day, yet are also aware that this is the first meeting she has chosen to attend although she's been on the ward for several days. You have assumed that she is anxious about groups, and thus are caught between wanting to help her and yet feeling uneasy about possibly threatening her in some way by calling upon her or encouraging her participation.

A therapist can also model modes of examining relationships by exploring his or her relationship with the co-leader. You may, for example, raise the question to the observers of whether you were too active, or shut out the co-therapist, or might have made a greater effort to follow leads opened up by the co-therapist.

For example, in one session a patient stated that she experienced one of the co-therapists as very cold and formal, and that she had a hard time feeling that he cared for any of the patients. That therapist responded that he did have a sense of wanting to be in control but at the same time regretted that it got in the way of his work. Some of the other patients agreed that he had a very formal style which they often experienced as aloofness. During the final phase the observers continued the discussion and agreed with the patients that this therapist created more distance between himself and the patients than did the other therapist in the group. The observers pointed out that whenever he was confronted by patients, he immediately began using polysyllabic and professional terms as a way, perhaps, of keeping the patients in their place. The therapist accepted this feedback and said that it was accurate and that he was feeling uncomfortable in the group. He pointed out how, for one thing, he did not have a great deal of group experience and felt uncomfortable working with a co-therapist who was extremely experienced in groups. The patients felt validated by his taking their comments seriously; they gained respect for the therapeutic procedure by witnessing the therapist open himself up for feedback; and they ended the session with more, rather than less, confidence in him as a therapist.

The final phase helps the reality testing of many patients. If members are confused and unable to make sense of some of the events of the session, it is enormously confirming for them to hear the observers make the same observations. Patients who feel that a group session is testy, adversarial, or ineffective, are "grounded" by hearing the therapists and observers make the same observation.

The input of the observers augments the potency of the group. The addition of several pairs of eyes and ears generates information. The observers note many things that the therapists have missed: nonverbal communication, patients who seemed disappointed, unfilled agendas, subtle transactions that took place off "center stage."

The observer-therapist discussion also helps to bring in the silent members of the meeting. The observers attempt to make some observation about each member and to guess at the experience of each of the silent members. This process opens the door for these patients to participate, even briefly, during the final ten minutes.

The observers' feedback is invariably given considerable weight. If, during a session, a member is told that he or she is impersonal or distant, that observation is made much more potent when observers make similar comments. Conversely, any negative comments by observers are particularly painful and often have enduring negative effects. Thus, it is important that the observers not be critical in a condescending way. Such statements as "the patient is playing games" or is "manipulative" invariably increase defensiveness and close down, rather than open, a patient to learning.

Observers, no less than therapists, must phrase their comments in such a supportive manner as: "The patient wants but fears closeness"; "There is something about therapy that frightens the patient"; "The patient seems to crave help but isn't yet clear about what kind of help would be best."

Occasionally observer criticism works paradoxically. I have witnessed many meetings in which the observers criticized the group for having not worked productively, and the group responded by becoming more cohesive than previously in the session and defending the work its members had done. (An attack by some outside group almost invariably strengthens the cohesion of any group; that's precisely why the ruler of a tottering political regime may often seek to strengthen his position by entering into a war with another country.)

Another important aspect of the final phase is that patients become acutely aware of the members who receive the bulk of the observers' attention. Patients want to be noticed and to be discussed, and they may feel slighted, neglected, or envious of those patients who receive most of the observers' attention. Therapists may then pursue the theme of each member's responsibility for what he or she receives from the observers. The equation is self-evident: if one is inactive during a meeting, it invariably follows that one will get relatively little attention during the "wrap-up."

A clinical vignette illustrates how profound wishes to be noticed and nurtured may be evoked by this final group phase. Paula, a thirty-eight-year-old patient, had effectively stymied therapy by her posture of extreme skepticism. She stated that everything in life, and especially everything that happened in the therapy group, was phony. She insisted on the phoniness of the feelings that the people demonstrated in the group. She knew that her feelings were phony because she created them capriciously; they were immaterial and not to be believed or taken seriously.

The therapist tried to reach Paula by speaking to her healthier side; he commented that, despite these pessimistic feelings, she still came to the group every day; obviously there was a part of her that wanted to get better. Why then, he wondered, did she persist in trying to defeat therapy? Why come faithfully to therapy every day and yet refuse to work? Paula then stated that she had worked in the group on a couple of occasions, but what was the point of it? Even when she did, her work was never acknowledged by the observers or the therapists in their final discussion.

The therapist noted that Paula stated this with a great deal of feeling and tears in her eyes. Here, at last, was a genuine feeling—one that Paula couldn't discard as phony or capricious! The therapist zeroed in on this perception, observing that Paula was deeply moved and asking her to share more of her feelings about receiving little attention in the final discussion. What did she make of it? What were its implications for her? Paula replied that she feared it meant that the therapists and the observers had put her into the "big C" folder ("C" for "chronic").

This revelation opened the door for her to share many of her innermost thoughts: her wishes to be noticed, to be rescued; her longing for the therapist to cradle and care for her; her sense of having been betrayed by figures upon whom she'd depended all her life; and her wish for, but fear of, intimacy. Paula subsequently worked far more productively in the group. By chance I had the occasion to treat her two years later as an outpatient, and she gratuitously referred to this particular group therapy session as a critical turning point in her therapy.

The Patients' Response to the Therapist-Observer Discussion

The therapist-observer discussion invariably generates considerable data, which it is the task of the final ten minutes of the group to respond to and integrate. Generally it is a period of great animation; there is more potential work on the floor than can possibly be accomplished.

There are two major directions that this part of the meeting can take. First, the patients may respond to the observers. Patients have a wide and deep range of affective responses to the therapist-observer discussion, and these ten minutes are often fully consumed by their sharing these reactions. Second, the final ten minutes is a time both for the patients themselves to process the meeting and to complete its unfinished business and for the therapist to touch base with any patients whom he or she feels may have been left out of the meeting.

Because the observers' comments frequently have a powerful impact upon the patients, it is particularly advisable for the therapist to attend to those patients who were most central in the "wrap-up" discussion. The therapist may simply ask what reactions they have to the observers' comments. Were the comments useful? Did members agree or disagree with the observers?

As the observers discuss the patients, it is fair game for the patients to turn the tables in the final ten minutes and discuss the observers and the therapists. Often patients comment upon the openness, or lack thereof, of the observers; patients may, for example, note that the climate of the discussion was more inhibited and uptight than the patient meeting. Sometimes they raise questions about the anxiety of the observers and inquire into the relationship between observers and therapists. I have heard patients engage the observers in a discussion of the latter's own performance anxiety, their uneasiness about being observed by the patients, or their concern about the therapist's evaluation of their comments.

The final discussion often serves as a projective test, and members may have a wide range of reactions to it. The patients' response to leader transparency is especially dramatic in this regard. Some patients so deeply distrust the staff that they suspect the therapists' behavior during their discussion. They accuse therapists of staging their discussion, of only pretending to ask the observers for advice, guidance, or feedback, of feigning uncertainty in order to lull the patients into blind trust.

It is obvious that some patients do not want to see the therapist as fallible, human, and potentially vulnerable. Whereas most patients appreciate the honesty of the therapist, some patients are unsettled by discovering that therapists, too, have "feet of clay." However, these reactions, like others, can be a springboard into a fruitful discussion of attitudes toward authority, of dependency cravings, of the yearning to remain young and protected forever.

The final ten minutes is a time for patients to process and evaluate their own meeting. The more they are able to do this, the more likely are they to assume more responsibility for their therapy in the future. The first step of such responsibility assumption is for patients to develop an explicit definition of good therapeutic work. Without this clear yardstick, it is difficult for them to know which direction to take. The therapist is generally the only person in the group who has a clear definition of what constitutes a good therapeutic "work" meeting, and it is the therapist's task to help members arrive at a satisfactory definition. The therapist may label some meetings as particularly effective and comment, for example, that this is the type of meeting he or she hates to see come to an end. The therapist may guide patients toward a definition by asking them to evaluate what parts of the meeting felt best to them or how a particular meeting compared with a previous one.

The therapist may circle the group and ask each member to evaluate the session, inquiring: What kind of meeting was it for you today? Did you get what you wanted to out of it? Who got the most? Who the least? What were your major disappointments with this session? If this were not three P.M. [the end of the session] but only two-thirty, what might you do to avert this disappointment?

The therapist is well advised to make contact with the silent members before the end of the meeting and inquire into their experience during the session. It is often helpful to explore their silence by asking if there were times in the session when they wanted to speak. What stopped them? Were they hoping for the therapist to call on them? *If* they had said something, what would it have been? (This last question is often miraculously facilitative.)

This line of questioning usually succeeds in helping silent members participate, at least in some limited way, in the group, and often a great deal of work can be done in a short period of time. For example, if—in response to this line of inquiry—a silent member, at the end of the meeting, offers some observation he or she almost made earlier about another member, the leader can immediately ask for a response from the other member or ask how it might have felt had the patient made that statement during the earlier part of the meeting.

Almost invariably the sequence of events is reinforcing for the patient. One may say that one was silent because everything one thought of saying had been said by someone else. The therapist can point out that, though that may be true, the fact remains that no one else really knew that this was the way that particular person felt. Therefore, one remains concealed from others—a state of affairs that patients will agree is not in their best interests. Not only can the therapist in this final phase engage the silent members in the meeting but, in so doing, can set the stage for their increased participation in the following session.

Conclusion

The current shape of this group therapy model evolved gradually over some four hundred meetings. During this period I made much use of trial and error and employed and then modified or dropped model after model. Throughout this time I have had considerable consultation from students and colleagues who observed almost all of my meetings and helped me analyze the meetings in debriefings afterward. I have had, in addition, considerable input from several other sources: consultation with the group members' individual therapists, with other members of the ward staff about the impact of the group on the patients, and with the group members themselves—at first informally and finally in a systematic research project.[8]

The present model has been used in hundreds of meetings by me and by my colleagues. It appears to offer a systematic, coherent, and effective structure for the group session. When beginning to lead inpatient groups, I, like most inpatient group therapists, had a sense of the group being out of control, of patients being too ill to profit from a group, of my being overwhelmed with the problem of the rapid turnover of membership. My impression is that the use of this model greatly enhances the effectiveness of the inpatient group. Even the less satisfactory meetings still offer patients something of value, which generally unfolds in the following meetings or elsewhere in their therapy program. Of course, there will always be occasional meetings that seem entirely unproductive. Generally, however, such meetings occur in an unusually unmotivated, resistant patient population, and the lack of work in the group is paralleled by its members taking little or no part in any of the ward therapeutic activities.

Chapter 6

The Lower-Level Psychotherapy Group: A Working Model

The lower-level psychotherapy group, while less complex than the higher-level group, is neither less effective nor less necessary in the inpatient group therapy program. Every acute inpatient unit will have patients who cannot function in a higher-level group: they may be too agitated, too confused, too fragmented or regressed to meet even the modest demands of the group I described in the previous chapter. But these patients can benefit from a therapy group specifically designed to meet their needs and to embrace their level of functioning. The task of this chapter is to describe a model of group therapy for these more poorly functioning patients. I offer this model, just as I did the one in chapter 5, not as a precise blueprint for others to trace but as a teaching vehicle to convey the application of a set of strategies and techniques. I developed this model of a lower-level therapy group (which I shall henceforth refer to as the "focus" therapy group) in conjunction with Vivian Banish, O.T.R., on the inpatient unit of the Stanford University Medical Center over several months of research and development.*

Selection of Patients

The rapidly fluctuating population on the contemporary acute inpatient ward makes it impossible to be precise about the numbers and categories of patients who might attend either a higher-level or a focus (lower-level) group. To take one example, consider the twenty-bed psychiatric inpatient unlocked unit at the Stanford University Medical Center. On this unit approximately five to twelve patients attend the daily higher-level therapy group. These patients are oriented; their attention span is such that they can concentrate on a meeting for seventy-five minutes. For the most part, they are not psychotic; they acknowledge that they are psychologically distressed and that they need and want help. If they are psychotic, even actively hallucinating, they are nevertheless verbal, appropriate, and capable of rational communication.

Of the remaining patients on the ward, there are always some who can attend no therapy group. The severity of their psychosis—either affective (generally manic), schizophrenic, or organic—is such that they are too fragmented, confused, or agitated to participate meaningfully in a forty-five-minute group

*I am indebted to Kathy Kaplan, O.T., and to Dr. Marc Hertzman, M.D., for allowing me to observe one of their meetings for regressed patients at the George Washington University Hospital, Washington, D.C. Their group served as the seed for the model I describe in this chapter.

session. Not only do these patients not benefit from a therapy group but their agitated, confused behavior disrupts the meeting for others.

The remaining patients, who may number between three and ten, can profit from the focus therapy group. These patients are generally psychotic and often floridly hallucinatory, delusional, and severely regressed. These are patients whose psychosis has overwhelmed most ego functions; often the patients do not express a sense of collaboration—that they and the therapists are allies working together to improve their (the patients') mental health. Not infrequently there will be in the focus group patients who, though not psychotic, are severely impaired and too phobic and anxious to meet the demands of the higher-level group.

These are crude distinctions. One would prefer to be more precise about selection criteria for both the higher-level and the lower-level groups. Indeed, one might prefer to have an elegantly constructed, staged group program with several levels of groups and specific entrance criteria to each. But the "revolving door," bustling character of the inpatient ward makes such precision impossible, and the great majority of inpatient wards must be content with a two-level system and these crude selection criteria.

The focus group works most effectively with a smaller number of patients than are in the higher-level group. Generally four to seven members constitute the optimal size, whereas the higher-level group can work effectively with as many as ten to twelve patients. The group boundaries, however, must be sufficiently elastic to accommodate rapid shifts in ward population. If, for example, it shifts because of an influx of admissions who are severely disturbed, the lower-level group must become larger and the higher-level group smaller. There are limits to the elasticity of a group's boundaries; once the higher- or the lower-level group reaches maximal size, then some members must be transferred to the other group, which must shift its level accordingly. If the ward is populated by patients who are severely impaired, the higher-level group must begin to function at a slightly lower level and the focus group must shift to an even lower level of functioning. Each of the level groups must have a flexible procedural structure that permits an upward or downward shift depending upon the needs of the ward.

This feature—the necessity to adjust the level of a group to accommodate change in ward composition—is even more pronounced in team group meetings (see chapter 2). It is for this reason that I have elected to describe models of the higher- and lower-level groups but not of the team therapy group. The composition and the character of a team group meeting can gyrate so wildly that it is not possible to provide a model sufficiently elastic to meet all clinical demands. The clinician, instead, must have a mastery of the techniques to deal with both well- and poorly functioning patients and be able to design team group meetings to accommodate the composition of the group each day.

General Principles

The basic principles of inpatient group therapy presented in chapters 2, 3, and 4 are entirely applicable to group work with severely psychotic patients. Therapists must merely adapt their their technique to the greater severity of illness,[1] but their basic goals and tactics are the same. Therapists must provide a supportive experience which patients experience as sufficiently pleasant and constructive to encourage them to continue therapy after leaving the hospital. Therapists must demonstrate to patients that talking helps; must help them identify problems that they can work on in future therapy; must help patients develop social skills that will permit them to become engaged with other patients on the unit and will serve them well outside of the hospital. Therapists must be active and must provide vigorous structure and support for the patients. They must develop an abbreviated time frame and attempt to be efficient and effective at all times. They must attempt to offer each patient some tangible benefit in each group meeting. They must be transparent and willing to be personal, not only to relate more honestly to the patient but to set a model that patients may emulate in relation to each other. Therapists must increase the effectiveness of the group by focusing, whenever possible, on here-and-now interaction.

Special attention must be paid to the task of providing severely psychotic patients with a supportive, pleasant, and constructive experience. Unless therapists particularly attend to this issue, the group experience of these patients is likely to be quite the opposite. Psychotic patients are often highly threatened by therapy group meetings. The basic task of the therapy group is too demanding for them. They are made anxious by being required, in the group, to interact openly with other individuals. Their attention span is too short; their ability to concentrate, to track themes, and to think clearly, too impaired; often their mentation is further obtunded by psychotropic medication. Their inability to engage in the group task often slows down the group, and consequently they often become pariahs. Becoming irritated with them, the members may hold the meeting "around" them, ignoring them. Severely psychotic patients are equally aware that they do not really fit in the group; that they are deviants, marginal members who are only tolerated and who block the progress of the group. It is all too easy, thus, for the group to become an experience of failure for severely psychotic patients; after a group session they generally feel more anxious and more unworthy than they did before the meeting.

The Group Meeting Must Provide Experience of Success

If the focus therapy group is to be therapeutic, it must provide an experience of success for severely psychotic patients. Group tasks must be designed that patients are capable of completing.

Since severely psychotic patients generally have marked impairment of attention span, special attention must be paid to the temporal dimensions of the group task. Patients with impaired concentration could not, for example, possibly focus on a twenty- to thirty-minute go-round of agenda formation. They could not keep the various agendas in their minds; these agendas would blur one with the other; the patients would become distracted by obsessive ruminations or by hallucinations. Long before the group task was completed, these patients would feel more confused and more anxious. An efficacious group therapy model must be constructed to take account of the fact that the severely psychotic patient is able to concentrate more effectively on several short tasks than on a single longer one.

Reduction of Anxiety

As psychotic symptoms represent an individual's final effort to ward off catastrophic anxiety, therapists must pay particular attention to the group members' anxiety levels. Focus group therapists have little margin of safety; their group members cannot tolerate additional anxiety without further exacerbation of psychosis. The leaders must strive continually to avoid any situation in the group which would elevate anxiety, and to attempt to provide a group structure and a group climate that ameliorate anxiety. The psychotic patient feels desperately isolated, and the group must address this isolation. Yet, since the psychotic patient experiences great anxiety when plunged into prolonged interaction with other individuals, the focus group must attempt to provide opportunities for social interaction that are undemanding, broken into brief time segments, and interspersed with periods of solo activity. Generally psychotherapists adhere to the belief that exploration and uncovering of the self are ultimately healing activities. The severely psychotic individual, however, is no candidate for self-exploratory therapy. The examination of painful areas in group therapy only heightens the psychotic patient's anxiety and is counterproductive. Group therapists must develop a healthy respect for the patients' defenses. When the regressed psychotic patient says, explicitly or implicitly, "I can't talk about my problem, it's too much for me to bear or to face directly," it is important for the therapist to accept the fact that the patient knows what he or she is talking about. Occasionally patients express these limits explicitly; but more often they communicate them nonverbally, through agitation, denial, avoidance, mutism, or aggressivity. An important part of the training of the group therapist who must work with severely psychotic patients is to change the assumption, developed in work with healthier clients, that one must ultimately face and deal with one's problems directly.[2]

Appropriate goal setting is vitally important to the morale of staff members who lead focus groups. The group work itself is not intrinsically demanding or complex, but unrealistically high goals invariably beget staff discouragement and demoralization. Limited and circumscribed goals and tasks must be designed and implemented. Therapists must derive their gratification from helping patients make small strides toward clarity and integration, and must realize that customary role definitions of "real" therapists (for example, as catalysts, explorers of the unconscious, interpreters, transference vessels, cognitive problem solvers) are not appropriate in brief psychotherapy of the severely psychotic patient. Therapists who cannot redefine their role will feel they are not fulfilling their role and will experience their group work as superficial and unsatisfying. I have rarely seen an inpatient staff whose members do not need to be reminded, from time to time, that therapy is for the patients, not for the staff.

Specific techniques to reduce anxiety are often indicated in the focus therapy group. Selected physical exercises or muscular relaxation are often useful. A spirit of safety and fun may be introduced by providing tasks that are clothed in the guise of games. Games may particularly engage deeply regressed patients and enable them to begin to take small risks and to interact with others. Games, however, have dark implications for many patients and must not be employed capriciously. Though they provide blessed light relief, fun, and safety, games may also convey a somber message. Even the most disorganized patients understand, at some level of awareness, that if the group sessions are composed entirely of games, then the staff has abandoned the therapeutic effort and believes that the patients are incapable of higher levels of functioning. Small wonder, then, that patients become resistant; they resent being patronized and are angered at the babyish, "sandbox" quality of such a group.

Hence games are to be used judiciously and sensitively. The focus group is capable of considerable therapeutic work; and games are an adjunct to, not a replacement for, this work.

Support, Support, Support

Although support is essential in all forms of inpatient group therapy, nowhere does it play a more central role than in the focus therapy group. Psychotic patients are confused, anxious, and highly threatened by being placed in a group. Unless the group offers immediate and tangible gratification, the patients will be too uncomfortable to be willing or able to engage in the group activity in a manner that will prove therapeutic.

Consequently, anxiety-dissolving support must be present at the very onset and flow continuously throughout a meeting.

The Lower-Level Psychotherapy Group

Every contribution of the therapist must be considered for its potential to support. It is the therapist's task to examine the behavior of every patient and find in it some positive aspect to express to the patient. The mute patient may be supported for having stayed for the entire session; the patient who leaves early may be complimented for having stayed twenty minutes; the patient who arrives late may be supported for having shown up at the meeting; the inactive patient may be reinforced for having made even a single comment or for having paid attention throughout the meeting. Statements that are unintelligible or bizarre may be recognized and labeled as attempts to communicate. Patients who give advice, even highly inappropriate advice, may be rewarded for their intentions to help and their willingness to express these intentions. In other words, patients must be supported anterior to risk taking; there must be "reward before effort."[3]

To give support requires not only that therapists adopt a support-oriented psychological set but also that they understand the patient deeply. Fatuous, "buckshot" support will be recognized as such and will prove countertherapeutic. The therapist must be sensitively attuned to a patient's internal state and able to reinforce even the slightest stirrings toward integration. The more that therapists know about the nature of the psychotic experience—the confusion, the catastrophic anxiety, the swirl of primary process, the succor of paranoia and delusion, the emptiness and compensatory grandiosity—the more will they be able to offer accurate support—support that the patient can experience as truly empathic rather than patronizing. I shall later provide many concrete examples of support as I describe the specific procedures of the focus group.

The Focus Group Meeting: Basic Arrangements

The focus therapy group I shall describe in this section meets daily (five times a week) for forty-five minutes. The attention span of the patients in this group is generally so impaired that a longer meeting is not advisable. The boundaries of this group should be more permeable than those of the higher-level group. Latecomers may be admitted; and a patient who is unable to stay the whole meeting may, of course, be excused. The preferred number of patients is approximately four to seven although, if necessary, more patients may be accommodated in the group. Unlike the higher-level group in which attendance may be made optional, attendance in the focus therapy group must be mandatory; otherwise, the majority of patients would either be reluctant to come or too confused to find their way unassisted to the group at the proper time.

Generally the staff is able to determine, at the time of admission, whether a patient can best function in the higher-level or the focus group and make the appropriate assignment at that time. Occasionally it may require as long as twenty-four hours to make that determination. For example, patients may be admitted in a confused psychotic state which clears very quickly. If the staff senses that such may be the case, it is often wise to hold off, for a short time, assignment to one of the groups. Often, if an initial assignments is made injudiciously, a patient will need to be transferred from the focus to the higher-level group. Whereas that may be a perfectly satisfactory arrangement on a ward with long-term hospitalization, on wards with very brief hospital stays it may unduly add to the group's instability.

Furthermore, transfer (or graduation) from the focus to the higher-level group may overly emphasize the different levels of patient integration served by the two groups. Ordinarily this is

The Lower-Level Psychotherapy Group

not a problem on the ward. It is uncommon for patients in the focus therapy group to wish to attend the higher-level group; they consider that group too demanding or too anxiety provoking and, given the choice, would prefer the focus group. The lower-level group may be spoken of by some patients in a disparaging way; but, in my experience, such comments are extremely rare. It is necessary, however, that thought be given to the name of the lower-level group. I have chosen to refer to it as the "focus group" to reduce patients' tendencies to compare the two groups. The word *focus* underscores the fact that one of the primary criteria for admission to the lower-level group is a patient's confusion, fearfulness, and/or limited attention span. One of the most important explicitly stated goals of the lower-level group is to help patients focus on specific tasks, primarily communicational and self-expressive, for relatively long periods of time.

Leadership of the focus group may come from any of the mental health disciplines: occupational therapists, psychiatrists, psychiatric nurses, activity therapists, recreational therapists, and so on. It is important, just as it is in the higher-level group, that there be one stable leader who will be there daily for at least a month's steady rotation. Co-leaders and students (and the group works well with as many as three staff members) may rotate in and out of the group at shorter intervals. It is important that the leaders be willing to participate fully in all of the group's activities; they must be as engaged and as self-disclosing as they expect patients to be. It strengthens the prestige of the focus group if psychiatrists (the discipline accorded the most prestige by the patients) rotate through the group as well —both the medical director and psychiatric residents.

The group is far less complex to lead than the higher-level group but does require a good working knowledge of the phenomenology of the psychotic experience. Group leaders must have a keen appreciation of task gradation: they must know which tasks are most and least demanding, which most appropriate for new members, which are particularly stressful to certain types of patient. It is important that several members of the staff be trained to lead this group so that the group will never have to be canceled in the event of illness or vacation on the part of the primary therapist.

Many of the group members of the focus group will be too resistant or too confused to arrive at the group punctually. Consequently the staff will need to round up most of the designated patients and escort them into the group room. Often it is useful to enlist the help of one or two of the better-functioning patients in the group to assist in this task. Patients who are napping before the group meeting should be awakened at least fifteen minutes before it starts. Patients who are very apprehensive about attending may be seated next to one of the therapists and be reassured that they may simply sit and listen and may leave early if they are too uncomfortable to stay for the entire forty-five minutes.

Plan of the Meeting

The focus group meeting is heavily structured, and the leader plans it prior to each day's session. The basic plan of a session is as follows:

1.	Orientation and preparation of patients	2 to 5 minutes
2.	Warm-up	5 to 10 minutes
3.	Structured exercises	20 to 30 minutes
4.	Review of the session	5 to 10 minutes

Orientation and Preparation

The length and comprehensiveness of the initial orientation and preparation of a particular group meeting depends upon whether there are new patients and upon the degree of intactness of the continuing members. The presence of confused patients necessitates an orientation even if no new patients are present that day. The goal of this phase is the same as for the higher-level groups: providing patients with a basic spatial and temporal orientation; decreasing anticipatory anxiety; instructing patients about the purpose and the procedure of the group; providing them with a rationale of how the group works; teaching them how best to make use of the group.

Here is an example of a typical orientation statement in a group meeting that has one or more new members: "I am [name], and this is my co-leader [name]. This is the focus therapy group which meets daily five times a week, Mondays through Fridays at two o'clock P.M. for forty-five minutes. We will meet every day in this room. We urge everyone to be on time, since we feel this group is very valuable, and we want to be able to use all of our forty-five minutes. We will try to remind you each day a few minutes before the meeting. The focus group's goals are to help you learn as much as possible about communicating with others: to help you learn how to concentrate, to learn to listen to others, to share important things about yourselves, to deal with shyness. We have planned some tasks for the group today, and we will start off with a warm-up task and then, after a few minutes of that, have another two activities, which we will describe to you. After that, we'll have a few minutes to review what we did in this meeting today."

Warm-up

This first phase of the group serves as a traditional ice breaker. The warm-up consists of one or more brief structured exercises which provide a gentle beginning to the group. It decreases anticipatory anxiety and permits each member to engage in brief, light, and nonthreatening interaction.

Here are some examples of warm-up structured exercises:

1. Any of a large number of physical exercises may be useful in opening the group and reducing tension. Members may be asked in turn to lead the group for a minute or so in some short physical exercise. The leaders participate as fully in this as any of the members of the group (just as the leaders participate fully in every one of the structured exercises in the group). A member may name a part of the body (such as shoulders, toes, or eyes) and ask the person on his or her right to lead an exercise involving this part of the body. To increase novelty and the degree of challenge, the members may be given more complex instructions about an exercise; for example, one may be asked to lead the group in an exercise involving a chair (that is, the exercise might be walking around one's chair three times or touching the leg of one's neighbor's chair twice).

The warm-up, no less than all of the other structured exercises, should be designed, whenever possible, to fit the mood of the group on a particular day. If one day it seems evident to the leader, for example, that the group is tense, he or she may design a physical exercise to deal with that tension. For example, the leader might ask each person to name a part of the body where each feels tight, and then suggest some exercise to help relieve that tightness. If, say, a member states that he or she feels tension in the neck, the leader may suggest a brief exercise (perhaps a head roll) to relax the neck. The leader might reduce tension in the chest by suggesting breathing exercises. When the leaders sense that a group is particularly resistant (for example, the members may have been reluctant to come in the room for the session, or several may have been late), then they may suggest an exercise that addresses that feeling. For example, they may ask the members to take turns leading the group in a nonverbal exercise that says "No"; and members may stamp their feet, shake their heads, turn their backs, or pantomime buttoning their lips.

2. A balloon or large rubber ball toss, in which the members throw a ball to each other and say the name of the person to

whom they are throwing. This exercise is appropriate only for poorly functioning patients and especially in meetings where there may be new patients and the members have difficulty remembering each person's name. The exercise may be made slightly more challenging and involve more interaction with additional instructions. For example, members may be instructed to say, each time they catch the ball, a brief comment about how they feel that day; or they may be asked to say something they like about each person to whom they throw the ball.

3. In another type of warm-up exercise, each member makes some observation about the other members. For example, one might be asked to comment about what one had seen the person on one's right doing earlier that day (or, if possible, during the last hour). If all the members in the group were present at the previous group session, they might be asked to look at each person and try to comment on how each looks different from the preceding day.

4. Members might be asked to make some short statement about themselves. A warm-up exercise that I use frequently is to ask each member to say briefly something about a good thing and a bad thing that happened to him or her that day, or about a good and a bad feeling that each has experienced that day. A typical round would include good feelings such as feeling bouncy, feeling good, having decided to leave the hospital, having called a friend on his birthday, having had a good therapy hour, having found a sock without a hole in it that morning; the bad feelings would include feeling oppressed by the rain, having hallucinations, being disappointed that one's doctor had increased one's medication, feeling hopeless, or feeling self-conscious at lunch.

Therapists should have at their disposal a series of such warm-up exercises and select those that seem most appropriate for the functioning of a particular group. Some exercises (such as the balloon toss or simple physical calesthenics) are most suitable for a group of patients who are functioning at a particularly low level and should be used accordingly. There will be times when the group is functioning at a higher level, and patients will feel patronized by exercises pitched at too low a level. Some groups must function at such a primitive level that the entire meeting will consist of safe and gentle warm-up exercises.[4]

Structured Exercises

The bulk of the remaining meeting is consumed by structured exercises. Generally two or three short (five- to fifteen-minute) exercises are used. If the group is unusually verbal and engages well in a discussion of some theme suggested by an exercise, one or two structured exercises will be sufficient.

Although each structured exercise often has several components, I shall, for expository purposes, categorize exercises according to their major thrust: (1) self-disclosure, (2) empathy, (3) here-and-now interaction, (4) didactic discussion, (5) personal change, and (6) tension-relieving games.

Self-Disclosure

Most of the structured exercises require some self-disclosure. It is important that therapists strive to make the process of self-disclosure a safe venture. The therapist may decrease the perceived threat to self-disclosure in a number of ways: by asking patients to disclose their strengths or interests rather than their shortcomings; by setting sharp limits on the amount of disclosure expected of each member; by full therapist participation in the self-disclosure exercise (this generally means that the patients in the focus group learn more about the leader's personal life than do patients in higher-level groups).

Though a large variety of exercises may be used, as a general rule the leader can increase the efficiency of the group by combining the act of self-disclosure with another major aim of the focus therapy group—increasing member interaction. The most

The Lower-Level Psychotherapy Group

effective type of exercise, in my experience, has been a pairing exercise which combines solo activity, dyadic interaction, and total group interaction.

The basic structure is as follows. Members are given a sheet of paper with two or three short sentences to complete. For example, a typical set of sentences might be:

1. One of the most important persons in my life is————.
2. One thing about me that people would be surprised to know is ————.
3. One thing I really enjoy is————.

Members are then given a few minutes to work on these sentences alone. When they have finished, each member is asked to pair up with one of the other members of the group or with one of the therapists. The therapists make the pair assignments according to some planned strategy. They may want patients to pair up who do not know one another well or who have not been paired before in any exercise. If a patient is particularly difficult to understand, then it may be desirable to pair him or her with one of the therapists. Or, the therapists may pair an extraordinarily shy patient with someone in the group who is particularly gentle and outgoing.

Each pair is instructed to exchange sheets, to read the other's answers, and to understand them as fully as possible by asking for clarification or for additional information. The therapists may offer guidance in conversational skills by providing worksheets with suggested questions one may use to clarify a partner's answers. After the pairs have interacted for a few minutes, the group re-forms; and each member of a pair reads aloud his or her partner's answers to the questions and tells the group anything additional he or she has learned about the answer to each question.

This basic structure has many advantages. First, although it is a single task, it consists of a number of briefer tasks: solo activity, questioning one's partner, explaining one's own answers to the partner, describing one's partner's answers to the rest of the group, listening to the other group members introduce their partner to the group. Patients whose attention spans are limited are able to attend to several short tasks far more successfully than to a single lengthy task. Furthermore, the changing nature of the task makes the exercise safer for the members than would be a period of continuous interaction with others. The time devoted to solo activity often provides the patients with a bit of safe, private time in the midst of the group. The exercise offers instruction in self-disclosure, creative listening, verbal expression, dyadic and group interaction. Many members are pleasantly surprised at being well understood by others. Some patients save their worksheets, which serve as a tangible record of their participation in the group.

I use some form of this exercise in the great majority of focus group sessions. It permits an infinite number of variations: all that is required is that the therapist construct different sentences emphasizing different themes. The exercise may be specifically built around some important theme for the group that day. If, for example, separation is an important issue—either because many members of the group are struggling with that theme in their lives, or because several members of the group are ready for discharge—then a set of questions around separation might be constructed; for example:

1. Someone I really miss is———.
2. The hardest separation I've ever had is———.
3. I handle separation by———.

If anger has been an issue for members, the group may deal with anger in the sentence completions with such items as:

1. The last time I got angry was———.
2. One thing that really irritates me is———.
3. When I get angry, I often———.

The Lower-Level Psychotherapy Group

If isolation has been an important issue for the group members, a set of questions around isolation may be posed:

1. When I am alone, I feel———.
2. The time in my life when I've felt most alone is———.
3. The time in my life when I've felt least alone is———.

Another variation on this theme is to present the patients with a list of values (for example, money, prestige, intimacy, fame, power, self-knowledge, popularity, or professional accomplishment) and ask them to select three of these values that they consider the most important. In the dyadic exercise each patient is asked to describe to a partner why these three are particularly important to him or her.

Some patients may express themselves better through art than through the written word, and simple pictures may be easily substituted for the sentence-completion task. Furthermore, drawing exercises provide variety and heighten the group's interest. For example, the therapists may provide the patients with a sheet of paper on which is drawn a blank coat of arms divided into four quadrants. Patients are asked to draw something in each quadrant which reflects these four themes (or, of course, any other four themes that seem appropriate to the needs and skills of the group): (1) one of my best accomplishments; (2) one of the nicest gifts I've ever received; (3) one of the most important persons in my family; (4) one of my keenest interests. The rest of the exercise may be handled in precisely the same way as the sentence completion, with pairing up and then each member introducing his or her buddy's coat of arms to the entire group.

A self-disclosure exercise that is slightly more demanding consists of dividing the patients into pairs and instructing one member of a pair to ask his or her partner one question repeatedly: "Who are you?" Each time the other gives an answer to that question, the questioner says, "Thank you," and then asks the question again. At a signal from the therapist, the members of the dyad switch roles, and the other becomes the questioner. When the group reconvenes, each member of the dyad reports to the group as many of his buddy's answers as he or she can remember, and introduces his or her buddy to the group. This is potentially a stressful exercise unless the therapist is careful to place strict temporal limits on the interaction. A period of questioning of sixty to ninety seconds is quite sufficient for each member of a pair.

There will be times when it is advisable to address important ward events even though they are intrinsically unsettling to patients. It may be helpful to focus the group's attention, for a limited time, on some major event on the ward, like a patient's elopement, an attempted suicide, or some physical assault. Even though this exercise asks individuals to express unpleasant feelings, it generally relieves anxiety since, without doubt, the members are internally preoccupied with these issues. Thus, the sentences to be completed might include such items as:

1. The fight on the ward last night made me feel————.
2. When Sandy tried to hurt herself yesterday on the ward, I felt ————.

Empathy

An essential ingredient in the development of social skills is the ability to empathize with others: to be interested in and to be able to identify with, reasonable accuracy, the feelings of others. Exercises that focus on the identification and expression of one's feelings about the internal state of another may be structured in any of a number of ways, but the basic strategy remains the same: avoid negative affect and critical feelings; encourage supportive interaction; focus on strengths. Exercise caution with highly paranoid patients who may consider empathy exercises invasive.

One exercise calls for each member to write his or her name

on a slip of paper, place it in a common box, and then to draw another member's name. Each person is asked then to make a statement about how he or she thinks that other person feels, and to express one thing that he or she has learned about that person in the group meeting that he or she had not known before.

Another variation calls for a collection of pictures clipped from magazines to be placed in the center of the room, with the instructions to members to sort through the magazine pictures and select one or two that each thinks the member sitting on his or her right might like. After the selections are made, each person shows the pictures and makes a statement about why he or she thinks that person might have liked them.

In another exercise the therapist distributes to the members sheets of paper on which has been drawn an outline of the human body, and asks them each to draw something on the outline of the body that they like about themselves. The members put their names on their papers, and then each paper is passed serially around the room. The task of each member is to draw in one thing that he or she likes about the person whose name is on each sheet of paper. When the papers return to their original owners, several positive things have been drawn in on the body outline, and each member is then asked to comment on his or her reactions to the things that are drawn. Members may, depending upon their capacity for abstract thought, complete this task in many different ways: a big smile to indicate a gentle disposition; a big ear to show that the person is a good listener; large hands to show a generous, giving disposition; a light bulb on top of the head to indicate good ideas. Other patients may respond more concretely and draw jewelry or certain clothes that a person wears.

A similar task is the strength-list exercise that I described in chapter 3 but will, for the sake of convenience, repeat here. After each member has put his or her name on a sheet of paper, along with two strengths that he or she perceives in himself or herself, the papers are passed around the room so that everyone can contribute one strength that he or she perceives in each of the others. The sheets are folded so that no member can see the strengths that have already been listed. At the end of the exercise, when each person has his or her own sheet back, all members share their lists with each other and their individual reactions to their own lists, especially to surprising items. If several members describe the same strength for a patient, the consensus carries considerable weight and may be effective in altering one's self-image.

A collection of various objects is required for another exercise. A tray of objects is placed in the center of the group, and each member is instructed to select a gift for the member sitting next to him or her. After the selections are made, each member is asked to present the gift and to describe to the group why he or she chose this particular gift.

Here are examples of typical responses from this exercise:

A gift of an arrowhead to a patient who came from Arizona.

A basket (to serve as a cradle) to a patient who was pregnant.

A seashell (from the therapist) to a patient who sometimes closed himself off but who had a lot of good and tender stuff inside.

A compass to a member who always liked to know exactly where he was going. (The therapist remarked that maybe this patient particularly wished a compass that day because of his uncertainty about leaving the hospital).

A key to a patient who was looking for a place to live (and the hope that he would find a home soon).

A pen to a patient who liked to write poetry.

A plant (to a therapist) because she liked to help others grow.

Another exercise requires a slightly higher level of functioning. The patients are requested to think of a metaphor—an animal (plants or inanimate objects may also be used) to represent oneself and another for the person sitting next to one in the group. It is important to explain this exercise carefully so that the members fully understand that they are to choose on the basis not of physical resemblance but of some trait of the animal which is similar to a trait of the person. Some examples of animals chosen: a deer for gentleness, a cat for seclusiveness, a dog for intelligence, a horse for strength, an angel fish for beauty, a cow for nurturance, a ram for stubbornness. After the selections are made, each member presents his or her choices and reasons for them. Other members of the group are invited to express agreement or disagreement with each member's choice.

Here-and-Now Interaction

Almost all of the exercises I have described are designed to facilitate interaction among the members. Furthermore, the final review of the meeting, which I shall discuss shortly, is also heavily focused on the here-and-now. The therapists may also, if they feel it appropriate for the group, use some structured exercises that explicitly focus upon the here-and-now.

The sentence-completion and pairing structure (see pages 291–93) may be modified into a here-and-now exercise. For example, appropriate sentences might be:

1. The person who knows me best in this room is———.
2. The person I most resemble in the room is———.
3. Something I envy about someone in the room is———.

The sentences may call the members' attention to some here-and-now event in the group. For example, in a group where the therapist was appearing for the last time, as she was rotating out of it, the members were asked to complete these sentences:

1. When I think of Liz leaving the group, I———.
2. It's not easy to tell Liz that I like her, because———.
3. Liz would be pleased if one year from now she knew that I ———.

If several members of the group are leaving the hospital and saying goodbye to the group, the sentence-completion task may focus on that event, with such items as:

1. What I've liked most about this group is———.
2. What I've liked least about this group is———.
3. One final gift I'd like to give to someone in the group is———.

Another particularly effective structured exercise that focuses on the here-and-now consists of offering pairs of members these instructions: "Find two ways in which the two of you are alike and two ways in which you are different." As in all these exercises, the pair is then asked to share what they have discussed with the rest of the group.

Didactic Discussions

The therapist who senses that many or all of the group members are struggling with a similar issue, may be helpful to them by offering a brief, guided discussion or short lecture to enable them to see that others share the same concerns and to encourage them to consider more effective modes of coping with these concerns. If they are to be useful, the discussions must include most or all of the members and be clear, brief, and relevant. An effective format combines a discussion with a prior solo or dyadic task.

For example, one procedure that has proven useful begins with a solo sentence-completion task. If "tension" is to be the topic, members are asked to respond to such questions as: (1) How do you experience tension? (Please list more than one way if possible.) (2) What do you do to try to relieve it? After a few minutes, when everyone has completed their written answers, the therapist begins the discussion by asking everyone to state their answers, and then he or she lists them on a blackboard. The patients thus have the opportunity to observe a wide vari-

The Lower-Level Psychotherapy Group

ety of ways in which tension is experienced as well as several modes, successful or unsuccessful, of coping with it. In the ensuing discussion the therapist emphasizes the similarity of members' experiences and also elicits comments and critiques about the various modes of coping. The same general structure can be a discussion of a number of other themes: for example, sadness, loss, loneliness, anger, rejection.

Personal Change

If several patients have worked in the group for a number of consecutive sessions, it may be appropriate to focus some structured exercises on personal change. The same basic exercise structure that I have described earlier may be used (solo sentence-completion followed, first, by dyadic discussion and, then, by a presentation to the large group) but with a content that directs the attention of the group toward personal change.

For example, the sentence completion tasks may include two or three of such items as:

1. Two things I want to change about myself are———.
2. Two things I like about myself and do not want to change are———.
3. The most important change I've ever made is———.
4. A change that I've made since coming to the hospital is———.
5. If I try to change, I worry that———.
6. An important change that I've seen someone in the group make is———.
7. A change that I would like to make in myself but do not think I can is———.
8. The reason it is hard for me to change is———.
9. Two differences between my personality now and my personality five years ago are———.
10. A trait of someone else's in the group that I would like to have is———.

Another format that has proven useful requires patients to answer these two written questions:

1. Two changes that I want to make in myself are————.
2. Some ideas I have about how I can make these changes are ————.

Following this solo exercise, the members are paired and instructed to read their partner's answers, to understand their modes of making changes and then to suggest other possible modes that might foster change. Following the dyadic discussion, each member presents his or her partner to the group by describing that partner's suggested modes of change and by stating any suggestions he or she may have made to that partner about additional modes of change. The group is highly encouraged to make further suggestions about modes of change. This is generally a long exercise and, if the group is highly verbal, consumes most of the meeting.

A typical sequence generated by this exercise: one patient, Will, stated that he was stubborn and that he should change by "rolling with the punches and compromising more." In the dyadic discussion his partner asked him for an example of his stubbornness, and Will described a typical problem that he had with his fiancée. His fiancée liked to dance but he refused to go to dances because he was a nondrinking alcoholic and did not want to be in places where alcohol was served. Consequently he and his fiancée often got into angry impasses in which both refused to budge. The group made many suggestions to Will: might he not drink some non-alcoholic beverage at a dance without telling people what it was? Could he not adopt some compromise with his fiancée by which he and she would alternate choosing what they would do in the evenings, so that neither would feel that they were being domianted?

Even though Will may have thought of some of these alternatives himself, he was gratified by the group's attempt to help him and felt much more engaged with the patient community following this meeting. During the group discussion the therapists were careful to support him heavily by commenting that he seemed to be making real attempts to change his stubbornness, as evidenced by the fact that he was willing to label himself stubborn and to seek and consider advice from other members.

Another patient stated that she wanted to change her ways of relating to people so that she could have more friends. Her suggested mode of doing this was to improve her physical appearance (in fact, her physical appearance was an issue since she was exceedingly untidy and poorly groomed). Her partner in the exercise was, by chance, a hairdresser who offered useful suggestions about ways to improve her appearance. Other people in the group gave advice to her about clothes, proper colors, et cetera; and one of them offered to take her on a shopping trip for new clothes.

Another patient stated that she wanted to change her shyness and be more open and assertive with others. She thought she might accomplish this by employing a speech teacher to help her speak more assertively. Her partner and the other members of the group offered other proposals. They reminded her of times in the group when she had been more assertive and less shy. The therapist suggested that possibly her soft way of speaking was related to her feeling unimportant, and that if the group could help her feel better about herself, her speech would change accordingly. She ended the exercise by asking members of the group to point out to her when her speech dropped in volume so that she could adjust it accordingly.

Tension-Relieving Games

It is important that patients in the focus group enjoy the session and look forward to the meeting each day. Games, judiciously employed, may facilitate this aim. Games may relieve tension, provide a light respite between more challenging tasks, increase member interaction, improve social skills, and augment group cohesiveness.

Earlier I discussed some caveats regarding the use of games. They must not signify to the patient that the staff, deeming the patient incapable of further change, has abandoned the therapeutic venture. The positive features of games may be enjoyed, and the negative consequences avoided, if therapists are judicious in their use and if they build into them a work component.

For example, a short game I have used often in focus groups entails a member leaving the room for a few minutes while one of the remaining members in the group alters his or her appearance in some small way. (One may take off spectacles or jewelry or exchange them or don additional jewelry from a box of props that the therapist provides; one may unbutton one's shirts, may role up one's sleeves, may exchange shoes; et cetera. Returning to the room, the designated person attempts to spot the change that has occurred.

This exercise, though it has a light, gamelike quality, is also obviously therapeutic work. At the very beginning of the exercise, each member is asked to go around the room and make a careful visual survey of every other member so as to be able to notice differences. The task increases group cohesiveness and member-to-member engagement; the members' attention is called to their habits of visual observation. The game encourages eye contact and increases each member's awareness of the others.

"Hangman," a common children's game, is often used in groups of poorly functioning patients. In the game, one member silently selects a word and places a number of dashes on a blackboard to indicate how many letters are in the word. The other members of the group attempt to guess the letters. When they are correct, the player writes in the letter; when they are wrong, he or she draws one segment of a gibbet and a stick figure victim until either the execution scene is completed or the word is guessed correctly.

"Hangman" becomes less of a "filler" and more relevant to therapeutic work if the therapist alters the instructions and advises the player to select as the word to be guessed some feeling—one that he or she either is personally experiencing or senses that someone else in the group is experiencing that day.

Another game exercise begins with the therapist placing in the center of the group, a collection of pictures clipped from magazines. The members are instructed to select two pictures: one of someone who they think likes them, and one of someone who they think dislikes them. After this selection each member shows his or her pictures to the rest of the group and briefly describes the reasons for selecting those particular pictures.

The therapists can effectively set the tone for this exercise (as they can for most exercises) by being the first to volunteer their pictures and their reasons for their selections. According to their assessment of the needs of the group, they can set a lighter "play" climate by choosing pictures for fanciful, comic reasons, or a more serious tone by selecting pictures for personal, autobiographical reasons.

In another game, a stack of cards is placed in the center of the room. On each card is written a short incomplete sentence requesting some safe personal disclosure. Some examples:

I feel happy when————.
One thing I like about myself is————.
I feel frustrated when————   .
I miss————.
The most active member of the group today was————.
The food in the hospital here is————.
I am very good at————.

The members are asked, in turn around the group, to select a card, read it aloud, and complete the sentence on it as quickly as possible, and point to someone else to draw a card. Even though the cards demand some self-disclosure, the fast pace of the game and the unpredictable selections of the members decrease personal threat and imbue the interaction with an air of lightness and play.

By no means do I intend these to constitute a comprehensive list of structured exercises. An inexhaustible supply of exercises is available both in the literature[5] and in the imagination of the focus group leader. Selection and presentation of the structured exercises are, however, only a small part of the group leader's task. I cannot emphasize strongly enough that the structured exercises represent only the unarticulated building blocks of focus group therapy. The group leader's therapeutic relationship with patients, and his or her technical skill and ability to support patients, to engage them and facilitate their engagement with one another, are the mortar that binds the bricks into a therapeutic edifice.

Review of the Session

The final phase of the focus group meeting is analogous to the final phase of the higher-level group where, with the help of observer and therapist input, the group reflects on its own process. Earlier, I emphasized that effective use of the here-and-now requires not only interaction but a second stage, a self-reflecting loop in which the participants of the group examine their interaction. The task of the final phase of the meeting in the focus group, no less than in the higher-level group, is to initiate this self-reflective stage and to encourage the group to review and evaluate its own session.

The structure of the focus group's final phase differs from that of the higher-level group. Poorly functioning patients are generally too agitated, too withdrawn, and/or too confused to integrate a detailed process commentary offered by therapists and observers. The review is far more effective if conducted by the members themselves according to a carefully sequenced, comprehensible blueprint.

One effective structure for the final review consists of a systematic review of all the parts of the meeting. The leader may go to the blackboard and ask the members to recall the first thing that occurred in the group that session. The members then try to recount not only the first exercise but the events even anterior to it; that is, when someone in the group changed his seat, or a new member introduced herself to the group. The therapist then asks not only for a description of the first exercise but for details of that exercise. For example, if the first exercise consisted of the group members each relating one good and one bad experience they had had that day, they are asked to try to recall some of these good and bad experiences. The same procedure is continued for all the other phases of the meeting.

Following this systematic temporal reconstruction of the meeting, the therapist guides the patients in an evaluation of the session. He or she helps patients express opinions about the most and the least valuable, the most enjoyable or the tensest part of the meeting, and to state some of their reasons behind these judgments. The provision of a legitimate forum to express negativity often decreases patients' resistance in subsequent meetings. Patients' positive and negative evaluations are not merely an academic exercise, since the therapist makes it clear that these evaluations will play a decisive role in shaping future meetings. If patients agree that a certain exercise was too threatening, too uninformative, or too patronizing, then the therapist takes their comments seriously and alters successive meetings accordingly.

Another phase of the review is a discussion about the members' observations of one another during the meeting. The therapist may frame a number of questions that are supportive and appropriate to that particular meeting: for example, Who was the most active member? the least active? Who was different from yesterday? Who took risks in the meeting? Who was the most supportive member? What new things did we learn about each member?

It is important that therapists participate in the review as fully as they participate in all other aspects of the meeting. They, too, describe what they have liked most about the meeting, and present their reactions to various events of the group. They may go around the room and comment on the positive contribution of each member.

This review of the meeting is useful to patients for several reasons. By supplying a self-reflective loop (that is, an investigation of process) the therapist facilitates the development of effective interaction. "Process checks"—whether they are built into a specific review phase of the meeting or into the flow of the meeting (for example, "Let's step back for a minute and try to understand what's happening in the group today")—almost invariably deepen the interaction, render it less threatening, and offer the members some cognitive framework by which they can transfer, to outside situations, what they have learned inside the group.

A systematic review is effective also in that it alleviates the confusion of many patients. By focusing their attention on the temporal sequence of the meeting, by urging them to remember what was the first, the second, the third, and the fourth part of the meeting, the therapist helps confused patients to organize their experience into an orderly temporal sequence. One confused patient remarked at the end of the review, "This is the first time I'll be able to tell my doctor what I did today."

The final review is also an exercise in responsibility assumption. Because their evaluations help to shape future meetings, the patients become more actively involved in their own therapeutic process.

The review process also increases concentration and attention span. Patients know that, during the final review, they will be asked to recount the events of the meeting; hence, they pay more attention to these events. In their first meeting some patients with impaired concentration may remember, at best, only the major events of the meeting—that is, say, that there were three different exercises in the session. Slowly, after a few meetings, they are able to fill in the parts of the meeting in finer detail.

The review process encourages patients to live, even for forty-five minutes a day, more completely in the present. Since they know that they will be asked to review the meeting in a comprehensive manner, they make an attempt to attend as fully as possible to their own participation and to that of the other members. The more that patients learn to live in the present, rather than in the future or the past, the more satisfaction will they derive from life, and the more successful will they be in engaging other individuals. The group therapist can be entirely explicit about this point to patients and indicate to them that much of their dysphoria stems from a dread of anticipated future events or from a re-experiencing of painful past events: the more they are able to stay focused in the present, the more control will they be able to exercise over their own anxiety.

Beyond Structure

I have, for reasons of pedagogic convenience, described the focus group session as a tidy succession of well-planned exercises. It is time now to make some compensatory remarks lest therapists mistakenly conclude that the role of the focus group leader consists merely of following, in a conscientious manner, some carefully planned recipe.

On the contrary, the focus group leader must exercise considerable clinical sensitivity and be flexible and skillful enough to alter the thrust, the pace, or the depth of every meeting to accommodate to the immediate clinical situation. The plan of the meeting must be used to provide structure and facilitate the work of the session, not as a rigid procedure that shackles the therapist. The therapist must retain flexibility and—throughout the meeting, in the midst of exercises, and between them—continually provide supportive, encouraging, or interpretive guidance.

For example, a young schizophrenic girl, whom I mentioned earlier in this chapter, had, with the help of another member, changed her hair style. In the following meeting she was agitated and highly distracted by auditory hallucinations accusing her of being a "slut." The therapist offered her considerable reassurance with a couple of quiet interpretive comments: "Everyone I've ever known has sexual desires," and "I'm wearing a pretty new sweater today and you have a new attractive hair style. My sweater doesn't make me a slut, and your hair style doesn't make you one."

Another patient was extremely self-castigating and negativistic in the group exercises. The therapist offered this interpretation: "Owen, I have an observation of you I want to share. When I came to get you to come to the group meeting at two o'clock today, you were talking on the phone to a friend. I know that you felt pissed at having to interrupt your conversation. I wonder if, throughout this meeting, you haven't felt annoyed with me and with the rigid ward schedule. Is it possible that you have dealt with your anger by turning it back on yourself and knocking yourself a whole lot during this session?" Owen's affirmative response was followed by an animated and constructive five-minute discussion in which other members aired their complaints about the strict ward schedule.

The therapist must be prepared to deal with disruptive events in the session and either mend the tears or, whenever possible, turn the disruption to therapeutic advantage. The same "grist for the mill" principles described in chapter 4 apply, except that the therapist must have more limited goals and proceed in a more gentle, cautious fashion. For example, three minutes after the beginning of a meeting, Mark, a young schizophrenic patient, inexplicably cursed and stomped out of the room. The remaining members were unsettled and puzzled by Mark's de-

The Lower-Level Psychotherapy Group

parture. The therapist channeled the event into a useful direction by commenting: "I happen to know from the staff rounds earlier today that Mark has been very upset because of some problems in his family. It's curious that, even though I know this, I still can't help feeling upset and a little hurt that Mark ran out of the meeting today. I somehow feel a little angry at him and also have been asking myself if I did something wrong in the meeting to upset him. I wonder if any other people in the room have similar feelings?"

In another meeting the group was engaged in a structured exercise that asked the patients each to draw something that would represent one of their regrets in life. A depressed patient, David, drew a picture of a graduation mortarboard and commented that his great regret was that he had dropped out of college in his junior year and had therefore never gotten his college degree. Suddenly Abby, a schizophrenic patient, interrupted, "David, you think that you are so smart, but I think you are the most unintelligent person on the ward." David looked obviously pained by Abby's comment, and the rest of the group looked embarrassed and puzzled about how to respond to the exchange.

The therapist decided quickly that there were two tasks that he should attempt to accomplish: first, to provide David with some support; second, to offer Abby gentle feedback about the consequences of her statement. The therapist proceeded to ask David to describe how Abby's comment made him feel. David, who was near tears, told the group that he had worried all his life that he was not as intelligent as others; hence, Abby's comment had hit a really sensitive area for him. The therapist then asked other people in the group about their opinions of David's intelligence. (The therapist had no concerns about this inquiry because David was obviously a highly intelligent person and was generally looked up to by the other members of the ward for this reason.) The group, as expected, gave David a great deal of support (as did the therapist).

This intervention (which took about five minutes) was obviously effective because ten minutes later Abby unexpectedly interrupted another exercise to tell the group that she had not meant what she had said to David at all and, in fact, the truth was she herself felt very stupid. David's comments about his regret at not having graduated from college had touched off painful feelings of regret in her for not having graduated from high school. Abby received considerable support from the group for her comment, and the members, in the final review, rated the meeting as very valuable.

Not infrequently the therapist may make helpful, succinct observations bearing upon some important issues that emerge in the session. In a debriefing interview patients described several useful comments they had retained:

"People really seem to like you a great deal. I hear them say that in the group all the time, but because you're so down on yourself, it's hard for you to believe them, and you keep insisting that others feel the same way about you that you feel about yourself."

"The job of a mother and a father is to help their children grow up strong enough, so they will be able to leave the family. It's not your job to stay home and try to keep your mother and father's marriage together."

"It's absolutely impossible for everyone to love you. There are always going to be people who are displeased with you. That's something that's hard to get used to, but it's a simple fact that we all have to face."

"Separations are always painful, but no relationship or friendship is forever. Separations always occur, and to stay away from being close with people because of anticipated separations is very self-defeating. It will sentence you to loneliness and isolation."

The focus group leader must be able to shift the level of the group up or down: up, if the degree of pathology is particularly severe; down, if the group is stable, and patients have indicated that they are able to work more intensively. The therapist's ability to determine the proper level of the group and to make the necessary technical adjustments requires considerable sensitivity and develops with clinical experience.

The therapist can shift the group to a lighter level by modeling more impersonal responses to exercise queries, by incorporating more game exercises, by prescribing more solo, parallel activities or more activities that call for indirect expression (for example, art, writing, movement) and de-emphasize here-and-now interaction. Or, the therapist can shift the group to a deeper level by employing the opposite strategies: by modeling a greater degree of self-disclosure; by using exercises that entail self-disclosure, member interaction, and the analysis of process. It is possible to increase depth by focusing on the here-and-now implications of any group interaction.

For example, consider the sentence-completion item: "I can't tell people I like them because————." To increase the here-and-now focus, the therapist can ask patients to comment whether their answer to the question also applies here in the current session. "To whom in the group would you like to say something positive? What are your fears about doing so?"

The therapist can deepen the here-and-now level of inquiry by being more personally revealing (for example, in describing bad experiences one day, the therapist might comment about feeling tense, or about having had an argument with a colleague, or about having slept poorly) and also by asking the group members to discuss how they feel about his or her having been so personal. Almost without exception, in their debriefing interviews, patients commented that they very much appreciated the therapist's honest self-disclosure. It made the therapist seem more human and encouraged them to participate more fully in the meeting.

The therapist can augment each patient's sense of personal responsibility in the focus group in ways very similar to methods employed in the higher-level group. In the final review the therapist may, for example, survey the amount of risk each patient thinks he or she has taken that day. The therapist who wishes to deepen the work might inquire whether the patient was satisfied with that degree of risk taking. Was it uncomfortable? Or would the patient like to take an even greater risk in tomorrow's meeting? If so, how would he or she like to be helped by the therapist? Would the patient like the therapist to call on him or her more frequently or be asked more questions? In the following meeting, the therapist can once again check to see whether he or she is following the patient's wishes correctly. This strategy allows the patient to monitor his or her own participation in the group; it enlists the patient as an ally and permits the patient to share in the responsibility for his or her own treatment.

Conclusion

I do not intend for either this model for lower-level groups, or the model for higher-level groups I described in the last chapter, to be regarded as some precise blueprint for other clinicians to follow: I close this book with the hope that these models illustrate general strategies that other therapists may apprehend and shape according both to their individual styles and to the requirements of their clinical settings.

Appendix

[A]. H. Davis and K. Dorman, "Group Therapy versus Ward Rounds," *Diseases of Nervous System* 35 (1974):316–19.

[B]. E. Arnhart, "Establishing Group Work in a Psychiatric Unit of a General Hospital," *JPN and Mental Health Services* 13 (1975): 5–9.

[C]. S. Lipkin, "Clients' Feelings and Attitudes in Relation to the Outcome of Client-centered Therapy," *Psychology Monographs*, p. 372; A. Goldstein, "Patients' Expectancies and Non-Specific Therapy as a Basis for (un)Spontaneous Remission," *Journal of Clinical Psychology* 16 (1960):399–403; and H. Friedman, "Patient Expectancy and Symptom Reduction," *Archives of General Psychiatry* 8 (1963):61–67.

[D]. E. Uhlenhuth and D. Duncan, "Subjective Change with Medical Student Therapists: II. Some Detriments of Change in Psychoneurotic Outpatients," *Archives of General Psychiatry* 18 (1968):532–40; and A. P. Goldstein and W. G. Shipman, "Patients' Expectancies, Symptom Reduction and Aspects of the Initial Psychotherapeutic Interview," *Journal of Clinical Psychology* 17 (1961):129–33.

[E]. Enormous problems bedevil the researcher who attempts to study the efficacy of inpatient group therapy. The ideal research design, approachable in the outpatient setting, calls for a comparison of the outcome of patients assigned to group therapy with the outcome of patients assigned to a "no therapy" control sample and to other forms of therapy, such as family, individual, or pharmacologic therapy. If this research is to be uncontaminated, there should be no crossover—that is, patients in groups should not receive concurrent individual or drug therapy; otherwise, the attribution of outcome to each of the various therapies becomes problematic.

Furthermore, the sample of patients receiving a specific type of therapy should receive relatively uniform treatment. If there are several individual therapists or group therapists in the study, each practicing widely divergent forms of therapy, then neither "group" nor "individual" therapy may be treated as separate cells; indeed, clinically the variability may be so great that one form of group therapy resembles individual therapy more than it does other forms of group therapy. Though statistical methods are available to assist us in assessing factors influencing outcome, such analysis would require massive numbers of patients and groups.

Consider the research conditions available on the acute inpatient ward. First, note that each patient is exposed to multiple forms of therapy: milieu therapy, activity therapy, psychotropic medication, individual therapy with a designated therapist, many informal one-to-one therapeutic sessions with members of the ward staff, discussions with other patients, art therapy, occupational therapy, community meetings, family therapy, and, of course, one or many of a large number of groups (see pages 4–5).

Appendix

Thus, group therapy is only one part of a comprehensive therapy program. If, for research purposes, some patients participate in the small therapy group and a control population does not, there may not be significant differences between the samples, because for some patients group therapy may account for only a small amount of the influence on outcome. Furthermore, it is possible that the "no group" control sample may pick up the slack of not being in a group and, for example, seek out additional, informal one-to-ones with staff or engage more deeply in any of the other therapeutic programs. (To a much lesser degree, the same phenomenon may occur in outpatient therapy, as "waiting list" control patients seek out informal therapy with friends, clergymen, bartenders, and so on.) Though the researchers may attempt to monitor the amount of informal therapy patients receive, it is a difficult task; and, especially in an extensive study, a great deal slips through the net.

The situation becomes even more confounded by the fact that, as I discuss in chapter 2, most wards have several different types of therapy group. Although these groups have widely differing names, they often overlap considerably in procedure and function. Thus, a "movement therapy" or a "rap" group may be a more effective interactional therapy group than the formal designated "talking" therapy group; and a patient may, for research design purposes, be excluded from the formal talking psychotherapy group but obtain the same experience in another group.

If researchers attempt to control for this crossover of function by barring the control patient from attending all groups on the ward, they may so greatly affect the patient's hospital experience as to make extremely difficult the interpretation of research results. The inpatient therapy group is enmeshed in an intricate therapeutic system in which all the elements are interdependent. To remove a patient from therapy groups may interfere with his or her treatment program in a number of ways.

To take one example, many patients receive much benefit from their relationship with other patients. The small therapy group often facilitates and repairs relationships among patients. A group therapy patient and a "no group" control patient may show significant differences in outcome. But are these differences due to the therapy group? Or, are they a function of their relationships with other patients—relationships that are facilitated and repaired in the small therapy group meetings?

Some researchers have tried to circumvent these obstacles by using a different experimental design: they have compared the outcome of patients who were hospitalized on a ward that offers a small therapy group program with those hospitalized on wards offering no therapy group whatsoever. But these projects, too, are plagued by problems of specificity. Are the differences specifically a function of the small therapy group experience or of other major differences that will be found between wards that sponsor a group program and those that do not? Wards that offer no groups generally rely heavily upon psychotropic medication, electroshock, and individual therapy with the admitting psychiatrist. The milieu is often intrinsically less therapeutic, and the ward staff less interested or less qualified to offer psychotherapy. If the staff is trained to offer therapy and is not permitted to do so by administrative decision, then it is very likely, as I discuss on page 35, that they will be a demoralized staff with high turnover and covert staff conflict, which will adversely influence outcome.

The research design that most effectively avoids the pitfalls of "group participation versus no group participation" is one that assigns patients to different types of small therapy group while keeping the remainder of their hospital experience constant. One might, for example, offer such groups as interactional groups, behavioral groups, gestalt groups, and problem solving groups and compare the results of each. Because inpatients constantly interact with one another and compare notes, the design is more effective if the groups are run consecutively rather than concurrently. In other words, the design would call for a ward offering only one type of group for a designated time —say, two months—and then offering sequentially each of the other groups.

Is such a design feasible? It requires enormous cooperation from the ward staff; furthermore, it contains its own set of methodological problems. For example, who leads the groups? If outside group therapists, trained in each of these modalities, are hired to lead the groups, they are at a disadvantage in lacking the considerable clinical information about the patients available only to the full-time staff. If the researchers ask the full-time staff to lead the groups, then the research is flawed because group therapists are asked to lead groups in styles personally uncomfortable or incompatible to them.

To my knowledge, there is only one inpatient project that approaches this more powerful comparative design (L. Beutler et al., "Comparative Effects of Group Therapies in a Short-term Inpatient Setting: An Experience with Deterioration Effects," *Psychiatry,* in press); and this project commits the error of requiring therapists to lead groups in styles unfamiliar to them.

Even if this design were perfectly executed, it would be encumbered by problems associated with the great heterogeneity of pathology and with the rapid turnover of patients and staff on an inpatient ward. As I write these lines, I am aware that yesterday my inpatient group was composed of eight patients, six of whom were depressed and profoundly demoralized, with much psychomotor retardation; while the other two were schizoid, with extreme timidity and self-consciousness. The group meeting, accordingly, was slow-moving and painfully cautious. I had to work extremely hard to elicit material and to keep the patients engaged. Only ten days previously, however, the same group consisted of eight borderline women (five with severe bulimia) and two depressed patients; the character of that group session was markedly different: the pace was lively; the atmosphere, crackling; members scrambled for group time; and my major consideration was to dampen affect and encourage more understanding of the group events.

The issue is that the composition and, thus, the character of the inpatient group fluctuate so wildly that research will be full of errors unless an extremely large sample of groups is studied and careful objective recordings are made of such variables as group climate, norms, leadership styles, affect levels, and types of interaction.

The leadership of the small group fluctuates greatly as well. Not only do leaders rotate quickly in and out of leadership roles, but the experience and the training of the leaders varies greatly. Often leaders are highly inexperienced: they may be, for example, first-year residents or newly graduated psychiatric nurses. Since no formal training in short-term inpatient group therapy is to be had anywhere in any training curriculum, group leaders are likely to be particularly idiosyncratic and uncategorizable in their approach. Thus, research that reports on the results of "inpatient group therapy" as though it were some uniform mode of therapy is of little value. Some leaders are skillful, sensitive, and effective; others, inept. To deny this in outcome research is to court serious error.

I have the same reservations about categorizations of leader style. Most research reports content themselves with an extremely brief, inadequate characterization of style (for example, "analytic," "nondirective," "gestalt," "insight-oriented"). Yet in an extensive 1972 group research project, my colleagues and I demonstrated that the official ideological labels that leaders assume convey extremely little information about a leader's actual behavior (M. Lieberman, I. Yalom, and M. Miles, *Encounter Groups: First Facts* [New York: Basic Books, 1973], pp. 226–67). The error is magnified by research inquiries that purport to compare such types of treatment as "insight groups" versus "support groups," provide no detailed information about types of insight or modes of support, and assume that there is no crossover of function (that is, an "insight" leader offers no support). And no research has ever addressed my personal pet peeve: how accurate is the insight? How well timed? All clinicians know that it is foolish to proceed, as some researchers do, to count "insight statements." There is accurate and inaccurate insight, and even accurate insight must be well timed and well worked through to be effective.

Acceptable research may avoid some of these pitfalls only by using large samples of patients, groups, and therapists, and making careful recordings by trained raters of leader behavior. A study extensive enough to meet these criteria would be enormously costly (the Lieberman, Yalom, and Miles study involved 18 groups and 210 subjects and cost approximately $250,000 in 1972 dollars). Thus, given inflation, the state of the current economy, and the reluctance of federal agencies to fund psychotherapy research, it is highly unlikely that the required definitive inpatient group therapy research will ever be done.

[F]. B. Rosen, A. Katzoff, C. Carrilo, and D. Klein, "Clinical Effectiveness of 'Short' versus 'Long' Psychiatric Hospitalization," *Archives of General Psychiatry* 33 (1976):1316–22.

These authors studied 126 patients shortly after public funds in New York restricted the length of hospital stay to 90 days. Those patients assigned to the short-term unit remained in the hospital an average of 86 days; those on the long-term wards, 180 days. The short-term units offered a group therapy program; the long-term units did not. The short- and the long-term patients were comparable, pre-therapy, in all criteria studied. The short-term (that is, group therapy) patients showed significantly greater improvement in social competence and in affective and cognitive functioning. Eighty-six days is not brief hospitalization by 1983 standards, but there is virtually no well-designed, analogous group therapy research on the acute ward with average hospital stays of four to twenty days. Consequently, we must rely on reasonable extrapolations of research data from related clinical environments.

[G] A. R. Alden et al., "Group Aftercare for Chronic Schizophrenia," *Journal of Clinical Psychiatry* 40 (1979):249–52; R. M. Prince et al., "Group Aftercare—Impact on a Statewide Program," *Diseases of the Nervous System* 77 (1977):793–96; J. L. Claghorn et al., "Group Therapy and Maintenance Therapy of Schizophrenics," *Archives of General Psychiatry* 31 (1974):361–65; S. A. Purvis and R. W. Miskimins, "Effects of Community Followup on Posthospital Adjustments of Psychiatric Patients," *Community Mental Health Journal* 6 (1970):374–82; S. P. Shattan et al., "Group Treatments of Conditionally Discharged Patients in a Mental Health Clinic," *American Journal of Psychiatry* 122 (1966):798–805; T. Borowski and T. Tolwinski, "Treatment of Paranoid Schizophrenics with Chlorpromazine and Group Therapy," *Diseases of the Nervous System* 30 (1969):201–2; M. I. Herz, et al., "Individual versus Group Aftercare Treatment," *American Journal of Psychiatry* 131 (1974):808–12; C. O'Brien et al., "Group versus Individual Psychotherapy with Schizophrenics: A Controlled Outcome Study," *Archives of General Psychiatry* 27 (1972):474–78; and L. Mosher and S. Smith, "Psychosocial Treatment: Individual, Group, Family and Community Support Approaches," *Schizophrenia Bulletin* 6 (1980):10–41.

This research literature provides compelling evidence that group therapy is an effective mode of aftercare treatment. Alden et al. demonstrate that group aftercare during a one-year follow-up was more effective than individual therapy in decreasing the number of hospitalizations and the mean duration of each hospitalization. Prince et al. reported similar findings: aftercare group therapy was more effective than individual therapy in maintaining chronic patients out of the hospital and within their own communities, and was as effective as individual therapy in keeping acute patients out of the hospital. Claghorn et al., in a controlled study, reported that group aftercare patients, compared with a "no group" control sample, showed significantly greater improvement in interpersonal functioning. Purvis and Miskimins and Shattan et al. demonstrated that aftercare group therapy decreased recidivism. Borowski and Tolwinski demonstrated that aftercare groups plus medication was far superior to medication alone. Herz et al. reported that group therapy was equally effective as individual therapy from the standpoint of patient outcome, but added that the therapists far preferred the group mode: staff morale was improved, therapists were willing to spend longer blocks of time with patients, and patients reported a greater sense of community and an opportunity for increased socializing. O'Brien et al., in a large randomized study, demonstrated that post-hospital group therapy was more effective than individual therapy in reducing the rehospitalization rate and psychiatric symptomatology and in increasing social effectiveness. All of these studies, incidentally, also used pharmacological treatment in both the experimental and the control samples. Mosher and Smith provide a comprehensive review of this literature.

[H]. S. Lipton, F. Fields, and R. Scott, "Effects of Group Psychotherapy upon Types of Patient Movement," *Diseases of the Nervous System* 29 (1968):603–5.

The subjects were sixty-seven Veterans Administration patients admitted to three wards: one ward with a group therapy program, two wards without one. The style of the group therapist is described as varying "from attempts to increase general insight on the part of the patients to attempts at increasing socialization on their part."

[I]. G. Haven and B. S. Wood, "The Effectiveness of Eclectic Group Psychotherapy in Reducing Recidivism in Hospitalized Patients," *Psychotherapy, Theory Research and Practice* 7 (1970):153–54.

The subjects were sixty-eight Veterans Administration patients on the same ward alternately assigned to group therapy (one hour twice weekly) or to no group therapy. Leader style was "eclectic, generally directive and oriented toward reality testing and relearning with the theme of assisting the patient to become more comfortable and effective interpersonally." The mean number of meetings attended was sixteen. The follow-up period for recidivism was one year. Thirty-three of the sixty-eight patients had a diagnosis of anxiety reaction, and it was this subsample that responded favorably to group therapy.

[J]. Approximately a dozen other inpatient group therapy studies have been summarized in major reviews: M. Parloff and R. Dies, "Group Psychotherapy Outcome Research," *International Journal of Group Psychotherapy* 27 (1977):281–319; Mosher and Smith, "Psychosocial Treatment" (see appendix [G]); and M. A. Lieberman, "Change Induction in Small Groups," *Annual Review of Psychology* 27 (1976):217–50.

These studies are not germane to our discussion on the efficacy of group therapy on the acute inpatient unit, because they study a chronic patient population: generally patients who have been hospitalized for years are then tested experimentally with a newly developed group therapy program.

Two studies, however, reported negative results of inpatient group therapy: E. Pattison, A. Brisserden, and T. Wohl, "Assessing Specific Effects of Inpatient Group Psychotherapy," *International Journal of Group Psychotherapy* 17 (1967):283–97; and N. Kanas et al., "The Effectiveness of Group Psychotherapy during the First Three Weeks of Hospitalization: A Controlled Study," *Journal of Nervous and Mental Disease* 168 (1980):483–92.

Pattison, Brisserden, and Wohl report a study of twenty-four Veterans Administration patients who were admitted to an acute ward for approximately twelve weeks. Half of the patients were randomly assigned to a therapy group; the other half participated in all of the other many therapeutic activities of a well-staffed ward. The style of the group leader is described only as "psychoanalytic, encouraging interaction by supplying minimal leadership." The authors state neither who the leaders were (that is, were they the researchers?) nor how frequently or for how long the group met. On a series of outcome measures

Appendix

(Inpatient Multi-dimensional Psychiatric Scale [IMPS], Rogers-Dymond Q-sort, Symptom Check List [SCL], 16PF), both experimental and control groups improved markedly; and there were no differences between the two, except that the *control* sample showed a greater improvement on self-esteem (Q-sort) and on guilt reduction (16PF), whereas the experimental sample showed a greater decrease in symptoms on the SCL and a trend toward greater improvement on the IMPS.

The test differences are small, and the authors very explicitly state that they "should be viewed with great caution since they merely reflect a few trends rather than weighty evidence." Since this research is often cited as evidence that inpatient group therapy is not effective, it is necessary to note that this research is so flawed that it yields no justifiable conclusions about group therapy efficacy on the acute inpatient ward. The sample size is small, and the population was a chronic all-male population. Only one group therapist was studied. The control population is, as the authors acknowledge, not an adequate control for a group therapy versus a "no group" therapy project, since the patients in the control sample received significantly more individual therapy.

What remains is only the authors' clinical judgment that inactive, psychoanalytic group leadership may not be indicated on an acute inpatient ward, and their recommendation that the goals and techniques of inpatient group therapy be modified to be more consonant with the goals of brief hospitalization. These impressions, as the rest of my text explicates, closely match my own clinical impressions.

Kanas et al. report a study of group therapy in a military hospital. Eighty patients were randomly assigned to one of three conditions: "no group" psychotherapy (but availability of individual counseling); an activity-oriented task group, in which patients worked together on a common project (generally some form of crafts) without discussing intrapsychic or interpersonal problems; and a therapy group that met for one hour thrice weekly. Aside from the three group therapy meetings each week, all the patients were equally involved in an active ward treatment program. Ratings of psychopathology were made (at admission and twenty days later) by these measures: the Global Assessment Scale (GAS), the Psychiatric Evaluation Form (PEF), staff ratings of patients, medication logs. The great majority of patients showed marked improvement, and ceiling effects made significant differences between the three conditions unlikely. Two findings emerged. First, overall, significantly *fewer* task group patients improved than in the group therapy or the "no group" therapy samples. Secondly, though the results of group therapy and "no group" therapy did not differ for the overall sample or for the nonpsychotic sample, the psychotic patients who were in group therapy did significantly more poorly than psychotic patients in the other two samples.

How can these results be explained, and what relevance do they have for the contemporary acute inpatient unit? Let me first consider the generalizability of the results. The research was done in a military hospital—a setting that confounds interpretation of results. Not only does this ward have the broad range of pathology found in all acute hospitals but also large numbers of patients admitted for reasons not found in civilian hospitals: some were veterans who were hospitalized for their disabilities to be evaluated; some were dependents; some were undergoing alcohol detoxification; some schizophrenic military personnel were hospitalized for administrative reasons for several months while awaiting discharge from the military. Furthermore, there are significant problems in treatment motivation in a military population: the secondary gains of psychiatric disability, both for those on active duty and for the retired personnel, are enormous. Kanas et al. provide some supporting evidence for this observation in their finding that the female dependents (who presumably had a different motivational set) did significantly better in group therapy than did the male population.*

It is extremely difficult to explain the finding that a low-keyed task group (that is, a group where patients select and engage in some craft activity "without discussing interpersonal or intrapsychic problems") resulted in significantly less patient improvement! That finding is so counterintuitive that it raises the question whether important uncontrolled variables were at play. Like all inpatient studies with a limited sample size, this research does not control for the multiplicity of treatments. All patients attended a large number of other treatment activities, and we cannot assay how potently some other treatment may have affected the patients.

The leaders of the psychotherapy groups were reported to have attempted to "help patients gain insight into intrapsychic and interpersonal difficulties by focusing on here-and-now interactions and expression of feelings. Principles and techniques described by Yalom were utilized." In a personal communication (1982), N. Kanas said that he meant that the leaders used techniques I described for long-term outpatient groups. The leaders also used some gestalt (for example, empty chair dialogue) and psychodrama techniques. At times, if the situation developed, open hostility was expressed in the groups. These groups were heterogeneous (that is, "team groups"), and the level of a group was pitched for the better-functioning patients. The psychotic patients were unable to perform the group task and were often left out or considered irritants or impediments to the group. This insalubrious group role of the psychotic patients is the most likely explanation for the groups' negative impact upon them.

These considerations suggest that we be cautious in accepting the authors' conclusions: "the results of this study raise serious

*N. Kanas, personal communication.

questions regarding the effectiveness of insight-oriented psychotherapy during the first three weeks of hospitalization, especially for acutely psychotic patients."

This research does not indicate that "group therapy" or "insight" or "interaction" is counterproductive, but indicates instead that group therapy that is not designed to meet the clinical situation and the specific needs of the group members is counterproductive. One of my reasons for undertaking the writing of this book was my conviction that many of the strategies and techniques I described in my text, *The Theory and Practice of Group Psychotherapy* (2nd ed., New York: Basic Books, 1975), are not applicable to acute inpatient work. The research by Kanas et al. supports that conviction.

It seems that the therapists in the Kanas et al. study made several technical errors: setting inappropriate goals for the group; encouraging too much affect expression, especially the expression of open hostility; permitting the group to scapegoat the more psychotic patients; providing, overall, far too little support for the group members (I discuss all these pitfalls in chapters 2 and 3). Indeed, it is not "inpatient group therapy" that Kanas's research criticized, since in his next two publications, he described a different leadership style for level meetings of psychotic patients which his research suggested was highly effective. The leaders in these groups used a far more gentle, supportive approach, avoided any expression of anger, encouraged expressions of other affects, encouraged member interaction, and helped members to test reality (N. Kanas and M. Barr, "Short-Term Homogeneous Group Therapy for Schizophrenic Inpatients: A Questionnaire Evaluation," *Group*, in press, 1983; and N. Kanas, M. Barr, and S. Dossick, "The Homogeneous Schizophrenic Inpatient Group: An Evaluation Using the Hill Interaction Matrix," submitted for publication, 1982).

These studies indicate that twenty-one of twenty-two psychotic patients found the therapy group to be helpful and valued it as a place to express feelings and to learn to interact with others. The Hill Interaction Matrix confirmed that the group was work-oriented, supportive, and effective.

J. Watson and J. Lacey ("Therapeutic Groups for Psychiatric Inpatients," *British Journal of Medical Psychology* 47 [1974]:307–12) provide additional data suggesting that traditional outpatient group therapy technique must be modified for the group situation.

They studied a small sample of twelve patients over eleven meetings and concluded that the techniques I described for outpatient groups (including a heavy emphasis—heavier than is my wont—on the catharsis and dissipation of intense affect) result in anxiety-provoking and unsatisfying inpatient group sessions.

[K]. Beutler et al., "Comparative Effects" (see appendix [E]).

L. Beutler, M. Frank, S. Scheiber, S. Calvert, and J. Gaines report a heroic attempt to conduct controlled inpatient group therapy research on the contemporary rapid-turnover inpatient ward. The authors studied 176 consecutively admitted psychiatric inpatients with diagnoses ranging from substance abuse to schizophrenia to bipolar affective disorder to adjustment reaction. Upon admission and completion of assessment scales, individuals were randomly assigned to one of the four research groups. Because of the limited size of the wards, only two groups were conducted at any given time. The therapists were drawn from staff nurses, psychiatric residents, clinical psychology interns, social work externs, and advanced psychology graduate students. One major methodological flaw in the study was that on a few occasions it was necessary to assign therapists a group style when their preference would have been to run the group in another style. All groups were supervised by experienced therapists. External observers rated the groups to make certain the groups were, in fact, being led in the style assigned to them. The outcome measures included the Minnesota Multiphasic Personality Inventory (MMPI), the Shipley

Institute of Living Scale, the SCL-90R, ward ratings completed by the nursing staff, and judgments of improvement made by each patient's primary therapist. Groups were offered twice a week; the average number of sessions attended by patients was 3.2. The results indicated that the patients in the psychodrama/gestalt group became worse. The process/patient-focused group was by far the most effective group.

The authors conclude that "the group emphasizing emotional support and group feedback tends to fare the best." This research is supportive of the general group techniques I describe in this text. It states that "social support and feedback to patients in crisis when treated on a short-term basis by relatively inexperienced people will be of greater value than techniques clumsily applied which exaggerate feelings and break down defenses."

[L]. See discussion on Pattison, Brisserden, and Wohl, "Assessing Specific Effects," and Kanas et al., "Effectiveness" (both in appendix [J]).

[M]. Kanas et al., "Effectiveness" (see appendix [J]); Watson and Lacey, "Therapeutic Groups" (see appendix [J]); and O'Brien et al., "Group" (see appendix [G]).

[N]. M. Zaslowe, J. Ungerleider, and M. Fuller, "How Psychiatric Hospitalization Helps: Patient Views versus Staff Views," *Journal of Nervous and Mental Disease* 142 (1966):568–76; E. Gould and I. Glick, "Patient-Staff Judgments of Treatment Program Helpfulness on a Psychiatric Ward," *British Journal of Medical Psychology* 49 (1976):23–33; C. Leonard, "What Helps Most about Hospitalization," *Comprehensive Psychiatry* 14 (1973):365–69; and R. Pasewark, J. Paul, and B. Fitzgerald, "Attitudes toward Industrial Therapy of Mental Hospital Patients and Staff," *The American Journal of Occupational Therapy* 23 (1969):244–48; and M. Leszcz, I. Yalom, and M. Norden, "The Value of

Appendix

Inpatient Group Psychotherapy: Patients' Perceptions," submitted for publication, 1983.

In 1981 my colleagues, Molyn Leszcz and Michael Norden, and I studied, at the time of discharge, sixty-eight consecutive patients who had remained in the hospital for longer than three days. Seventeen patients were excluded from the study. (Seven paranoid patients and five borderline patients refused to cooperate; five patients were too confused to be included in the sample.) The other fifty-one patients comprised the experimental sample.

The Stanford psychiatric unit is a twenty-bed open unit which heavily emphasizes groups in the treatment program. Every patient attends a "team" (heterogeneous) group meeting in the morning, and the better-functioning patients attend an optional "level" (homogeneous) group in the afternoon. The team group meets five times a week, and the higher-level group four times a week. At the time of the research, no lower-level group was offered; but shortly afterward, a daily "focus" group (see chapter 6) was begun.

The aspect of our research most germane to this current discussion was a sorting task in which each patient was presented with fifty poker chips and asked to distribute them among eleven boxes. Each box represented one aspect of the ward treatment program: individual treatment with psychiatrist, talking with other patients, one-to-one treatment with the nurses, the morning team therapy group, medication, the after noon optional therapy group, ward activities, community therapy meetings, family therapy meetings, occupational therapy, alternative groups (art therapy, movement therapy, et cetera). The patients were asked to assign the poker chips according to how helpful each of the treatment modalities had been to them.

Twenty of the patients attended only the morning team group meeting (that is, they were not functioning at a sufficiently high level to attend a somewhat more demanding afternoon optional group). These were the patients with the major psychotic disturbances. Their rank-order of ten ward therapeutic activities is as follows (they ranked only ten activities since they did not attend the afternoon level group):

		Average Rank
1.	Individual therapy with psychiatrist	3.0
2.	Team psychotherapy group	3.65
3.	Discussions with other patients	4.35
4.	One-to-one talks with the nurses	4.57
5.	Alternative groups	5.11
6.	Ward activities	5.25
7.	Medications	5.87
8.	Community therapy meetings	6.38
9.	Family therapy group meetings	6.7
10.	Occupational therapy (crafts)	7.16

Thirty-one patients attended both meetings: the higher-level optional group therapy meeting and the team group meeting. The ranking of these thirty patients was as follows:

1.	Individual therapy with psychiatrist	2.69
2.	The level psychotherapy group	3.06
3.	Discussions with other patients	4.06
4.	The team psychotherapy group	4.5
5.	One-to-one talks with the nurses	4.69
6.	Medication	5.38
7.	Ward activities	6.74
8.	Family therapy group meetings	6.96
9.	Community therapy meetings	7.6
10.	Alternative groups	8.04
11.	Occupational therapy (crafts)	8.08

In addition to the chip-sorting ranking of the ward activities Leszcz, Norden, and I obtained other data, which is reported in various sections of this text.

Patients were asked to do a similar chip-sorting task for ten curative factors (see chapter 2): instillation of hope, altruism, advice, understanding, vicarious learning, expressing feelings, assumption of responsibility, universality, interpersonal learn-

Appendix

ing, cohesiveness. Following the two or three chip sortings (if patients attended both the team and the level groups, the researchers asked them to do a curative-factor chip sorting for each group), the researchers conducted a semistructured interview using the following protocol:

1. *Analysis of chip sorting tasks:* Reasons why a patient considered items helpful or unhelpful.

2. *The team group:* Were you pleased with your participation? What would you have liked to have done differently? Did you have enough time in the group? Should the leaders have ensured better distribution of time in the meeting? The team group is compulsory—how did that affect you and the group? Should certain patients have been excluded from the group meetings? Which patients? How were they disruptive to the group? Were there times it would have been better for you not to come to the group—that is, to choose not to come or to be asked not to come? What would it have been like to have been excluded from the group? Were you a central member of the group? Did anything harmful occur in the group?

3. *The level group:* Were you pleased with your participation? What would you have liked to have done differently? Did you have enough time in the group? Did leaders ensure that there was equal distribution of time? The afternoon group is optional —did that have any influence on you or upon the work of the group? Should certain patients have been excluded? Which patients? How were they disruptive to the group? Were you a central member of the group? Did anything harmful occur in the group? What is your evaluation of the agenda format and of the final "wrap-up"? (See chapter 5.) Can you give examples of helpful comments by observers? How do you feel about the therapists criticizing themselves or being criticized by the observers?

4. *General comparisons between the team and the level groups.*

5. *Leadership:* What aspects of leader behavior facilitated or hampered the group? What are your feelings about leadership

activity, structured approach, transparency, relationship between co-leaders, leader turnover? Or, about seeing the leaders
in other roles on the ward?

6. *Setting:* What are your feelings about the short-term nature
of the group? Did the rapid turnover in the group affect the
work of the group? How did living with the other group members throughout the whole day influence the work of the group?
Were there important things going on with patients that specifically did not get talked about in the group?

[O]. Note that in this study, "individual therapy with psychiatrist" was ranked first. Also note that the research was performed on a ward in which patients saw their individual psychotherapist four to five times weekly. However, even though
individual psychotherapy was the most popular choice, only 40
percent of the patients ranked one-to-one therapy with their
psychiatrist first (or tied for first and second). Seventy percent
of the patients with a major affective disturbance rated one-
to-one therapy with their psychiatrist as the most important;
and approximately 25 percent of the remaining patients in the
study ranked individual therapy as the most important choice.

[P]. E. Gould and I. Glick ("Patient-Staff Judgments," see appendix [N]) studied forty-four patients who had been in the
hospital for thirty days or longer. They interviewed the patients
twenty-four hours before discharge and asked patients to rank-
order twenty treatment activities from "most helpful" to "least
helpful." They also asked the ward staff to rank-order the same
activities for "most patients" and for "neurotic" and
"psychotic" patients. Unfortunately the authors do not present
any information about the specific nature of the group therapy
offered by the ward. The staff rated group therapy highly for
"most" and for "neurotic" patients (second of the twenty treatment activities) but only sixth for the "psychotic" patients. The
patients gave the highest average ranking to "individual ther-

apy with their doctor." Closely following this was "talks with nurses and technicians," "group therapy," and "talks with other patients." A breakdown by diagnostic category reveals that group therapy is ranked as the most important therapy modality by patients with a character disturbance and as the second most important modality by nonschizophrenic paranoid patients. Paranoid schizophrenics rated the group as less important (fifth of the twenty ward activities) than any of the other diagnostic categories.

Gould and Glick analyzed the data according to length of hospitalization. They noted that patients with the shortest hospitalization (ninety days or less) rated group therapy as the most important of the twenty treatment activities. This finding is particularly significant, since virtually all the patients we attempt to treat on the contemporary inpatient unit would fall into the short-term category.

[Q]. Leszcz, Yalom, and Norden, "Value of Inpatient Group Psychotherapy" (see appendix [N]).

[R]. Ibid.

[S]. Eighteen months after Leszcz, Yalom, and Norden's research, another project on the same ward (I. Yalom and L. Gonda, unpublished data, 1983) studied (with the same chipsorting technique) a small sample ($N = 12$) of poorly functioning patients who attended both the daily team group therapy meeting and the daily lower-level (focus) therapy group. Their rank orders:*

	Average Rank
1. Individual therapy with psychiatrist	2.9
2. Level psychotherapy group (focus group)	3.4

*Only nine activities were ranked. "Alternate groups" and "family therapy group meetings" were eliminated from rankings because several patients did not attend these activities.

3. Team psychotherapy group   4.1
4. Ward activities   4.2
5. Medication   4.8
6. Discussions with other patients   5.1
7. Community meetings   6.2
8. One-to-one talks with the nurses   6.5
9. Occupational therapy   7.2

See also Kanas et al., "Effectiveness" (see appendix [J]); and Beutler et al., "Comparative Effects" (see appendix [E]).

[T]. D. Strassberg et al., "Self-disclosure in Group Therapy with Schizophrenics," *Archives of General Psychiatry* 32 (1975):1259–61.

[U]. P. May, "When, What, and Why? Psychopharmacotherapy and Other Treatments in Schizophrenia," *Comprehensive Psychiatry* 17 (1976):683–93.

[V]. M. Linn et al., "Day Treatment and Psychotropic Drugs in the Aftercare of Schizophrenic Patients," *Archives of General Psychiatry* 36 (1979):1055–66.

[W]. B. Corder, R. Corder, and A. Hendricks, "An Experimental Study of the Affects of Paired Patient Meetings on the Group Therapy Process," *International Journal of Group Psychotherapy* 21 (1971):310–18; and J. Otteson, "Curative Caring: The Use of Buddy Groups with Chronic Schizophrenics", *Journal of Consulting and Clinical Psychology* 47 (1979):649–51.

Corder, Corder, and Hendricks designed a program in which they assigned each patient a partner with whom he or she was required to spend thirty minutes a day talking about problem areas. The researchers found that the patients involved in this "buddy" program required less staff care; had higher morale, greater interaction, and greater intimacy with staff and other patients; and made more frequent helpful comments to other patients.

Appendix

Otteson, in a related study, assigned each group patient a buddy who was directed to expend his or her energies helping the other patient get discharged from the hospital. Each buddy was instructed to talk to his or her assignee and also to exert pressure on the ward staff to augment the help that assignee received from the staff. The results showed that significantly more members of this buddy-oriented group were discharged than were from a "no treatment" control sample or from a traditional therapy group.

[X]. T. Main, "The Ailment," *British Journal of Medical Psychology* 30 (1957):129–45; and A. Stanton and M. Schwartz, *The Psychiatric Hospital* (New York: Basic Books, 1954).

References

Chapter 2

1. I. Yalom, *The Theory and Practice of Group Psychotherapy* (New York: Basic Books, 1975); D. Whitaker and M. Lieberman, *Psychotherapy through the Group Process* (New York: Atherton Press, 1964); E. L. Pinney, *A First Group Psychotherapy Book* (Springfield, Ill.: Charles C. Thomas, 1970); H. Mullen and M. Rosenbaum, *Group Psychotherapy* (New York: Free Press of Glencoe, 1962); H. Kellerman, *Group Psychotherapy and Personality: Intersecting Structures* (New York: Grune & Stratton, 1979); C. Sager and H. S. Kaplan, eds., *Progress in Group Family Therapy* (New York: Brunner/ Mazel, 1972); and H. Kaplan and B. Sadock, eds., *Comprehensive Group Psychotherapy* (Baltimore: Williams & Wilkins, 1971).
2. Yalom, *Theory* [1].
3. Ibid., pp. 3–104.
4. Ibid.
5. I. Yalom, *Existential Psychotherapy* (New York: Basic Books, 1981).
6. Yalom, *Theory* [1], pp. 77–83.
7. I. Youcha, "Short-term Inpatient Group: Formation and Beginnings," *Group Process* 73 (1976):119–37.

The numbers in brackets refer to the original complete citation of a reference in each chapter.

References for pages 53–88

8. J. Maxmen, "An Educative Model for Inpatient Group Therapy," *International Journal of Group Psychotherapy* 28 (1978):321–38.
9. Ibid.
10. T. Main, "The Ailment," *British Journal of Medical Psychology* 30 (1957):129–45; and A. Stanton and M. Schwartz, *The Psychiatric Hospital* (New York: Basic Books, 1954).
11. M. Leszcz, I. Yalom, and M. Norden, "The Value of Inpatient Group Psychotherapy: Patients' Perceptions," submitted for publication, 1983 (see appendix [N]); and E. Gould and I. Glick, "Patient-Staff Judgments of Treatment Program Helpfulness on a Psychiatric Ward," *British Journal of Medical Psychology* 49 (1976):23–33.
12. K. Arriaga, E. Espinoza, and M. Guthrie, "Group Therapy Evaluation for Psychiatric Inpatients," *International Journal of Group Psychotherapy* 28 (1978):359–64.
13. Leszcz, Yalom, and Norden, "Value of Inpatient Group Psychotherapy" [11]; and I. Yalom and L. Gonda, unpublished data, 1983 (see appendix [S]).
14. Leszcz, Yalom, and Norden, "Value of Inpatient Group Psychotherapy" [11].
15. Yalom and Gonda, 1983 [13].
16. N. Kanas, M. Barr, and S. Dossick, "The Homogeneous Schizophrenic Inpatient Group: An Evaluation Using the Hill Interactional Matrix," in preparation; and N. Kanas and M. Barr, "Short-term Homogeneous Groups for Schizophrenic Inpatients: A Questionnaire Evaluation," *Group,* in press.
17. Leszcz, Yalom, and Norden, "Value of Inpatient Group Psychotherapy" [11].
18. Kanas and Barr, "Homogeneous Groups" [16].
19. Leszcz, Yalom, and Norden, "Value of Inpatient Group Psychotherapy" [11].
20. Ibid.
21. H. Levine, "Milieu Biopsy: The Place of the Therapy Group on the Inpatient Ward," *International Journal of Group Psychotherapy* 30 (1980): 77–93.
22. H. Kibel, "The Rationale for the Use of Group Psychotherapy for Borderline Patients on a Short-term Unit," *International Journal of Group Psychotherapy* 78 (1978):339–57.
23. R. Klein, "Inpatient Group Psychotherapy: Practical Considerations and Special Problems," *International Journal of Group Psychotherapy* 27 (1977):201–14.

24. Leszcz, Yalom, and Norden, "Value of Inpatient Group Psychotherapy" [11].
25. Ibid.
26. Maxmen, "Educative Model" [8].

Chapter 3

1. M. Leszcz, I. Yalom, and M. Norden, "The Value of Inpatient Group Psychotherapy," submitted for publication, 1983 (see appendix [N]).
2. D. Zlatin, "Member Satisfaction in Group Process in Structured vs. Unstructured Groups with Hospitalized Psychiatric Patients," unpublished doctoral dissertation, University of Maryland, 1975.
3. A. Schwartz et al., "Influence of Therapeutic Task Orientation on Patient and Therapist Satisfaction in Group Psychotherapy," *International Journal of Group Psychotherapy* 20 (1970):460–69.
4. B. Bednar and T. Kaul, "Experiential Group Research: Current Perspectives," in S. L. Garfield and A. E. Bergin, eds., *Handbook of Psychotherapy and Behavior Change* (New York: John Wiley, 1971), pp. 769–815; I. Yalom et al., "Preparation of Patients for Group Therapy," *Archives of General Psychiatry* 17 (1967):416–27; S. Budman et al., "Experiential Pre-Group Preparation and Screening," *Group* 5 (1981):19–26; and E. Gauron and E. Rawlings, "A Procedure for Orienting New Members to Group Psychotherapy," *Small Group Behavior* 6 (1975):293–307.
5. M. Orne and P. Wender, "Anticipatory Socialization for Psychotherapy: Method and Rationale," *American Journal of Psychiatry* 124 (1968):88–98; and R. Hoehn-Saric et al., "Systematic Preparation of Patients for Psychotherapy," *Journal of Psychotherapy Research* 2 (1964): 267–81.
6. I. Yalom, *The Theory and Practice of Group Psychotherapy* (New York: Basic Books, 1970), pp. 286–300.
7. J. Heitler, "Clinical Impressions of an Experimental Attempt to Prepare Lower-class Patients for Expressive Group Psychotherapy," *International Journal of Group Psychotherapy* 29 (1974):308–22.
8. J. Houlihan, "Contribution of an Intake Group to Psychiatric Inpatient Milieu Therapy," *International Journal of Group Psychotherapy* 27 (1977):215–23.
9. S. Zyl, C. Ernst, and R. Salinger, "Role Expectations: A Significant

References for pages 119–126

Concern for the Nurse-Therapist," *JNP and Mental Health Services* 5 (1979):23–27.

10. B. Rauer and J. Reitsema, "The Effects of Varied Clarity of Group Goal and Group Path upon the Individual and His Relation to His Group," *Human Relations* 10 (1957):29–45; D. Wolfe, J. Snock, and R. Rosenthal, "Report to Company Participants at 1960 University of Michigan Research Project" (Ann Arbor, Mich.: Institute of Social Research, 1961); A. Cohen, E. Stotland, and D. Wolfe, "An Experimental Investigation of Need for Cognition," *Journal of Abnormal Social Psychology* 51 (1955):291–94; A. Cohen, "Situational Structure, Self-Esteem and Threat-Oriented Reactions to Power," in D. Cartwright, ed., *Studies in Social Power* (Ann Arbor, Mich.: Research Center for Group Dynamics, 1959), pp. 35–52; and A. Goldstein, K. Heller, and L. Sechrest, *Psychotherapy and the Psychology of Behavior Change* (New York: John Wiley, 1966), p. 405.

11. J. Authier and A. Fix, "A Step-Group Therapy Program Based on Levels of Interpersonal Communication," *Small Group Behavior* 8 (1977): 101–7.

12. R. Vitalo, "The Effects of Training in Interpersonal Functioning upon Psychiatric Inpatients," *Journal of Consulting and Clinical Psychology* 35 (1971):166–71; C. Whalen, "Effects of a Model and Instructions on Group Verbal Behaviors," *Journal of Consulting and Clinical Psychology* 33 (1969):509–21; and S. Angel, "The Emotion Identification Group", *American Journal of Occupational Therapy* 35 (1981):256–62.

13. E. Coche and A. Douglas, "Therapeutic Effects of Problem-solving Training and Play-reading Groups," *Journal of Clinical Psychology* 33 (1977):820–27.

14. C. Anderson et al., "Impact on Therapist on Patient Satisfaction in Group Psychotherapy," *Comprehensive Psychiatry* 13 (1972):33–40.

15. M. Lieberman, I. Yalom, and M. Miles, *Encounter Groups: First Facts* (New York: Basic Books, 1973).

16. W. Crary, "Goals and Techniques of Transitory Group Therapy," *Hospital and Community Psychiatry* 19 (1968):389–91; M. Weich and E. Robbins, "Short Term Group Therapy with Acute Psychotic Patients," *Psychiatric Quarterly* 40 (1966):80–87; and L. Gruber, "Group Techniques for Acutely Psychotic Inpatients," *Group* 2 (1978):31–39.

17. C. Truax and K. Mitchell, "Research on Certain Therapist Intrapersonal Skills in Relation to Process and Outcome," in A. Bergin and S. Garfield, eds., *Handbook of Psychotherapy and Behavior Change* (New York: John Wiley, 1971).

18. Lieberman, Yalom, and Miles, *Encounter Groups* [15], pp. 226–68.

19. I. Yalom and G. Elkin, *Every Day Gets a Little Closer: A Twice-Told Therapy* (New York: Basic Books, 1974).
20. M. Hertzman, *Inpatient Psychiatry: Toward a Restoration of Function* (Human Sciences Press, forthcoming).
21. A. Richmond and S. Slagle, "Some Notes on the Inhibition of Aggression in an Inpatient Psychotherapy Group," *International Journal of Group Psychotherapy* 21 (1971):333–37; Crary, "Goals" [16]; I. Youcha, "Short-term In-patient Group: Formation and Beginnings," *Group Process* 7 (1976):119–37; N. Kanas and M. Barr, "Short Term Homogeneous Group Therapy for Schizophrenic Inpatients," *Group,* in press (1983); and Gruber, "Group Techniques" [16].
22. Gruber, "Group Techniques" [16].
23. Yalom, *Theory and Practice* [6], pp. 204–17.
24. Ibid., p. 214.

Chapter 4

1. I. Yalom, *Theory and Practice of Group Psychotherapy* (New York: Basic Books, 1970), pp. 12–44, 121–70.
2. M. Lieberman, I. Yalom, and M. Miles, *Encounter Groups: First Facts* (New York: Basic Books, 1973), pp. 365–68.

Chapter 5

1. I. Yalom, *Existential Psychotherapy* (New York: Basic Books, 1980).
2. M. Leszcz, I. Yalom, and M. Norden, "The Value of Inpatient Group Psychotherapy," submitted for publication, 1983 (see appendix [N]).
3. I. Yalom, *The Theory and Practice of Group Psychotherapy* (New York: Basic Books, 1975), pp. 459–67.
4. H. Chertoff and M. Berger, "A Technique for Overcoming Resistance to Group Therapy in Psychotic Patients on a Community Mental Health Service," *International Journal of Group Psychotherapy* 21 (1971): 53–61; and E. Gould, C. Garrigues, and K. Scheikowitz, "Interaction in

References for pages 264–304

Hospitalized Patient-led and Staff-led Psychotherapy Groups," *American Journal of Psychotherapy* 29 (1975):383–90.
5. E. Berne, "Staff-Patient Staff Conferences," *American Journal of Psychiatry* 125 (1968):286.
6. Yalom, *Theory and Practice* [3], pp. 440–45.
7. I. Yalom and J. Handlon, "The Use of Multiple Therapists in the Teaching of Psychiatric Residents," *Journal of Nervous and Mental Disease,* 141 (1966):684–92.
8. Leszcz, Yalom, and Norden, "Value of Inpatient Group Psychotherapy" [2].

Chapter 6

1. K. Kaplan, "Directive Groups: A Therapy for the Acute Psychiatric Patient," submitted for publication; L. Gruber, "Group Techniques for Acute Psychotic Patients," *Group* 2 (1978):31–39; H. S. Leopold, "Selective Group Approaches with Psychotic Patients in Hospital Settings", *American Journal of Psychotherapy* 30 (1976):95–102; M. J. Horowitz and P. S. Weisberg, "Technique for the Group Psychotherapy of Acute Psychosis," *International Journal of Group Psychotherapy* 16 (1966):42–50; I. Youcha, "Short-term Inpatient Groups: Formation and Beginnings," *Group Process* 7 (1976):119–37; J. Grobman, "Achieving Cohesiveness in Therapy Groups of Chronically Disturbed Patients," *Group* 2 (1978): 141–49; T. Cory and D. Page, "Group Techniques for Effecting Change in the More Disturbed Patient," *Group* 2 (1978):150–54; A. Druck, "The Role of Didactic Group Psychotherapy in Short-term Psychiatric Settings," *Group* 2 (1978):98–109; M. Hertzman, *Inpatient Psychiatry: Toward Rapid Restoration of Function* (New York: Human Sciences Press, forthcoming); and W. Crary, "Goals and Techniques of Transitory Group Therapy," *Hospital and Community Psychiatry* 12 (1968):37–41.
2. Youcha, "Short-term Groups" [1].
3. Grobman, "Achieving Cohesiveness" [1].
4. Kaplan, "Directive Groups" [1].
5. J. W. Pfeifer and J. E. Jones, *Handbook of Structured Exercises for Human Relations Training,* 6 vols. (California: University Associates, 1973–75), G. Corey, M. S. Corey, P. Callanan, and J. M. Russel, *Group Techniques* (Monterey, Calif.: Brooks/Cole Publishing Co., 1982); W. Schutz, *Joy:*

Expanding Human Awareness (New York: Grove Press, 1967); H. Otto, *Group Methods to Actualize Human Potential—A Handbook* (Beverly Hills, Calif.: Holistic Press, 1970); H. Lewis and H. Streitfeld, *Growth Games* (New York: Bantam Books, 1970); A. J. Remocker and E. T. Storch, *Action Speaks Louder: A Handbook of Nonverbal Group Techniques* (Edinburgh, London, New York: Churchill Livingston, 1979); K. T. Morris and K. M. Cinnamon, *A Handbook of Nonverbal Group Exercises* (Springfield, Ill.: Charles C Thomas, 1975); and B. Reuben and R. Bubb, *Human Communications Handbook: Simulations and Games* (Rochelle Park, N.J.: Hayden, 1975).

Index

administrative community meetings, 20

agenda filling, 243–59; general strategic guidelines for, 244–52; issues beyond the agenda and, 252–56; problems of, 257–59

agenda go-round, 212–42; advantages of, 215–16; agenda formation in, 241–42; described, 211; final-product agendas in, 226–27; options in, 213–14; patient agenda formation in, 216–20; resistance to, and responsibility assumption, 227–35; therapist techniques in agenda formation, 222–26; transforming interpersonal agenda to here-and-now agenda, 220–26

aggression of therapist to patient, 140–41, 197–99

Alden, A. R., 320

altruism: facilitation of, through here-and-now approach, 178; in outpatient group therapy, 42

ancillary therapy, see specialty groups

anger, 145–53; agenda formation for expression of, 222; expressing early forms of, 148–50; "gentling" of,

153–54; of group leaders, 140–41, 197–99; patient difficulty with, 144; see also conflict

anorexia nervosa, selfishness and, 151–53

anxiety: toward agenda formation, 257–59; from confronting existential issues, 228–30; from feedback, 189–94; here-and-now approach and, 184; in lower-level groups, 279–82; patient ejection or transfer from ward and, 101–2; preparation for group therapy and, 119–20; relieving iatrogenic, 59–62; role of structure in relieving, 108, 121–22; therapist self-disclosure and, 162–63

Arnhart, E., 313

art therapy, 6–8

assertion, agenda formation and, 221

Banish, Vivian, 276

Barr, M., 326–27

Beutler, L., 317, 327–28, 334

blind spots, feedback and, 188

343

Index

externalization and agenda formation, 230

family, and outpatient group therapy, 42, 314
favoritism, 138–40
feedback: agenda formation and, 222; in here-and-now approach, 187–94; patient-to-patient, 178; in review sessions, 304–7; therapist self-disclosure and, 166, 170–72; in wrap-up sessions, 259–73
Fields, F., 321
"fishbowling" format of group therapy, 264
Fitzgerald, B., 328
focus in group therapy, 19–24; common themes in, 21–23; then-and-there problems in, 20–21, 177–78; *see also* here-and-now approach
focus therapy groups, *see* lower-level inpatient groups
fragility of patients, 184, 187
Frank, M., 327–28
Friedman, H., 313
friendship in inpatient group therapy, 92
Fuller, M., 328
funding, for research, 319

Gaines, J., 327–28
games in lower-level groups, 282, 301–4
Glick, I., 328, 332–33
Global Assessment Scale (GAS), 324
global criticism, 160
goals: of inpatient group therapy, 52–62; of outpatient group therapy, 40; of staff, for lower-level groups, 281–82; *see also* agenda filling; agenda go-round
goals groups, 8
Goldstein, A. P., 313–14
Gonda, L., 333–34
Gould, E., 328, 332–33

group leaders, 14–19, 318; anger of, 140–41, 197–99; anxiety of, and structure, 121–22; focusing inpatient group by, 19–24; forms of address of, 116n; interdisciplinary rivalry of, 13, 14–19; of lower-level inpatient groups, 285–86; modeling of, 154–56, 163–65, 266–68; motivation of, 86; nurses as, 3–4, 7, 14, 18–19; other sources of patient information and, 94–99; psychiatric residents as, 6–8, 14, 17; self-disclosure of, 102, 154–56, 161–72, 259–73, 290, 311–12; social workers as, 6, 11; specialty therapists as, 1–2, 6–8, 76, 314–15; structure of lower-level groups and, 307–12; structure of therapy sessions and, 107–25; style of, 29, 112–15, 124–25, 252, 318–19, 321, support of patients and, 125–44; techniques of, in agenda filling, 244–52; techniques of, in agenda formation, 222–26; training of, 3, 13–15, 17–19, 23–25, 318; wrap-up sessions and, 259–73
group therapy, *see* inpatient group therapy; outpatient group therapy

Haven, G., 321–22
Hendricks, A., 334
here-and-now approach, 23–24, 47–48, 173–208, 325–26; agenda formation and, 220–26; bizarre, disruptive incidents in, 194–207, 308–9; cohesiveness and, 17–48, 177–78; described, 173–74; in lower-level group exercises, 297–98, 311–12; rationale for, 174–79; special considerations of, 184–94; therapist self-disclosure and, 102, 154–56, 161–72, 259–73, 290, 311–12; two stages of, 179–83
Herz, M. I., 320, 321
higher-level inpatient groups, 110, 209–74; agenda filling in, 243–59; agenda go-round in, 212–42; composition of, 68; conclusion on, 273–74; final phase in, 259–73; orienta-

345

Index

preparation: in higher-level inpatient groups, 115–17, 210–12; of lower-level inpatient groups, 286–87; of patient for group therapy, 117–20
Prince, R. M., 320
private practitioners: "calling out" of patients from group therapy, 10, 155–56; individual therapy and, 30–31, 86–87, 320–21; tension between nurses and, 18–19
problem solving in group therapy, 20–21, 177–78
process illumination in here-and-now approach, 181–83
projective identification, 157–58
Psychiatric Evaluation Form (PEF), 324
psychiatric residents: as group leaders, 6–8, 14, 17; role of, in group therapy, 6–8; tension between nurses and, 18; training of, 17
psychotic patients: disruptive incidents and, 203–7; group therapy for, 29, 30, 32; psychotherapy and, 54; therapist self-disclosure and, 162–63; in team groups, 64–66; see also lower-level inpatient groups
Purvis, S. A., 320–21

"rap" group, 315
reality testing: of borderline patients, 129–31; wrap-up sessions as aid to, 268
recreational therapy, 6
relaxation therapy, 8
relevance of here-and-now approach, 184–86
resistance to agenda formation, 225–41; communicating needs in, 231–32; externalization and, 230; fear of growing up and, 239–41; identifying area of change in, 230; isolation and, 220, 236–37; learning to take care of oneself and, 232–35; need for dependency and, 237–39
responsibility assumption, 43; resist-

ance to agenda formation and, 227–35; review sessions as form of, 305–7
review sessions, lower-level group, 304–7; see also wrap-up sessions
rivalry as source of conflict, 146–47
Rogers-Dymond Q-sort, 323
role reversal in conflict resolution, 158–59
romantic pairing in inpatient groups, 93–94
Rosen, B., 319

Scheiber, S., 327–28
schizophrenic patients: evaluation of group therapy by, 31, 32; making contact with, 133–34, 136–37
Schwartz, M., 335
SCL-90R, 328
Scott, R., 321
self-disclosure of patients, in structured exercises, 290–94, 303–4
self-disclosure of therapists, 102, 154–56, 161–72; advantages of, 163–69; barriers to, 161–63; feedback and, 166, 170–72; in lower-level groups, 290, 311–12; types of, 162–63; in wrap-up sessions, 259–73
self-dissection, 160
selfishness and anorexia nervosa, 151–53
separation, anxiety and, 101–2
Shattan, S. P. 320–21
Shipley Institute of Living Scale, 327–28
Shipman, W., G., 313–14; 16PF (outcome measure), 323
Smith, S., 320, 321, 322
social microcosm, therapy group as, 46–47
social skills, 33–35; development of, in outpatient group therapy, 42; empathy and development of, 294–95; here-and-now approach and, 48; therapist self-disclosure as model for, 164–65

Index